Last Season of Innocence

Last Season of Innocence

The Teen Experience in the 1960s

Victor Brooks

ROWMAN & LITTLEFIELD PUBLISHERS, INC.
Lanham • Boulder • New York • Toronto • Plymouth, UK

Published by Rowman & Littlefield Publishers, Inc.
A wholly owned subsidary of The Rowman & Littlefield Publishing Group, Inc.
4501 Forbes Boulevard, Suite 200, Lanham, Maryland 20706
www.rowman.com

10 Thornbury Road, Plymouth PL6 7PY, United Kingdom

British Library Cataloguing in Publication Information Available

Library of Congress Cataloging-in-Publication Data
Brooks, Victor.
  Last season of innocence : the teen experience in the 1960s / Victor Brooks.
    p. cm.
  Includes bibliographical references and index.
  ISBN 978-1-4422-0917-6 (cloth : alk. paper) — ISBN 978-1-4422-0918-3 (electronic)
  1. Teenagers—United States—History—20th century. 2. Nineteen sixties. 3. United
States—History—1961–1969. I. Title.
  HQ796.B696 2012
  305.2350973—dc23

2011051199

∞™ The paper used in this publication meets the minimum requirements of
American National Standard for Information Sciences—Permanence of Paper
for Printed Library Materials, ANSI/NISO Z39.48-1992.

Printed in the United States of America

Contents

~

Introduction

Not too long ago, one of my children returned from an excursion to the local bookstore with the exciting news that he had spotted a new release that focused on the year 1959, the period I emerged into full preteen middle school status, with adolescence clearly looming on the near horizon. Less than a half hour later, I settled into a comfortable chair with an impressive-looking book with a lime-green cover and began a journey backward in time, courtesy of author Fred Kaplan.

The book, *1959: The Year Everything Changed*, was fast paced, well written, and generally enjoyable, but to my disappointment focused on individuals and events that barely registered in my experience as a suburban child living in a house with three younger siblings and a neighborhood teeming with Baby Boomers. Narratives about Norman Mailer, Lenny Bruce, and Miles Davis, debates over the issue of book censorship, and innovations in jazz music might have been the center of conversation among older, hipper people or could even have caused a ripple in a typical business office, but my fellow Boomers and I clearly lived in a parallel universe. As the fifties were about to transform into the sixties, we experienced an alternative world to that of most adults. It was an environment where the real excitement was DC Comics' introduction of Superman's fellow Kryptonian survivor, his cousin Supergirl, who the Man of Steel, in a move many young readers openly questioned, forced into a dreary orphanage existence as mousy Linda Lee, with only cameo roles as a gorgeous blond crime fighter. This was a world of boys debating whether television hero Wyatt Earp's Buntline Special pistol was a better weapon than the Rifleman's fast-firing rifle, while girls considered the advantages and disadvantages of the brand-new Barbie dolls in comparison to much-younger-looking dolls already in their collections.

The children and preteens of 1959 were oblivious to the jazz revolution Kaplan describes, when Alvin and the Chipmunks' "Christmas Don't Be Late," Annette Funicello's "Tall Paul," and Eddie Byrnes and Connie Stevens's "Kookie, Kookie, Lend Me Your Comb" were readily available on cool transistor radios with earplugs. The chronicler of John Cassavettes's stunning new filmmaking technique in *Shadows* described an alien entertainment device in a film industry that allowed Boomers to settle in their movie theater seats and watch Pat Boone and James Mason battle subterranean dinosaurs in *Journey to the Center of the Earth* and John Wayne, Dean Martin, and Rick Nelson stand up to ten times their number of outlaws in *Rio Bravo*.

Reading this otherwise interesting book clarified my growing realization that the narrative of the period from 1959 to 1969 tends to be divided between two vantage points: the activities of the dominant adult society and their leaders, such as John Kennedy, Lyndon Johnson, and Richard Nixon, and the impact of the nominal leaders of a dynamic youth culture, such as Mario Savio, Tom Hayden, and John Lennon, who spent a major part of the sixties as members of the twenties age group. The problem with these two primary emphases in most chronicles of that decade is that they largely marginalize the experiences of tens of millions of preteens and teenagers who, thanks to the Baby Boom, became the catalysts for massive changes in popular music, television programming, fashion design, and much of the general popular culture of the period. They also formed such a massive cohort of school students that much of the educational establishment of the United States underwent significant alterations.

The sixties decade was a period of enormous promise for those young people who spent the majority of it as young adults, as they often gained a level of power and respect usually only granted to more mature individuals, while at the same time receiving tacit permission to maintain a lifestyle that continued to be very youth oriented. In effect, they now had a unique ability to wield influence while still being able to act like "kids" until very late in their twenties, or sometimes even beyond. These young people, who generally experienced adolescence primarily during the 1950s, became the recognized spokespersons for youth culture and empowerment during the sixties and then tended to eventually become the cultural caretakers of the era through their historical and cultural publications, memoirs, or music. These young people include scholars such as Todd Gitlin, journalists Tom Brokaw and Ed Bradley, actors Warren Beatty and Faye Dunaway, and musicians Paul Simon, Bob Dylan, and Barbra Streisand, most of whom graduated from high school in either 1958 or 1959 and then spent most of the sixties as young adults. Yet, as they were often lauded or envied by the younger members of an emerging "kids generation" that increasingly extended from about ages ten to thirty, emerging Boomer generation members such as Patty Duke, Stevie Wonder, Hayley Mills, and Kurt Russell were beginning to emerge as the authentic purveyors of adolescent dreams during the sixties decade.

This book is intended to be a new chronicle of the 1960s through the perspective of individuals who lived through that decade, primarily as adolescents or preadolescents, and those journalists, scholars, and other adults who held major responsibility for interpreting those young peoples' experiences to the adult world. One motivation for my chronicle is the almost unbelievable reality that kids and teens made up nearly 40 percent of sixties-era Americans, who by their sheer energy and presence gradually enticed their elders into at least sampling a portion of their fashions, hair styles, and viewing and listening choices, something that would have been unthinkable in most earlier decades yet became increasingly common in the decades that followed the sixties.

This is a narrative of the sixties world that focuses primarily on the topics and themes of interest to the adolescents who experienced that era. These include home life, social life, the high school and college freshman experience, the music scene, youth-oriented television and films, shopping habits, and relations with adults. The book is a combination of a thematic and a chronological narrative as it progresses from 1959, the portal to the sixties decade, and concludes with a consideration of how the 1960s has been perceived from the seventies to the twenty-first century. The two topics of popular music and television and films underwent such enormous changes during the decade that I have written separate chapters focusing on the first half and second half of the decade, while most of the other themes span the era in one chapter.

I must make special note at the outset that I spent most of the sixties as a teenager and all of the decade as a full-time student, from junior high school at the beginning of the era to the initiation of graduate school at the very end. Much of my adolescent experience during this period was the same strange and wonderful, exciting and baffling experience that was shared by most other people who were neither small children nor adults in the "soaring sixties." Beyond the fact that I am a college professor who teaches young people about being young in the 1960s, my own otherwise rather normal adolescence during that era was mildly spiced by a few moderately different experiences that will hopefully add a bit of insight to this chronicle.

For example, I experienced two very different forms of high school for almost exactly equal periods, as a family housing move transferred me from an all-boys Catholic high school with over four thousand pupils to a public, combined junior-senior high school, where my not-entirely-appreciated assignment to the top honors section placed me in classes where girls outnumber boys by two to one and where enrollment was so diminutive that my senior class graduated exactly ninety-one students. While neither of these high schools was really "typical," the combination of the two certainly broadened my perspective of the diversity of the secondary school experience.

My adolescent experience attending two different types of Philadelphia suburban secondary schools was broadened further by summer vacation activities. Most summers were equally divided between several weeks at the Jersey Shore, like an East Coast version of *Gidget* or the Beach Party films with boardwalk, beach, and ocean, and the remaining weeks visiting maternal grandparents in a small city in central New York, with a white Victorian house, porch swings, the sound of multigenerational conversation on warm summer evenings, and the gentle reminder of having both an accent and a suntan not common to those parts. Interspersed during those summers were special family excursions on transatlantic ocean liners that provided substantial communication with European teens and their fashions, music, and opinions, from Britain at the peak of the Beatles' reign to the edges of Eastern Europe, with an adolescent population that often condemned American adult politics while dreaming of the teen lifestyle that the United States had largely originated.

Writing a book on teen life in the sixties is particularly challenging and interesting in light of the experience of parenting three twenty-first-century adolescents, substantially reinforced by a toddler who will achieve his own teen status sometime in the 2020s. Fortunately for me, all of my children are at least moderately interested in sixties films, music, fashion, and television and reinforce the idea that this project might actually produce a "cool" book at the end.

The reality of a home environment being a single parent with all male offspring makes me specially aware not only of the uniqueness of Fred McMurray and *My Three Sons* in television programming but, more importantly, of the fact that half of sixties teens were not of my gender. My own possible bias is mitigated somewhat on a number of fronts. First, I spent the 1960s living in a household with two younger sisters, very verbal and self-assured identical twins who were vocal about the advantages and drawbacks of their adolescent experiences and kept me attuned to what was similar and different about teenage girl life. Second, the vast majority of sixties teen magazines, which form a major element of my research materials, are either mostly or totally oriented toward a female audience and provided features on almost every element of the teen experience important to that era's girls. Thanks to eBay, I am now the owner of far more sixties teen-life and fashion magazines than most other males of my age group. Finally, in my interviews of sixties-era teens, I have discovered that females consistently offered a broader panorama of their experiences, thoughts, hopes, and fears than most males and are often more noticeably enthused about this project.

Villanova University, my academic home since I was only six years removed from my own teen experience, has offered a stimulating environment that is ably led by its president and fellow sixties teen, Reverend Peter Donohue, O.S.A. Consistent encouragement has emanated from Vice President for Academic Affairs Reverend Kail Ellis, O.S.A.; outgoing Dean of Arts and Sciences Dr. John Doody and his newly appointed successor, Dr. Jean Linney; and the chair of the Department of Education and Counseling, Dr. Edward Fierros. Their support would have been of little avail without the superb typing skills, editorial assistance, and timely content suggestions of another fellow sixties teen and invaluable departmental asset, Anne Feldman.

Since this is a book about children and families, special dedication must go to Lillian Ginter Brooks, with whom I shared all-too-brief memories of the parenting experience; Matthew, Gregory, and Stephen Brooks, who proved that the teen experience for parents can be far more joy than angst; and to Liam Brooks, who is angelically holding his Blankey Dog "Alfonso" and watching the Nick Junior channel two feet from my desk, blissfully unaware that he is a member of the 2020s teen generation. I hope that he and his fellow toddlers will experience all of the wonder and little of the trepidation of the fascinating and wonderful sixties teens who populate this book.

June 2011
Norristown, Pennsylvania

CHAPTER ONE

~

Teen Life in 1959

The Gateway to the Sixties

As Americans prepared to greet the last year of the decade already being described as the "fabulous fifties," most families settled in for an evening with their usual Wednesday-night television formats. During the past nine years, television set ownership had soared from under 10 percent to over 90 percent of households, and now the actors, panelists, and game show hosts of *Ozzie and Harriet, The Donna Reed Show, Wagon Train, The Price Is Right,* and *I've Got a Secret* were virtual presences in most homes on a typical Wednesday evening. Then, as the late local news ended, network cameras shifted to festive on-site New Year's Eve celebrations dominated by Guy Lombardo and the Royal Canadians fronting the activities at New York's Waldorf-Astoria Hotel. The festive atmosphere encouraged many parents to dispense with earlier bedtime curfews for their children, and, as the famous lighted ball began its descent on Times Square, the 40 percent of Americans who were either teenagers or children were well represented on living room couches and floors. Huddled around the flickering box that had become the centerpiece of the American living room, an incredibly young population welcomed 1959 and, perhaps, began to wonder how the now-looming sixties decade would change their society and their lives.

Even before the last year of the fifties began, there was an increasing volume of predictions that 1959 would serve as a portal to a "soaring sixties" that seemed replete with promise of progress. There was increasingly ample cause for such optimism. Only a year earlier, the Soviet Union seemed destined to rule the cosmos as two Sputnik satellites crisscrossed the globe emitting their curious, cricketlike chirps. Then, after a disastrous launching pad explosion of the American Vanguard satellite system in January 1958, the army funded the Explorer Project, which made space a competitive field as a tiny but sophisticated American satellite joined its burly Russian counterparts in orbit.

Now, in the early winter of 1959, American news magazines and television networks began to run features on the selection of the first seven men who would someday challenge Soviet cosmonauts for access to the heavens. Soon a hugely publicized press conference would introduce these real-life Flash Gordons and Buck Rogerses as American astronauts, and every minute aspect of their lifestyles and backgrounds would be reported in order to discern their true nature. Cover features on the astronauts were soon followed by cover features on their wives, who looked much more like typical American women than beauty queens or real-life Dale Ardens or Wilma Deerings set to accompany Flash or Buck against Ming or Killer Kane. Meanwhile, as many Americans dreamed of the experience of space exploration, some of them were beginning to experience the first step in that direction, as First Lady Mamie Eisenhower presided over the launch of the Jet Clipper *America*, the first Boeing 707 passenger liner to make a nonstop flight across the Atlantic Ocean at an altitude that many passengers believed was on the threshold of "outer space."

Twenty years earlier, the World's Fair held in Flushing, New York, had drawn millions of wide-eyed spectators to a promised "World of Tomorrow," which was depicted in the moderately distant future of 1960. Now, with those vaunted sixties only months away, most if not all of the exotic exhibits had become part of everyday life. The Westinghouse Pavilion's talking, cigarette-smoking robotic-mechanical man would be routinely pushed further ahead on the horizon, perhaps achieving reality in the generically named "Robot" on *Lost in Space*, set in the late 1990s, or even as Rosie the Robot in a *Jetsons* world of the 2060s. However, President Eisenhower's Interstate Highway bill was already turning most stretches of clogged thirty-five-mile-an-hour roads into seemingly futuristic limited-access freeways that could be traveled at nearly twice that speed in cars with rocketlike fins that made boxy 1930s sedans look hopelessly outdated.

One of the "must see" exhibits at the World of Tomorrow had been the demonstration of television broadcasting, which was hinted at as a major possible diversion in the world of two decades hence. People who had experienced that exhibit could now only nod, either with trepidation or smugness, that television was indeed nearly universal, with the added features of remote control and color telecasting now available, if still limited, realities. Those relatively few American viewers who settled in their easy chairs as they watched the 1959 Tournament of Roses Parade and Rose Bowl football game in "living color," armed with a channel surfing remote control to pick at other options, were enjoying an expensive (over four thousand dollars in 2010 currency) experience that would be far less exotic a decade later.

Amazingly, the "futuristic world" predicted at the 1939 World's Fair was actually a far more conservative vision than the real world of twenty years later. The transition year between the fifties and sixties was a world of Cinerama theater, sparkling, spacious supermarkets with automatic opening doors, transistor radios, and sleek, powerful streamlined cars. It was even a world in which primitive computers were beginning to take baby steps toward relieving humans of the drudgery of pencil-and-paper calculations. Columnist and author Fred Kaplan describes 1959 as "the year when the shockwaves of the new ripped the seams of daily life . . . when the world as we know it begins to take form." Some of those seams that were about to be ripped were largely in that frayed condition due to the stark reality that America now had considerably more residents under twenty than over forty, and millions of them were adolescents or preadolescents who on some levels saw those ripping seams as more an opportunity than a disaster.

In 1959 the first cohort of seventy-six million Baby Boomers were turning thirteen years of age, and adult Americans viewed these emerging adolescents with a mixture of good humor and fear. The young people just ahead of them had already brought the marriage age for girls down to just over nineteen and had made Elvis Presley, and rock and roll in general, a controversial anthem for an occasionally dark-sided youth culture. One adult concern was that if the relatively small number of pre-Boomer teens were already causing a "youth problem," what would happen when the far-more-numerous Boomers segued into teen status during the upcoming sixties decade? Actually, many of the objects of this adult concern were spending their final year before the new decade dealing with conflicting sentiments of excitement, fear, and confusion as they attempted simultaneously to understand and react to the challenges and concerns of the adult world of their parents, teachers, and adult authorities, the still-new experience of adolescence that was dominated by their older siblings and neighbors, and their just-emerging sense of identity.

The most daunting reality that faced virtually all Americans at the end of the 1950s was the lurking possibility that the Cold War could turn into a thermonuclear holocaust that would end American society as most people understood the term. By 1959 the sheer terror of Stalinism had been replaced by a more human face, but that face belonged to Soviet party leader Nikita Khrushchev, a person who combined moderate reform in his own nation with mercurial, bullying, blustering showmanship toward the West, particularly the arch rival United States. Khrushchev actually spent part of the summer of 1959 touring America, alternatively praising farmers in Iowa and threatening nuclear Armageddon to stunned California leaders. The chairman's antics included rhythmically banging his shoe on his desk in a United Nations session, threatening to "bury" America after the triumph of Soviet socialism, and pouting like a spoiled child when security issues forced the cancellation of a tour of Disneyland.

During 1959, emerging teenagers could go to the movie theater and watch the film version of Nevil Shute's stunningly intense novel of nuclear Armageddon, *On the Beach.* This film, which this author considers the most depressing movie ever viewed, chronicles the lives of Australian civilians and the crew of an American nuclear submarine in the aftermath of a nuclear war that has annihilated all of mankind beyond that continent, with a cloud of deadly radioactivity scheduled to arrive to kill the survivors in several weeks, a dismal prospect that provokes everyone to carry a suicide pill to be swallowed upon arrival of the deadly nuclear executioner.

Similarly, a television program enormously popular with teens and pre-teens, Rod Sterling's *Twilight Zone,* was peppered with episodes that depicted the effect of nuclear war on characters that included a substantial number of adolescents or preteen boys and girls.

In an eerie conjunction of fiction and reality, the release of *On the Beach* coincided with New York governor Nelson Rockefeller's espousal of a mandatory fallout shelter program that would not only require shelters in all new construction but also order retrofitting of existing homes with a "safe room" based on federal government policies that every American family should be able to fend for itself for at least two weeks after a nuclear attack. Journals that carried articles on Rockefeller's proposal also insisted that their surveys of public opinion unearthed massive resistance to such compulsion as morbid. As one article noted, "Over five hundred million dollars have been spent by the Civil Defense Office on informational pamphlets and films, but our population is almost totally ignorant on how to behave in case of nuclear war. Most hope to either die quickly or expect some authority to keep us alive."

A particularly grim calculus of Civil Defense outlays suggested that an additional twenty billion dollars in fallout shelter construction could cut the number of fatalities by twenty-six million and leave over one-quarter of Americans still more-or-less alive after a massive nuclear strike. Relatively nonsensationalist worst-case scenarios suggested that as few as one in nine Americans might still be alive even two weeks after a nuclear war, a scenario that reduced the national population back to the level of the 1840s. A *Life* magazine editorial intoned, "The number of individual survivors and their morale will determine whether the United States could survive as a nation after a nuclear war," as it somewhat morbidly calculated "We all won't be dead, that is sure."

By 1959 even eleven- or twelve-year-olds could be seen on school playgrounds debating the pros and cons of surviving a nuclear war that killed most other people. Children and preteens almost mimicked adult conversations as they debated whether a life without most friends or relatives would be worth living. Even mainstream comic books began to enter the nuclear holocaust debate. DC Comics' science fiction anthologies, such as *Mystery in Space* and *Strange Adventures*, began featuring more post–nuclear war story lines, one of the most publicized of which was "The Atomic Knights," featuring a handful of characters who survive the nuclear war of 1997 by discovering special suits of armor that provided immunity against most forms of radiation. In the bleak world of those young men and women, fireflies are now one of the most predominant species, and most of the action takes place in eerie ruins of a once-flourishing twentieth-century culture. Critics of preteen and teen culture who saw young people as clueless and shallow would have been surprised if they had taken the time to eavesdrop on adolescent conversations that so strongly mirrored the many adult dialogues of this era.

One of the major ironies of growing up at the end of the 1950s was that the technological advances that had made the extinction of human life at least somewhat feasible had also produced a growing list of breakthroughs that offered the possibility of ending drudgery and furnishing leisure and entertainment that would have been unheard of even a decade earlier. One of the iconic photographs of 1959 appeared in a national news magazine and displays facing images of thirty-one bank clerks tallying figures with adding machines and, opposite, the console of a $217,000 Visual Record Computer, which "automatically reads, sorts and records 15,000 checks a day." The accompanying article, titled "Relief from Drudgery in Banks," noted that the two-and-a-half ton "electronic computer" featured on the photo "can now do in a minute what would take a single clerk and hour to accomplish with far fewer errors. As the new automated computing machines invade offices and factories, thousands of people will be freed from boring, monotonous jobs to take on more creative, rewarding work."

Another "futuristic" innovation that was just beginning to gain widespread public attention in 1959 was the introduction of credit cards as a reliable substitute for cash payments. Department store credit was already relatively common by the late 1950s, but the concept of going cashless in a wide variety of venues was still in its infancy. As the 1960s approached, the first major credit card company, Diner's Club, was facing major competition from the new American Express Card, which had already enticed six hundred thousand people to pay a five-dollar annual fee to charge purchases at thirty-two thousand institutions worldwide. One journalist marveled that plastic credit was growing so rapidly that "if a credit card member looked around far enough, he could charge tickets to a White Sox baseball game, walk into a movie theater in Corpus Christi, Texas, and secure credit in a Reno, Nevada, casino."

The president of rival Diner's Club was even more bullish on credit cards transitioning from relative novelties to a vital part of purchasing activities. "Twenty years from now, there will only be two classes of people, those who have credit cards and those who want them," while by the beginning of the twenty-first century, "There might be a universal credit card anyone can use to buy almost anything." Two subsets of this just-emerging credit explosion were articles in news magazines that the FBI was beginning to investigate a new type of criminal, the "credit card thief," while magazines geared toward teen readers were featuring forums on whether adolescents were mature enough to use their parents' credit cards, or, if enrolled in college, whether candidates should be able to obtain cards to gain their own (limited) credit identity.

If computers and credit cards represented lifestyle changes for adults and possibly even young people in the world of the day after tomorrow, at least three solidly entrenched consumer products were undergoing major transformations as the sixties were about to begin. Transportation, home appliances, and communications were all assuming an aura of "the future is now" in 1959. Progress in each of these areas was followed as much by young people as their elders, as Americans openly wondered where this magic transformation of consumer culture would lead, while advertisers diligently took their dreams a step further toward actual purchases.

One of the most common shared dreams of American adults, adolescents, and children at the transition from the fifties to the sixties was either driving or riding in the latest model automobiles, which seemed to have reached near perfection in power, style, and comfort. Young people who viewed numerous television-aired films from two or three decades earlier often laughed aloud at the ungainly, boxy, and seemingly uncomfortable automobiles, which now seemed as dated as straw hats and plucked eyebrows. Cars of that earlier era were seen by the young as boxes on wheels compared to the tail-finned, accessory-laden ground transportation rockets that cruised the new freeways and expressways. Most male teens, and not a few females, could easily identify the difference between a 1958 and 1959 Chevrolet and Ford based on grillwork, positioning of dual headlights, and size of fins. The domination of black as a major automobile color was seen as permanently ended by two-tones, pastels, and brightness to match the NBC colorcast peacock. In many states, nearly half of new cars were convertibles, and cheap gasoline made any excuse to drive a good one.

Safety-conscious twenty-first-century drivers would cringe at splashy, colorful magazine ads that show beaming parents rolling down the highway in their finned chariots with children sitting on their mother's lap or hanging precariously out of the sides with not a seat belt in sight, yet lax driving safety seemed as safe as chain smoking in the magical world of the era's advertising.

While massive sales of the finned land rockets produced at least some possible opportunity to sample the latest in auto technology at some point, the most spectacular real-life transportation adventure of preteens and teens was to ride into the stratosphere on one of the new jet airlines. At the dawn of the Jet Age, air travel was fearfully expensive, but most kids at least knew someone who knew someone who had made it aloft, and those individuals were happy to regale those who were tethered to the ground about what jet travel was really like. For the small minority of teens who did experience jet flight, the trip was most likely far more magical than today. This was still an age of very personalized onboard service, short check-in lines, and above all an absence of security issues, in which X-ray machines were seen only in doctors' or dentists' offices, and people dressed up to fly as a natural offshoot of the adventure and pleasure of the experience.

If aerodynamic cars and jet passenger planes were harbingers of "the future" in transportation, an array of new appliances for home use seemed to be forming a chain of progress that promised to extend directly into the sixties and toward the new century a few decades beyond. As late as 1950, more than half of American homes were still heated by coal. Most washing machines still featured an external, semimanual wringer that was both tedious and dangerous to operate, and air conditioning was an experience mainly enjoyed in movie theaters.

One of the major factors in the booming prosperity of the 1950s was the ability of manufacturers to provide, and the willingness of consumers to purchase, a steady stream of relatively "hi-tech" products that reduced drudgery and increased enjoyment for most families. However, even at the end of that decade, much like fifty years later, individual households contained a fascinating mix of cutting-edge and semiobsolete appliances, largely determined by a combination of budget priorities, particular individual interests, special needs of one or more family members, and even geographic location of the household.

For example, by 1959 room air conditioners, central air conditioning sys-tems, and automobile air conditioners were all available, although none of these items could be considered inexpensive. Parents, often with some input from children, would have to determine whether any of these appliances was important enough and affordable enough to secure a place in that family. Adults shopping for a new automobile in a family with a number of teens or preteens might choose a more glamorous convertible coveted by their children and forgo a conventional car equipped with air conditioning in the interest of family excitement and happiness. Parents with children suffering from severe asthma or allergy issues might put a premium on several room air conditioners or even a then greatly expensive central air system, even though they lived in a northern state and in a neighborhood where everyone else relied for cooling on much cheaper electric fans. In another context, rather expensive automatic washer-dryer combinations that might appear rather ostentatious to some neighbors might easily emerge as a necessity for a family that recently added twins to the household, while a relatively unusual single-child family a few houses away might view an equally expensive color television as a responsible purchase in order to entice playmates to watch TV with their son or daughter.

Among the enormous variables when studying any domestic environment in history, especially when children are involved, are both the uneven nature of technology literally from one home to the next and the fact that available technology from a particular time may or may not have been in a particular home, which is more often a miniature museum of artifacts from a variety of decades. Therefore, watching a popular television situation comedy from the late 1950s might give a hint of what technology was at least available to families of that time, but this does not mean that an average American family had access to the same level of appliances or services. A large enough sampling of 1959 households would definitely produce families with color television sets, central air conditioning, room-to-room intercom systems, large freezers, and state-of-the-art stereo systems, even in relatively middle-class neighborhoods. Many of the very popular split-level houses of the era still look more "futuristic" than a twenty-first-century colonial "McMan-sion." However, much of the state-of-the-art technology existed side by side with perfectly serviceable appliances from earlier decades, and late fifties America was not yet really a "throw-away" society. A home with a remote-control color television in a very modern-design living room might have a ringer washing machine in the basement, simply because it still worked well. The adults, and even more so the adolescents and children, of the end of the 1950s reveled in discussing and reading about a future that, barring nuclear holocaust, seemed to offer comfort, speed, and excitement. One advantage of living in a society that, perhaps more than today, still continued to hold on to its past as well was that young people could see the process of change before them simply by roaming from room to room in their own houses and, ironically, by turning on that most modern of home conveniences, their television set.

One of the most significant changes in home-centered leisure activities between 1949 and 1959 was the transformation of television from a limited-use curiosity to the dominant evening recreation option for the vast majority of American families. By the last month of the fifties, between 90 and 95 percent of American households had access to at least one television, and an increasing minority of homes now possessed two or more sets, as first-generation twelve-inch models found their way into bedrooms or recreation rooms when they were displaced by the new twenty-one-inch versions that were state-of-the-art for the time.

Television opened a window on a far wider world for most American families of this time and allowed a form of vicarious time travel back to eras such as the Old West and forward into the age of space exploration, while adding a deeper dimension to contemporary life. Ten years earlier, television was primarily focused on a series of live dramas and variety programs such as *Texaco Star Theater* featuring Milton Berle, *Arthur Godfrey's Talent Scouts*, *Studio One*, and *Kraft Television Theatre*, supplemented by boxing and wrestling matches and local news. While some live drama, comedy, and variety programs could still be found in the prime-time grid in 1959, the dominant feature of television during the next decade would be in filmed series churned out by the dozen on the back lots of the three major networks from their bases in Hollywood.

The last year of the fifties represented a milestone of sorts for network television programmers as that fall a never-to-be-equaled twenty-nine prime-time Western dramas found their way to viewers' homes. In a time of Cold War uncertainty, with a fear of collectivism imposed on the rest of the world by Krushchev's Russia or Mao's China, the late fifties and early sixties Western glorified the American values of individuality, fair play, and the general triumph of good as sets representing the 1870s or 1880s somehow transmitted modern messages from characters regaled in Stetson hats and handlebar mustaches. This was a world of *Bonanza*, *Gunsmoke*, *Maverick*, *Have Gun—Will Travel*, and *Wyatt Earp* that would fascinate American families from pre-schoolers to senior citizens and then find its way to television screens from London to Hong Kong. Almost any nineteenth-century decade or locale was loosely defined as a Western, from the 1840s saga *Riverboat*, which featured adventures as far east as Pittsburgh, to *The Alaskans*, based on turn-of-the-twentieth-century gold prospectors. Modern issues often found their way into Western plot lines; for example, Christopher Colt of *Colt .45* was essentially a secret agent fighting villains who were almost proto-communists, Lucas McCain was a widowed single parent of a precocious son who could have played with Fred MacMurray's children on *My Three Sons*, and Zorro pitted democratically inclined Don Diego against a largely totalitarian police state imposed by the Spanish on early Los Angeles.

However, a trio of very popular new programs that first aired in the fall of 1959 offered that era's viewers a glimpse of possible future American issues. *One Step Beyond* and *The Twilight Zone* offered plots in which inhabitants of a society yet to come dealt with crises and complications that transcended any single decade. *Men into Space*, an expensive, tautly written CBS entry featured movie star William Lundigan as the commander of a team of astronauts who make the first successful landing on the moon in 1969. Plotlines had no bug-eyed monsters or alien invaders, with much of the drama revolving around real-life space exploration crises, such as experienced by Apollo 13, as American viewers were, in effect, braced for both the triumphs and the tragedies of a space race that was expected to be an ongoing adventure into the foreseeable future.

While the impact of teen-oriented programming on sixties adolescents will be discussed in more detail in two subsequent chapters, this chapter is a relevant place to introduce some of the more general myths and realities relating to the viewing activity of this demographic group just before the new decade dawned.

First, while adolescents tended to be, and still are, attracted substantially to programs that feature teen actors and issues, this reality in no way suggests that members of this age group simply got up and left the room when another genre began flickering on the screen. In a society with a limited number of television sets per home and a limited number of broadcast networks, an almost villagelike atmosphere emerged as family groups gathered in a living room or recreation room and watched television together, often engaging in more individualized activities as they watched. For example, many teen boys were attracted to the action and climactic resolution of the numerous Western series often cast with either primary or secondary figures little older than the teen viewers themselves. Western drama stars such as Clu Gulager, Steve McQueen, Michael Landon, or Doug McClure were often irreverent and even immature in their demeanor, a situation that related to more than a few adolescent fans. Adolescent boys and girls together often formed a large part of the fan base for almost look-alike Warner Brothers detective dramas

77 Sunset Strip, Hawaiian Eye, and *Surfside Six,* all of which devoted considerable airtime to late teen / early twenties regulars, along with a parade of troubled, in-danger clients who were little beyond adolescence themselves. Major teen idols of the sixties, such as Edd (Kookie) Byrnes, Connie Stevens, and Troy Donahue roamed Los Angeles, Honolulu, and Miami in sports cars during programs and were mobbed in public appearances nationwide. Boys and girls in steady relationships still found television viewing in either parent's living room a cheap date with free refreshments, with movie theater attendance reserved for more special formal dates. Even programs seemingly beyond the pale of teen interest—Lawrence Welk, Perry Como, or Mitch Miller—snagged some adolescent viewers by featuring an occasional pop music performer or playing toned down versions of rock and roll hits.

The third element of the triad that dominated 1959 television, along with Westerns and variety/musical programs, was the ever-popular situation comedy, which normally included some form of traditional or nontraditional family driven by a comic tension between adults and young people or among the adults themselves and the children themselves. In some respects, the year 1959 was the peak year for the iconic situation comedies that would be remembered and analyzed in future decades. In effect, this was an unusual year in which programs that were ending their primarily fifties runs, such as *Father Knows Best, The Danny Thomas Show (Make Room for Daddy),* and *The Bob Cummings Show (Love That Bob),* aired for a brief time alongside emerging new shows such as *The Donna Reed Show, Leave It to Beaver,* and *Bachelor Father,* which aired the majority of their episodes in the early sixties. In 1959 each of these programs had a significant adolescent presence while, interestingly, three of these six shows featured plotlines that deviated somewhat from the conventional family arrangement of the era. *The Danny Thomas Show* featured a transition for Thomas from marriage to widower status and then back to a second marriage; Bob Cummings was a bachelor/ surrogate father to his teenage nephew, Chuck, son of his widowed sister; and in *Bachelor Father* John Forsythe was a playboy with sole responsibility for orphaned teen niece, played by Noreen Corcoran. Of the three remaining programs, *Father Knows Best,* which was nearing the end of its long run, featured the most teen-oriented plots, considering all three children were now in some form of early, mid-, or late adolescence, while the young people on *Donna Reed* and *Leave It to Beaver* were just a little bit younger, with parents a shade less experienced with adolescent issues than the now very seasoned Jane Wyatt and Robert Young of *Father Knows Best.*

While all six of these comedies drew significant teen audiences, based on the presence of adolescent actors, articles and letters to the editors in 1959 teen-oriented magazines reveal a trio of comedies that had virtually no teen presence, yet were discussed regularly in school cafeterias or similar venues. These enormously popular programs include the just emerging *Dennis the Menace*, which featured talented young Jay North as a relatively young boy (although older than his comic strip persona); *Oh Sussana!* with comedienne Gale Storm as a harried cruise director; and *The Phil Silvers Show*, featuring that comedian as a fast-talking, conniving motor pool sergeant in a gentle satire of the peacetime army. Gale Storm and her program particularly enthralled adolescent girls, as she held both a relatively powerful yet "dream" job in which she routinely bested her chief nemesis, crusty, somewhat sexist Captain Huxley. In turn, so many adolescent boys regularly followed the comic antics of Sergeant Bilko on *The Phil Silvers Show* that it also morphed into a very widely read comic book that often featured adventures beyond the confines of the company motor pool.

Another phenomenally popular television genre that had, on the surface, minimal adolescent presence yet still was a major topic of conversation in 1959 junior and senior high schools were the headline-grabbing quiz shows that were engulfed by one of the most high profile scandals of the just-ending decade. During the 1950s, quiz shows and game shows morphed from relatively small-stakes daytime programs to prime-time events, such as *The $64,000 Question, The $64,000 Challenge*, and *Twenty-One*. These shows all featured seemingly ordinary but interesting contestants placed in an "isolation booth" and pitted against an equally formidable and interesting opponent for stakes that could be worth over a million dollars in 2010's purchasing power. However, in order to tweak ratings and drama, the producers began to rig the contests by supplying favored contestants with the answers ahead of time. Sloppy preprogramming security, combined with the wrath of disgruntled losers, produced a scandal that surged as far as congressional hearings, with the primary victim becoming Carl Van Dorn, a young Columbia University literature professor who gained wealth and a regular slot on the *Today Show* in his somewhat tainted rise to quiz show royalty. Van Dorn insisted that a major reason for his actions was an intention to prove to often-maligned, gifted teens and children that brain power was as attractive as athletic prowess, a concept that had numerous supporters in post-Sputnik America. The congressional hearings ended Van Dorn's television and academic career and, for a considerable time, reduced game shows to small-prize daytime contests. However, far more adolescents than socially ostracized, gifted teens were affected by the fall of Van Dorn and the quiz show empire.

Many Americans who believed that the now-disgraced game shows had always been a symbol of a crass, demeaning popular culture quickly shifted their energies to what some perceived to be an even greater threat to morality: the still rather new genre of rock and roll music. Just as quiz show producers were exposed rigging their product, investigation of the popular music industry revealed a new catch phrase, "payola," in which record companies bribed radio and television "disc jockeys" to provide maximum airplay to favored songs and artists. Since numerous alleged or real scandals were already leaking concerning many of the genre's top stars, the bribery angle provoked many adults to call for the virtual banning of rock and roll with the hope that teens would eventually develop an interest in a more socially acceptable music genre.

As the sixties loomed ever larger on the horizon, the most socially challenging, rebellious aspects of rock and roll seemed destined to end with the outgoing decade as an assortment of causes, from military conscription to auto and plane crashes to scandalous romantic relationships, either permanently or temporarily ended the careers of the first generation of rock and roll stars. By 1959, Buddy Holly and Richie Valens were dead, Elvis Presley was in Germany wearing military fatigues, Jerry Lee Lewis was castigated for marrying his thirteen-year-old cousin as his third bride, and Little Richard was considering a call to the ministry. Yet these titans of the still new genre were somehow being at least temporarily replaced by performers who were able to push the age threshold for interest in rock and roll to the preteen, elementary school level and open enormous opportunities for adolescent performers to become narrators of the teen experience.

The expansion of the demographics of "teen music" actually began early in the summer of 1958. As children and teenagers romped through church and school carnivals, made their first forays on local beaches and welcomed the end of the school year, two unlikely artists dueled for recognition as the number-one-selling pop record artists. Sheb Wooley, who was primarily oriented toward country music, released a pop-oriented record that was essentially a satire of the commercialism of rock and roll. The "Purple People Eater" chronicled the adventures of a "one-eyed, one-horned" space-traveling alien who simultaneously coveted a food menu composed exclusively of "purple people" while dreaming of becoming a member of a human rock and roll band. His ability to turn the horn on top of his head into a credible saxophone earns him a slot in a combo that secures a spot on a televised dance party and fabulous royalties for Wooley in real life. An equally unlikely rock star emerged that summer from the mind of producer David Seville, who used a clever series of overdubbed nonsense phrases in a dialogue between a lovestruck young man and his unlikely counselor, who is a jungle resident shaman. "Witch Doctor" featured scenarios as unlikely as Wooley's horn-headed alien, which Seville embellished at the end of the year into a franchise that continued into the twenty-first century.

Seville expanded the nonsense verse concept into three characters, Simon, Theodore, and cantankerous leader Alvin, known as the Chipmunks, into a blockbuster holiday song simply titled "The Chipmunk Song (Christmas Don't Be Late)," in which the stubborn Alvin answers queries about his Christmas gift list by insisting he still wants a Hula Hoop, which had been the most publicized craze of the previous summer and had now essentially become a national joke as piles of unwanted hoops cluttered toy stores.

Record store owners began noticing a huge spike in preteen and even child record purchases thanks to the "Purple People Eater" and to the "Witch Doctor/Chipmunks," and record company executives now began to realize that the relative downturn in teen record sales caused by the temporary or permanent elimination of major stars could be largely counteracted by expanding the target age group downward. Record industry publicists began latching onto this new preteen, early adolescent subgenre of "novelty tunes," but during 1959 it became even more difficult to separate "novelty" and "mainstream" teen music. This final year of the fifties saw the emergence of fourteen-year-old Dodie Stevens with her huge hit, "Pink Shoe Laces," TV horror movie host John Zacherle's "Dinner with Drac," and college student/ singing duo Jan and Dean's "Baby Talk." Each song featured the catchy beat and lyrics of traditional rock and roll but featured satirical lyrics that poked gentle fun at the seriousness of very young romance.

Soon young television and film stars were flocking to recording studios to diversify their careers as Annette Funicello, Hayley Mills, and Connie Stevens often merged visual and audio media with tie-ins. For example, Mills publicized her comedy about separated identical twins in *The Parent Trap* with her overdubbed duet "We Go Together," while Stevens poked fun at the hair combing fetish of young *77 Sunset Strip* star Edd (Kookie) Byrnes in her duet "Kookie, Kookie, Lend Me Your Comb." For young adolescents of 1959 who would primarily experience their teen years in the next decade, much of their orientation to rock and roll would come more from these probably misnamed "novelty" sources than from the more serious-minded romantic ballads of the fifties. Some of the early icons of the genre were merely temporarily dormant and would reinvent themselves in the upcoming decade, adding sixties teens to their base audience of fifties adolescents. Jackie Wilson, Chuck Berry, and most certainly Elvis Presley would find the upcoming decade and its teens a fertile ground for new hits and audiences. A second group, most notably Jerry Lee Lewis and Little Richard, would become revered as "founders" of the new music and always find guest spots on national and local music programs. Yet even by 1959 they were perpetually in "oldies" mode, caught forever in a time warp of "signature songs" that always had a 1950s copyright. The third group, Buddy Holly, Richie Valens, and Eddie Cochrane, all of whom died in 1959 or 1960, would gain permanent legendary status as they were forever young, dying at an age only marginally older than their fans, leaving grieving teen widows who might have sat next to any other adolescents in a typical classroom.

Each of these three categories of rock and roll performers—the often very young and often female "novelty" performers, the living "founders" of the "beat," and the dead martyrs etched into visual and auditory amber—were in a state of confluence as the old decade neared its end and the new decade loomed ever larger.

Several thousand miles from congressional investigations of "payola" in rock and roll and magazine editorials predicting that this vulgar music was doomed to extinction, people living under a far different social and political system viewed American teen culture as the first wave of a hopefully peaceful and prosperous future. During the summer and early autumn of 1959, a temporary truce was called to the Cold War as fifty thousand Russians per day trooped into a Moscow fair that was simply called the American Exhibit. Within shouting distance of the Kremlin, ordinary Muscovites were guided by young Americans through a technological wonderland of plastic baby bottles, frozen foods, and multicolored kitchen appliances. An enormous new IBM computer, the RAMAC, featured a huge screen with four thousand questions about American life that could be selected and answered by the multitude of visitors.

Yet American news magazines gushing about the impact of their nation's technological wizardry on this Marxist audience admitted with obvious mixed feelings that "the longest lines and largest crowds gather to see rock and rollers in sporty sweaters and skirts give rock and roll dance exhibitions," admitting that "Thousands of Russians were lured here by teen fashion and the big beat of the music."

By 1959, in the shadow of scandals, adult outcries, and often inaccurate or exaggerated films, American teenagers had developed a distinctive appearance, musical taste, and vocabulary that overshadowed even the decidedly youth-oriented Jazz Age and swing years. During the final year of the fifties, the first contingent of Baby Boomers had become teenagers, and tens of millions more would follow into that status in the upcoming decade. The portal to one of the most "teenage intensive" decades in history was now opening. It remained only to discover how that era would affect American adolescents and the adults and children who would be interacting with them.

CHAPTER TWO

~

Teen Family Life and Social Life

As nearly 180 million Americans greeted the arrival of the soaring sixties in January of 1960, political leaders, census officials, and educators were already discussing ways in which the tidal wave of rising teenagers could be accommodated in a nation that was not particularly prepared to deal with them. The surge in teenagers was not exactly a crisis in the traditional sense, as expected rises in teen consumption would become a major linchpin in maintaining a vibrant economy, but for the parents of preteens and adolescents, simply finding the money and room for their burgeoning progeny would be a major challenge for the entire decade.

Five decades later, in a society with generally larger houses and smaller families, the domestic environment of sixties teenagers, their younger siblings, and their parents would seem relatively cramped and overcrowded. The postwar housing boom had already produced millions of new dwellings with many more on the way, but the average new home of that era had perhaps one-half of the floor space of a comparable 2010 model. By modern standards, bedrooms and bathrooms would seem somewhat cramped, halls narrow, and ceilings low. Basements and cellars, a fixture of Victorian architecture, had given way to concrete slabs, and the highly touted two-car garage was often so jammed with power mowers, bicycles, and baby carriages that even one auto could not be squeezed inside. A combination of thin walls, ascendant one-floor house plans, and entertainment devices seldom equipped with headphones often produced a noise level in which young children, adolescents, and parents all took equal responsibility for a constant din.

Added to the simple fact that a 1960s family, on average, had 50 to 100 percent more children than their 2010 equivalent, teen (or adult) complaints about a house being too quiet was not a likely primary concern.

The domestic environment of a typical sixties teenager tended to exist against a backdrop of sharing, negotiation, and compromise, all on higher levels of frequency than several decades later. A fairly typical family household of the 1960s contained between three and four children, which, unless it contained rather young parents, stood an excellent chance of housing one or more preteens or teenagers. Since the social mores of the time frowned upon the idea of boys and girls sharing a bedroom much beyond the stage of infancy, and most average- to above-average-size families could not provide every child with his or her own room, many teens spent much of their adolescence with a roommate, or perhaps even two, of very different ages than themselves. One of the most popular sixties situation comedies, *Leave It to Beaver*, utilized this situation to excellent effect, as Wally and Beaver Cleaver, who are perhaps five years apart in age, share a bedroom, pairing first a boy and an early teen and later a preteen with a fully developed teenager, who exhibits a very realistic combination of love, advice, and exasperation with his younger sibling. This scene was repeated with multiple variations throughout the sixties. Sometimes the paired siblings were girls; sometimes three relatively similarly aged siblings shared quarters; and sometimes the roommates had much more significant age differences than did the Cleaver kids. Yet all of these situations required more sharing and compromise and perhaps offered more bonding than single-occupied rooms. Since many sixties families living in relatively cramped conditions were eager to move into more spacious quarters when and if finances permitted, a switch to a larger home could often initiate a property settlement "divorce" between two roommates who now found themselves in separate bedrooms. For more than a few teens, "custody" of the old room television and record player became an uncomfortable preview of the adult experience of marital separation.

Thus two of the most readily discernable differences between teen home life in the 1960s and five decades later were the realities of less overall privacy that teens often crave and a greater expectation of sharing communication and entertainment devices, such as telephones, television sets, and sound equipment. Growing up in households containing nearly twice as many children as their twenty-first-century equivalents produced an incursion on adolescent desire for privacy that sometimes prompted a need to discover personal space somewhere other than the bedroom. A relatively unused portion of an attic, basement, or even porch or garage often served the need for personal space when a bedroom contained one or more potentially prying siblings. The twenty-first-century ritual of shutting out unwanted adult intrusions by simply shutting the bedroom door and donning earphones or headphones was simply not as practical in this time, yet there is no indication that teens were any less drawn to some private space free of unwanted incursions.

The often volatile exercise of sharing entertainment and communication devices was actually a more major issue in the early years of the sixties than it would be later in the decade. A fairly typical family home in 1960 featured two telephones, one usually located in a public domain of the kitchen, living room, or entrance hall and a second in the parental bedroom; one television set, usually located in the living room; and one sound system, also most likely located in the living room. In the very recent past, perhaps the previous two to three years, a growing number of teenagers had gained access to a transistor radio or a small portable record player designed to play 45 rpm "singles." These two devices, sometimes combined with teen children inheriting the family's "cast off" twelve-inch first-generation television set, constituted the bedroom entertainment and communication array of relatively fortunate teens at the very beginning of the decade. The transistor radio was usually the most prized of these devices, as it was very portable, had an earphone jack for personal listening, and was still quite expensive, worth over two hundred dollars in 2010 currency. A typical teen used his or her transistor radio two to four hours a day everywhere from bedrooms to beaches. On the other hand, the portable 45 rpm record player, while still coveted, usually suffered from a lack of speaker capacity, which produced a sound just as "tinny" as the transistor radio and was usually incapable of playing the just emerging array of 33 rpm long-play albums. The teens who wanted to play LPs or use the telephone were usually required to use devices still primarily under direct control of parents.

During the first half of the sixties decade, many teens found that access to communication and entertainment devices substantially improved due to a number of significant technical and advertising breakthroughs. First, providers of telephone services and equipment began to understand the enormous desire of preteens and adolescents to have access to phone devices free from what was generally considered to be adult intrusion, which meant, in essence, any parent within listening distance of a "private" conversation. Telephone expansion continued with a massive television and magazine advertising campaign offering attractive prices for the installation of a separate phone line for use of younger patrons and an attractively designed "princess" phone for preteen or adolescent daughters, which featured slim styling, multiple color variations, and illuminated dials. While there was no male equivalent of a princess phone for teenage boys, there is little evidence that they appreciated parental "intrusion" on conversations any more than their female counterparts, and many of them were just as appreciative of receiving their own line, even with a generic black device.

At the same time that the phone companies discovered the profitability of providing personalization of teen communications, television and music appliance corporations were heading in the same direction. For example, early in the sixties, the General Electric Corporation scored a major breakthrough in portable television technology. Portable televisions had emerged in the late 1950s as cheaper, more mobile versions of the heavy, expensive "consoles" that often became the centerpiece of family living room furniture. However, "portable" televisions were initially relatively heavy devices that were moved room to room on wheeled stands and not particularly easy to lift by hand. The breakthrough GE model largely substituted thin plastic for metal housing and reduced the weight to a truly portable ten pounds and the price down to ninety-nine dollars. Thousands of these "super portables" were soon found in teenagers' bedrooms, and the earphone jack capability allowed many adolescents to simply bypass adult viewing choices on the living room console.

At about the same time as the new generation of cheap, portable televisions emerged, music appliance manufacturers began offering relatively cheap, teen-oriented portable stereo systems, which usually featured a turntable, now capable of both single and LP use and equipped with small, mobile speakers that could be located in a wide variety of places. Now parents could regain total control of the more expensive sound system for their show-tune albums or swing records while teens retreated to other venues to listen to their own music. These technological and marketing breakthroughs did not totally end the "sharing" dilemma in still rather overcrowded homes, but they did tend to reduce parent/teen conflict over entertainment and communications—no small victory for both sides.

If 1960s teens had to accept less privacy and more sharing than their twenty-first-century counterparts, they could console themselves with the realization that a combination of three demographic realities that marked their particular generation of American families combined to produce a certain uniqueness in the sixties teen experience compared to earlier or later generations.

The first reality is that during the 1960s a majority of American preteens and adolescents lived in an environment where at least one parent was routinely available when the kids arrived home from school. A combination of the general economic prosperity that pervaded most of the decade and the social and cultural milieu in which most sixties parents had spent their own childhoods and adolescences made it possible for very large numbers of parents, usually mothers, either to devote their primary energies to domestic and family issues, or, at the very least, to arrange their work schedules around children's school schedules. While there were numerous exceptions to this situation, much of the adolescent experience in this decade revolved around a reality of parental accessibility for aid in school projects, attendance at school events, transportation for nondrivers, and even aid in some home-work assignments. Even in an ongoing teen quest for privacy, the availability of parental aid, advice, and concern was generally conceded to be more of an asset than a liability.

The second reality of teen family life in this decade was that well over four of every five teenagers spent their adolescence in a two-parent house-hold. While there is no way to gauge whether the majority of these intact marriages were particularly happy, most serious studies of adolescent devel-opment do agree that two-parent households prove very advantageous to student success in school. The sixties would be the last decade before the American divorce rate began to soar toward the 50 percent level, so the teens of that decade often benefited from a combination of a relatively prosperous economy and relatively stable family life, neither of which is as much in evidence five decades later.

A third reality of the sixties teen domestic experience is the fact that a very significant number of adolescents were able to accomplish a feat that their parents had not—they would graduate from high school. The 1960s represents the first full decade in which acquiring a high school diploma became a "normal" part of the teen experience. As will be seen in a later chapter, the discrepancy of educational accomplishment between sixties young people and their parents would sometimes provoke generational con-flict and incivility, but in a broader sense, the rise in possession of a high school diploma from under 50 percent of the population to nearly 90 percent of that decade's adolescents was a vital factor in the promotion of affluence and status in subsequent decades of the American experience. Some sixties teens could be amazingly arrogant in their condescending attitude toward less academically credentialed parents, and some of those parents could be exasperating in displaying a "martyr" complex over their lack of educational opportunity compared to what was available to their children. Yet the ten-sions that arose in this dispute should not mask the genuine accomplish-ments of this particular teen cohort.

While much of the adolescent experience outside the school consisted of interaction with parents and siblings, social relations with peers occupied an increasingly prominent place in the teen cosmos with each year further removed from childhood. While most teens and parents in relatively advanced societies experience the bittersweet, sometimes-confusing process of transformation from child to "adult in training," families in the 1960s dealt with at least some issues that were rather different than the experience of either five decades later or five decades earlier. Some of these realities might have tended to smooth the inevitable transition; others, perhaps, made the process more complicated or stressful.

Two of the major aspects of adolescent social life in the 1960s that were both quite new and substantially different from many of the realities of the twenty-first century were the institutionalization of "going steady" as the most important and sought-after relation among teens, and the noticeable tendency for young people to marry before they ended their teenage years. While the next chapter will focus on the impact of the American high school experience on these realities, this chapter will focus on teen social life outside of the direct impact of the secondary school.

One of the most challenging aspects of parenthood of adolescent children in the 1960s was the need to understand a teen social life that, in some ways, had altered enormously since the time those adults were adolescents themselves. A generation earlier, when sixties parents were teens, terms such as "stag lines" at dances and "playing the field" in dating, combined with strong association among groups of boys or groups of girls and ongoing economic distress, all tended to delay serious romantic relationships, especially for adolescents who expected to graduate from high school. Now rituals that seemed alien to adults yet natural to teens produced concern among parents, educators, and specialists in adolescent psychology. Just as a generation or more earlier, preteens and early adolescents sought admission to or simply formed a peer group of the same gender and then, in most cases, selected one or two "best friends" from the slightly wider circle.

However, almost simultaneous with that process, sixties adolescents, encouraged by dances for many young teens, the lyrics of popular music, and sometimes even their parents, started a process of finding a "steady" relationship that could run in length from a matter of weeks to years. Magazine advertisements of this period mirror the mixed messages of the time. They show groups of boys or girls sometimes having fun separately, sometimes together, especially in ads for soft drinks, snack foods, or entertainment products, while featuring romantic "steady" couples in personal grooming and many fashion ads. A television program, such as *Leave It to Beaver*, shows Wally Cleaver palling around with Eddie Haskell and Lumpy Rutherford, but it seems that he is mostly marking time between his quests for new dating relationships.

Similarly, an episode of *The Patty Duke Show* evokes the startled surprise of Patty's parents when her geeky preteen brother graduates from ant farms and equally geeky male friends to a quest for steady status after being smitten by a pocket-size girl at a sixth grade dance.

Sixties parents were often fascinated yet confused about the ability their teenage children developed in balancing some form of relationship with same-sex friends with a time-consuming relationship with an opposite sex "steady." The energy required for this balancing act is a major plotline for the hugely successful *Grease*, which is set only a few months before the onset of the sixties and chronicles Danny Zuko (played by John Travolta) in his attempts to maintain a steady relationship with the prudish Sandy Olson (Olivia Newton-John), simultaneous to leadership of a somewhat hell-raising group of black-leather-jacketed semihoodlums. The unanswered backstory to this plot might well be the questions of how many previous times Danny Zuko has initiated the same balancing act.

The prominence of going steady in sixties teen social life can be discerned easily in the numerous articles and letters to the editor in the broad spectrum of teen magazines published during that era. One subject that repeatedly emerges is the related questions of the proper age to initiate the search for a steady and ways to maximize success in this process. Surprisingly, the huge volume of articles and letters on this topic provides such diverse possibilities that no particularly cogent answers actually emerge. The apparently expert advice of one sage who tacitly accepts some form of steady arrangement in junior high school is apparently totally contradicted in a later issue of the same magazine by a dissenting opinion that sixteen or seventeen is a more proper time to begin dating. Some articles advise girls to aggressively pursue potential "steady material" boys; others roundly criticize any form of female pursuit.

Even if a teen boy or girl could navigate the treacherous waters of contradictory "expert" advice on finding a steady, there was considerable divergence on proper symbols to advertise that sought-after condition. Exchange of school rings or school sweaters might be appropriate for upper high school grades, while younger steadies might have to make do with matching charm bracelets or exchange of school photos. One recurring fad during this decade was the practice of the steady boys and girls dying their hair the same color, with the preferred tint being different from either person's natural hue.

There is little doubt that steady status was the social coin of the realm for much of the sixties and was seen by teenagers as a utilitarian necessity in a decade in which during several years the single most common age for new brides was eighteen. What is less clear is the determination of parental level of acceptance or opposition to a rather ritualistic relationship that had been far less prevalent in the parents' own years of adolescence.

National news and opinion magazines of the early to mid-1960s carried numerous articles concerning the impact of going steady on a demographic group many journalists still termed "teen-agers." There is little evidence on the extent to which adolescents read these features, but it is quite evident that the theme of parental disapproval of at least some types of steady relationships was enormously useful for American popular songwriters. Parental disapproval of some elements of teen romances became a virtual subgenre of rock music of the early sixties. This trend began with at best a cloak of historical camouflage when Johnny Preston scored a major hit in the new decade with "Running Bear," a tale of two American Indian adolescents who had the bad luck to belong to rival tribes and drown in their vain attempt to meet in the middle of the river that represented the tribal boundary.

General parental opposition to the youthful age of steadies became a predictable hit maker, ranging from Bobby Soxx and The Blue Jeans' "Not Too Young to Get Married," Del Shannon's "Keep Searchin' (We'll Follow the Sun)," and Tommy James and the Shondells' "I Think We're Alone Now." Romantic entanglements among couples who belong to a different social class was a convenient vehicle for "parental protest" records, such as Dickey Lee's "Patches," which suggests a poor girl–rich boy, parentally induced breakup that results in a double suicide, while Joey Powers's "Midnight Mary," Billy Joe Royal's "Down in the Boondocks," and the Shangri-La's "Leader of the Pack" all suggest an opposite economic gulf that results in a secret marriage, in the Powers song, or the death of the male protagonist, in the Shangri-La's tale. Perhaps the best a parent could hope for in the world of parental-disapproval rock songs was indirect responsibility for disasters, such as in J. Frank Wilson's lament in "Last Kiss" that he swerved into a fatal accident for his female love while "driving his Daddy's car," without commentary on parental support or opposition to the ill-fated relationship.

Parental disapproval themes were a reliable path to a significant rock and roll hit in what were essentially three-minute audio knockoffs of *Romeo and Juliet*, but a perusal of journal articles, relevant television programs, and print and television advertising reveals more tacit approval of teen social mores than denunciations. For example, a surprisingly large number of photographs of teen couples in articles concerning the impact of going steady shows a boy and girl sitting on a couch or sprawled on the floor, albeit doing homework and watching television, surrounded by nonchalant adults and children more intent on watching *Rawhide* or *Leave It to Beaver* than in criticizing the teens. A surprisingly high percentage of parents interviewed admitted that they preferred knowing who was dating their son or daughter, and knowing where they were at the moment was more important than forcing the child into a more surreptitious relationship.

Another way in which parents could, at least indirectly, monitor either teen steadies or groups of teens who hoped to find steadies was by providing young people with that archetypal sixties housing upgrade: the family recreation room. Period television programs, television commercials, and magazine advertisements are replete with references to this new concept in home design. Manufacturers of everything from sound systems to tile flooring invariably seemed to depict their product in a recreation room environment in which the major variations seem to be in whether the beaming, telegenic inhabitants are all members of one family from parents down to youngsters or several obviously steady couples dancing, playing ping-pong, or sorting through records. Virtually every significant soft drink company—Coca Cola, Pepsi Cola, Royal Crown Cola, 7UP, Hire's Root Beer, and Canada Dry—essentially utilized the same tableaux, with the exception that everyone was enjoying only the advertized soft drink. In fact, even primarily "adult" magazines such as *Life* and *Look* seem to have employed as many soft drink ads in recreation rooms for photogenic teens as cigarette ads for only marginally older "young adults." The implicit video and print message is that recreation rooms of some type were the rooms where teens "wanted to be" and where adults tacitly wanted them. The implication was that a workable compromise between parents and teens, especially those in dating relationships, was an environment where adults largely remained in living rooms watching television or even socializing by playing bridge or listening to state-of-the-art stereo systems while teens played records or ping-pong in a separate room just out of range of but still loosely under parental supervision. This basic premise even carried over in warmer seasons or warmer climates to the sixties boom in outdoor barbeque areas, swimming pools, and teen-oriented recreation facilities such as basketball courts. Here again numerous television and print advertisements strongly suggest that parents were willing to forgo direct supervision in return for the knowledge that teen behavior would be relatively restrained.

Despite numerous articles critical of going steady, in almost every print medium from news magazines to parents' and religious periodicals it appears that many parents to some degree accepted the reality that teen preoccupation with finding and keeping steady girlfriends or boyfriends could not be eradicated. A large number of parents admitted to their peers that the steady relationships that their teens had formed did offer some positive attributes, such as the ability to learn more about their child's steady partner and the willingness of many couples to save limited funds by remaining close to home much of the time, as long as entertainment facilities were available and adults were not overly intrusive.

One of the paradoxes of sixties teen culture is that teen-oriented magazines repeatedly featured letters to the editor and articles stressing the willingness of adolescent couples to both save money and placate parents by spending considerable amounts of free time in one or the other of the family homes, while numerous popular songs and films supported by national news magazine articles proclaimed the ascendency of a "car culture" among young people. How could teens be playing records in the basement recreation room if they were simultaneously "cruising" streets and highways that seemed perpetually clogged with other adolescents?

The simplest answer to this apparent paradox is that teens of the era were essentially engaged in both activities, sometimes in the same afternoon or evening, while the equally valid, complex answer is that the highest demand for automobile utilization was actually among teens who wanted to have a steady boyfriend or girlfriend and were using a car in a quest for that special person.

Teens and automobiles had become a natural combination from the time that Jazz Age adolescents realized a cheap, used Model T Ford could be the key to escaping adult oversight as a young couple interacted on the front porch swing. The affluence of the 1950s enhanced this relationship as motorized vehicles ranging from powerful sedans to custom-made "hot rods," and even motorcycles, implied power and freedom from adult supervision. Most aspects of the teen-auto alliance were simply enhanced in the even more affluent sixties as auto manufacturers scrambled to dazzle young motorists with seemingly rocket-propelled, low-slung "sports cars," ranging from extremely pricey Jaguar XK-Es, Corvette Stingrays, and Ford Thunderbirds to slightly more functional Chevrolet Camaros and Ford Mustangs.

During most of the decade, particularly between 1960 and 1965, one of the most significant music genres for most teens was "car songs," which included gentle satires on driving, for example the Playmates' "Beep Beep" and Paul Evans' "Seven Little Girls Sitting in the Back Seat"; pride-of-ownership themes, including the Beach Boys' "Shut Down" and "409," the Rip Chords' "Hey Little Cobra," and Ronny and the Daytonas' "G.T.O."; and "teen opera" car tragedies, such as Jan and Dean's "Dead Man's Curve" and J. Frank Wilson's "Last Kiss." Sometimes even a "less is better" theme prevailed, as in the Hondells' romp on a motorbike in "Little Honda" or the Beach Boys' offer to provide substitute experiences for a girl who has been forced to surrender use of her Thunderbird to her father in "Fun, Fun, Fun." Some form of car chase pervades almost every teen high school film, from *The Explosive Generation* in 1961 to *Maryjane* in 1968.

Most of the decade's car songs and films evoke a sense of competition, showing off, adventure, and daring, laced with occasional tragedy. Yet for most of the era's teens outside of such anomalies as the most densely populated centers of New York City and a few other very large urban downtowns, access to an automobile was simply a necessity for an adolescent social life, even if the only car available was a decidedly unsporty parental station wagon or a cheap secondhand car well past its prime.

Boys and girls who had formed steady relationships were certainly willing to save limited funds and gain a certain sense of parental affirmation by doing homework on the floor in a family living room or playing records in the recreation room. Yet a car was still very desirable for a number of activities ranging from driving to various venues to "show off" their partner to presumably envious friends, to attending movies, dances, or school athletic contests or, most notably, securing some level of privacy for the couple.

Ironically, while sixties steady couples viewed access to an automobile as an instrument to function independently of their respective sets of parents, many of their adolescent activities were somewhat unconsciously emulating married adults as teens settled into committed relationships that often evolved into virtual trial marriages. Automobiles that theoretically offered teen couples the opportunity to escape adult supervision in many respects offered teens little more than the opportunity to simply act like married couples. Television programs, documentaries, and films of the era all quite frequently show teens in a supermarket with the boy pushing a shopping cart as his girlfriends loads in items for purchase, bored-looking boys impatiently waiting for their girlfriends to decide on clothing purchases standing over adult men looking just as unenthused, or bored-looking teen girls watching their boyfriends make purchases in a sporting goods store blending with married women barely concealing their own exasperation with their husbands' very similar activities.

Also, while automobile availability theoretically provided an opportunity to escape the prying eyes of parents, many times the car was simply being utilized to travel to venues where groups of boys and girls split off into male and female circles that talked and acted not that much differently than their parents, with the major difference being the background music playing on the sound system.

One of the ironies of the impact of the automobile on dating couples of the sixties is that while dramatic films and television programs often imply that accessibility of a car is a form of rebellion in which the young couple seeks intimacy in the privacy of a local "lover's lane," or even uses the car to elope and get married against parental wishes, most television documentaries and magazine photo essays depict teen couples using the auto to do far more mundane activities, from shopping to attending social events that look startlingly similar to what the adults are doing at the same time.

If teen steady couples viewed an automobile as a vehicle to attain privacy, evoke envy, or mingle with similarly committed couples, access to a car was often far more important to the social life of teens who had either never achieved the security of "steady" status or were attempting to achieve this status once again. Until fairly late in the decade, sixties film, television, and literature tended to portray uncommitted single adults as either slightly bizarre or objects of pity by the overwhelming majority of the population that was, at least officially, "happily married." Throughout at least two-thirds of the decade, "normal life" meant "married life." Television programs featuring single, professional characters—Mr. Novak, Ben Casey, Dr. Kildare—strongly implied that the character's singleness was temporary, as evidenced by the steady stream of possible matches in other regular characters or guest stars. Most of the now-burgeoning suburbs were dominated by married couples, interspersed with a few divorced or widowed individuals who were actively seeking to restore their marital status.

This "couples" orientation was so pervasive that even as parents exhorted their teens to "behave themselves," they were also tacitly matchmaking by organizing "at home" parties or chaperoning school dances that often involved preteens. Friends, neighbors, and relatives were often less than discreet in asking parents of teens what was "wrong" with their son or daughter who seemed either unable or unwilling to enter adolescent social life, with even less discreet admonitions directed at the teens themselves. In most areas of the United States, the search for that "steady" partner who would confer social acceptance on a teen involved some level of access to an automobile. George Lucas's semiautobiographical chronicle of teen life in early sixties small-town California captures the central role of the car in adolescent dating rituals. The action in *American Graffiti* takes place almost exclusively from dusk to dawn on one September night in 1962, as teens endlessly cruise the streets of a small city, ever vigilant to the prospects for potential partners. The passenger configuration in the autos changes almost constantly, as boys and girls switch vehicles and pass on information of the possible current location of likely matches with stops at the drive-in restaurant to recharge for the next round of flirting.

American Graffiti, which was released in the early 1970s, accurately depicts one of the ironies of sixties "car culture," the fact that there were more adolescents eager to drive than there were automobiles to accommodate them. Access to a car offered unattached teens access to meeting places beyond school and immediate neighborhoods. These venues included drive-in movies, where teens often spent as much time socializing as viewing the film, dining locations including drive-in restaurants, diners, and ice cream stands, and the increasingly lucrative and well-attended dances run by local disc jockeys, which contributed a major supplement to radio station incomes. During the second half of the decade, the rapid emergence of enclosed shopping malls initiated a soon-to-be iconic teen meeting place, but again, many of these emporiums were primarily accessible by automobile.

The 1960s was roughly the midpoint of a now nearly century-long process of movement toward automobiles as the primary transportation mode in the United States. During the decade, American families were in the process of transition from one car to two cars, as the postwar suburbanization of the nation and the ever-diminishing public transit options in many locales were encouraging consumers to seriously consider availability of an automobile for both husband and wife. However, the United States had not begun to approach the reality of the 2010s experience where there are almost as many automobiles registered as there are licensed drivers. Compared to contemporary design and manufacturing standards, the powerful, finned vehicles of the late fifties and sixties tended to have shorter spans of serviceability, thus producing a smaller pool of drivable vehicles.

One significant route to automobile accessibility for teens in the 2010s is for parents to pass on what have now become "second tier" cars to their teen children as the parents purchase new vehicles for themselves. Many sixties teens had to settle for borrowing one of the parental cars when and if the parents were not using them. Thus, even though sixties teen life was often quite automobile dependent, the logistics of car availability were far more complex and often resulted in ride sharing among two or more friends. The 1960s was still an era of substantial amounts of "double dating," with two couples dependent on availability of what were primarily parental vehicles or, in the case of boys or girls attempting to find potential girlfriends or boyfriends, the need to engage in group excursions, which could significantly complicate the process of meeting suitable companions. For example, a boy attempting to establish common ground with a new female acquaintance at a diner or record shop could often be subject to the whims of the friend who drove him there and who might now be getting bored as he realized that there were no likely prospects for his own consideration. In turn, a double date could be complicated when the two boys, who might be close friends, would find themselves attempting to maintain civil relations with two girls who were not nearly so friendly with each other. Teen magazine advice columns from this era are filled with queries or complaints revolving around what was essentially an ongoing reality, that America's burgeoning car culture still had gaping holes when it came to automobile accessibility for the nation's exploding teen population.

One of the most common ways for teens, especially teen boys, to fill this looming car availability gap was to purchase an automobile for themselves. Attempts to secure funds for a personal vehicle were regular plots or subplots for television comedies and teen films, but parents, teachers, and authorities on adolescent development were not always amused by this process. Teens who chose to remain in school could never hope to purchase new cars on part-time job wages, and therefore many adolescents were thought by adults to be jeopardizing academic success by being sucked into a dual trap in which they worked significant hours that should have been utilized for academic pursuits in part-time work to earn money for a car, but then spent additional time in repairing or restoring a car that was effectively beyond its prime driving life. One ongoing sixties parental nightmare was a form of addiction in which a child, usually a boy, spent so much time working for a car and then repairing that car that academic success was shortchanged and college admission became more problematic.

For most sixties teens, family life and social life represented two often interchangeable portions of a third that defined their lives between the onset of adolescence and the beginning of the college experience. The third pillar of this triad, also somewhat interchangeable with the other two experiences, was probably the most familiar symbol of the teen experience to Americans and even foreigners. This was the institution called the high school. It permeated and defined the adolescent experience of this decade to an enormous degree. The sixties was the first decade that the vast majority of American teens not only attended high school but graduated with a diploma. In a world where even advanced societies largely dismissed most adolescents at fifteen or sixteen with rather nebulous "school" certificates and provided relatively few nonacademic activities for those who remained, the American high school of this decade was an all-encompassing experience that most teens experienced to the fullest. Even family life and social life often seemed dependent on what went on beyond the entrance to High School, USA.

CHAPTER THREE

~

High School, USA

Barely two years after the nation's secondary schools had been the focal point for public outrage and fear in the wake of the Soviet launch of Sputnik satellites, high school administrators girded themselves for a new crisis that had been years in the making but still offered no easy solution. At the beginning of the 1960s, as the children born before the onset of the Baby Boom streamed out of high schools to accept relatively plentiful seats in college or career opportunities, a massive tide of their younger siblings was inundating a secondary school system only marginally prepared to accommodate them.

For the first time in American history, virtually an entire generation of adolescents would not only enter high school but complete their course of study all the way to graduation. Those sixties teens would begin high school only half a step out of childhood and graduate with an unsure step toward some level of adult experience. They were about to enter a unique place, a private world within a world where the pressures of learning and social life and maturing would all be focused. They were boys and girls who were enjoying the excitement of a wonderful moment called youth, but they would be experiencing those emotions in a wider society that was undergoing its own transformation. These sixties teens entered high school clutching at a childhood that was slipping away too fast while seeking to enter a more adult universe that still seemed just out of reach.

Because of their numbers and their residence in a decade where the entire nation was increasingly obsessed by youth, the high school experience of the sixties teens would be even more parsed, more investigated, and more photographed than their already iconic fifties counterparts. The first part of an ongoing series on teens and high school in a September 1963 issue of *Life* magazine introduced the first class of seniors who had experienced high school entirely in the sixties decade. "There they stand for their class portrait, a crop of high school seniors—earnest, brash and vulnerable, trying to choose a face to show to the camera. Someday, much later, they will find the picture with a small smile and an ache of how young they looked then. And back will come the special time when life keeps changing and changing, and everything, good or bad, is supercharged."

That supercharged atmosphere experienced by high school students of most generations would be even more noticeable in the sixties decade, as demographic, cultural, social, and technological changes would all conspire to make the world of a student in 1961 dramatically different than that of a younger sibling attending the same school in 1969. Therefore, this chapter will focus primarily on the high school experience during the first half of the decade, while an exploration of the second half will follow later.

One interesting way to explore teen life in an early to midsixties high school is to employ a twenty-first-century vehicle, a "virtual tour" of a typical high school and its denizens about midway through the first half of the sixties. The date of this tour will be Monday, October 1, 1962, in an autumn in which the Yankees and Giants will soon be dueling in the World Series, the AFL and NFL are still rival leagues, the new CBS program *The Beverly Hillbillies* is the surprise hit of the new season, and "Sherry," the first significant release by a new group called the Four Seasons, is dueling for top record status with "Monster Mash" by Bobby "Boris" Pickett.

A twenty-first-century "virtual visitor" to one of the approximately twenty-five thousand high schools then in session would probably notice the first impacts of the Boomer surge through the architecture of the school, which would often be either a very new building or contain a large new wing attached to the original structure. Another initial shock for this twenty-first-century visitor would be the comparative lack of security concerns when entering or strolling around the building. While the entrance might include a "visitors please report to the main office" sign, a reasonably well-dressed visitor could probably bypass that office, unless he or she were in a high-crime-area school, and stroll the halls until a concerned student or faculty member asked if the visitor needed help in locating a specific room. On the other hand, a profusion of black-and-yellow signs would quickly inform a visitor of the nature of the most highly perceived danger to the welfare of the students in that era. These signs directed boys and girls to the school fallout shelter in case of nuclear attack, and before the month of our tour was over, most students would pay substantial attention to that location as America and Russia teetered on the brink of thermonuclear war over Cuba.

The sheer physical energy and the conversations laced with teen-oriented dialogue would be quite familiar to this twenty-first-century visitor, but phrases such as "awesome," "hot," or "oh, my God!" would be replaced with "boss," "bitchin'," or "sharp," interspersed with a few carryover slang terms from the 1950s such as "cool," "far out," and "crazy."

The same blend of familiarity and difference would emerge after a perusal of the fashions worn by these early sixties teens. By 1962, many, but not all, of the classic 1950s fashion statements had disappeared from everyday teen use. The poodle skirt, which was still very popular as late as 1959, had been replaced with shorter skirts, often paired with knee socks. Some boys still roamed school halls with black leather jackets, peg pants, and cleat shoes, but this look was an endangered, if not quite extinct, species. Pompadours could still be seen in the halls, but early sixties commercials encouraged boys to "stop using that greasy kid stuff," and shorter hairstyles, such as the "Princeton" and "Caesar," which required less combing and maintenance, were rapidly gaining attention.

Since very few high schools allowed boys to wear jeans, T-shirts, sweatshirts, or sneakers during class hours, most boys were adopting a style that looks quite similar to adult male "business casual" fashions of today. This look included collared long or short sleeve sport shirts, dress shirts with or without a tie, colorful "Banlon" (golf) shirts, and some form of chino/khaki slacks, supplemented by corduroys in schools that would allow them.

Both boys and girls of the period extensively used sweaters as a major part of their wardrobes, with pullovers dominant for both genders. Many schools had numerous formal and informal "dress-up days," including the last day before a major school break, such as Christmas, numerous class picture and yearbook photo shoots, and pep rally days in which boys donned dress shirts, ties, and dressy sweaters or sport coats and girls wore dresses with stockings and dress shoes. While some teen fashion changes over a five decade interval are to be expected, many items in a 2010 teen's closet were already familiar to adolescents in the 1960s. Hoodies, flip-flops, jeans, message-oriented T-shirts, and "designer" sneakers were all available as early as 1962. However, the gap between what was considered "school wear" and "leisure wear" for both boys and girls was far greater in the early sixties than today.

While differences in teen jargon and fashion would be obvious to almost any twenty-first-century "virtual tourist," a far more important distinction might not be recognized as quickly. High school students of the 1960s would seem as exuberant, energized, and youthful as their counterparts five decades later, but a careful observer might notice there were proportionately more of these young people crowding the halls than their 2010 equivalents. The stark reality of a 1962 high school was that despite years of surging birth rates, the nation had not fully prepared to accommodate substantially larger cohorts of high school students. New schools and classrooms had certainly been constructed, and districts attempted to hire at least some additional teachers. Yet a great number of taxpayers, school administrators, and even parents tacitly admitted that at least part of the numbers crisis could be solved by simply putting more teenagers in each classroom.

Earlier in the twentieth century, high school classes had often been relatively small because relatively few teenagers attended high school and even fewer graduated. Now nearly every adolescent enrolled in high school. And nearly 90 percent of them graduated. The result was that while a typical 2010 high school features a ratio of seventeen students to each member of the institution's instructional staff, the ratio in the 1960s was nearly double that at thirty-three to one. This meant nearly twice as many homework assignments to peruse, twice as many examinations to grade, and twice as many students to identify and engage. In return for these frequently onerous duties, an average teacher in 1962 made $4,995 a year after obtaining both a Bachelor's and Master's degree, while a similarly aged counterpart with only a high school diploma made just over $6,000 a year in the private sector.

If that teacher with thirty-three students in a class seemed either distracted or exhausted as he or she segued from one group of teens to the next, it was quite possibly due to the fact that seven out of ten teachers held one or more jobs outside their high school duties.

A national news magazine of the time featured a cover story on the plight of underpaid high school teachers and focused on an early middle-aged physics teacher in a Portland, Oregon, secondary school. A comparison of monthly take-home pay with even minimal comfort expenses for his family in a small, mostly unfurnished bungalow revealed a startlingly large gap that could only be closed with a variety of part-time jobs, including driving a bus for adult fans to the high school's away basketball games, driving a tour bus twelve hours a day every Saturday and Sunday, and teaching three nights a week at a local television repairman school.

A lighter, yet actually more biting, satire on lack of pay for teachers was a feature article in an issue of *Mad* magazine. The illustrated story depicted an after-school costume party for teachers, sponsored by the local school board. On closer examination, the article reveals that the "costumes," including a bus driver, maid, and street cleaner, were all actually for the moonlighting jobs waiting for the faculty after the party—a blatant slap at stingy school officials shortchanging their teachers.

Given the community parsimony, it is small wonder that as late as October of 1962, there were still over two hundred thousand teaching positions listed as unfilled throughout a nation that five years earlier, in the wake of Sputnik, had acknowledged that better pay for teachers was one of the linchpins of creating a school system to compete with the Russians.

Our virtual visitor to a high school of 1962 could go to the school library and read a large selection of national magazine articles attempting to explain the roots of the great teacher shortage and to offer possible solutions. A contemporary article in *Life* magazine titled "How We Drive Teachers to Quit" explained that "by 1967 half of the already shorthanded American teacher contingent would be gone, including the best minds, the ones best able to ignite and fan the enthusiasm of their students. Their ambitions and self-respect will take them into business and other professions. They will leave behind an increasing population of tired time-servers."

The students in this representative 1962 high school would be trapped in a demographic crisis that at this point showed no signs of abating. During the previous summer, over 125,000 teachers had submitted their resignations, while all American colleges combined had only produced 100,000 new teachers. Meanwhile, the addition of another bumper crop of Boomers to the overall student population had created a demand for 30,000 more teachers than needed in the 1961–1962 school year. A fall 1962 survey by the University of Illinois of its recent class of certified teachers revealed that 40 percent were so dismayed by poor pay prospects they never even applied for a teaching job, while 30 percent of the remaining graduates quit teaching within two years.

The *Life* article cited a three-pronged dilemma facing teachers that prompted many to exit early. First, only 21 percent of teachers were currently making the $7,000 a year that was considered a reasonable middle-class income in 1962. Most new teachers that year were fortunate to enter with a $3,000 to $4,000 initial salary, which almost guaranteed financial shortfalls, even if supplemented by moonlighting. Second, most communities provided teachers with very little prestige and sometimes went out of their way to demean their school faculties. A Connecticut school district advertised to parents that their teachers made excellent evening and weekend babysitters for their children and seldom failed to appear because they were all so desperate for the extra money. An Arizona district required teachers to stand in front of supermarket entrances to plead for passage of a school bond issue to entering customers. A Los Angeles high school mathematics department chair, who had spent three hundred hours of his leisure time devising a new curriculum, had his pay docked when he left school during a free period to purchase materials for the new classes with his own money. Third, teachers were buffeted by conflicting demands that could not possibly be met in their entirety. A combination of know-nothing school boards, insecure and inadequate principals, doting parents, and rebellious or apathetic children pushed teachers toward a series of frustration, petty worries, and accumulated anger that drained many otherwise enthusiastic teachers of their energy.

According to psychologist Dr. Solomon Rettig, who was conducting extensive research on high schools' student-teacher academic interaction, the prognosis for a stimulating learning environment was rather poor in many classrooms. Not only were teachers exhausted from multiple part-time jobs and ever increasing class size, "They are choked, have no freedom of expression. They are not being stimulated nor are they stimulating others."

By the time that our twenty-first-century visitor left the 1962 high school library, he or she would probably have been very confused about what was *really* going on in a typical classroom of the sixties. Five years after Sputnik, one high school teacher complained that the classroom atmosphere was now worse than five years earlier. Her learning environment was poisoned by "dull, bored, even belligerent students, including boys who come into the room late yelling, which encourages other kids to get up out of their seats, form groups and yell even louder. I go home sick every night and have lost all sympathy for the kids." A somewhat more sympathetic teacher insisted that, thanks to her school's administrators, "You're not supposed to teach kids to think but to be robots. My students are expected to sit still and keep their eyes always on you."

On the other hand, a senior researcher for the Educational Testing Service shifted the blame for dull classrooms to the teachers. "The average English teacher is barely literate, capricious in judgment, hard to decipher and eager to misinterpret." Critics of American high school history and social studies programs noted that less than half of world history teachers had taken even one course in European history, less than one in ten had studied any Asian, African, or Latin American history, while in some school districts, as many social studies teachers were certified in physical education as in history or government.

These suggestions that the five-year anniversary of Sputnik had left American high schools even more dysfunctional than in 1957 were often contradicted by other articles that insisted that improvement, even if spotty and erratic, was clearly evident from one end of the nation to the other. *Fortune* magazine detected a "re-emphasis on the intellectual aims of education, and in their search for new ways to transmit knowledge, some schools are once again learning that there must be something to transmit." A *Harper's* article chronicled the efforts of a Harlem secondary school to send their disadvantaged students to plays, operas, and concerts to make them feel that they had something in common with New York City's cultural life. A period *Life* article followed up on a Sputnik-era article that focused on the plight of gifted students in schools unequipped to deal with them. The main subject of that feature, Rockwell Iowa's preteen Barry Wickmann, had been portrayed in the earlier article as a lonely and utterly bored sixth grader who was so out of step with his school's expectations that he almost had to repeat that grade despite a 162 IQ. Now, a sixties high school student, Wickmann's situation had improved markedly. "Since then, a massive concern for all the nation's Barrys has moved more and more schools to push more gifted students toward advanced studies. Now brilliant minds are coddled and courted the way that potential great football players have been for decades. Barry is, at last, finding a feast for his fine mind."

For better or worse, high school students in October 1962, now over-whelmingly Baby Boomers, were confronting academic experience largely the product of events from almost exactly five years earlier. An increasing atmosphere of urgency, that somehow the school was now the front line of the Cold War or the space race, permeated much of the academic element of the high school experience. Whatever themes or activities were consid-ered most "purposeful" in the classroom were sure to gain preference, even if some students, and even more of their parents, were not quite sure exactly what these new activities were expected to accomplish. This era was a period of fairly significant curricular criticism and experimentation, as traditional textbooks, teaching methods, and even grade assignments came under fire. Almost every "major" subject was undergoing some form of revision, and even more peripheral disciplines and activities gained added stature if they could be even remotely linked to American security in the age of Sputnik.

The most publicized, misunderstood, and even feared curricular develop-ment in the early to middle 1960s was the emergence of mathematics and science as the royalty of the high school curriculum and national debate as to how these two fields could be made understandable to the average teenager. During much of the previous decade, since math and science teachers were in even shorter supply than most other subject areas, a large number of high schools had tacitly allowed a significant percentage of their students to opt out of many requirements in these areas, especially if the students were not interested in going to college or were applying to a university that had rela-tively liberal guidelines on the nature of secondary courses required. Now at least some portions of the educational reform movement were insisting not only that should more students take more math and science courses, but that the way they learned these skills should be radically altered, with much of the instruction focused on a concept termed the "inquiry process."

For example, the "New Math" concept in 1960s high schools emerged from an organization called the School Mathematics Study Group that had strong ties to the University of Illinois and Massachusetts Institute of Technology research initiatives. Encouraged by the post-Sputnik demand for reform, an increasing number of high schools bought into the SMSG concepts, which featured new textbooks and methods revolving around the "discovery" method. By 1962 a growing number of high school mathematics courses were developed around the idea that students could become budding mathematicians by being made aware of the excitement of mathematical structure, precise use of language, deductive proof, and the process of discovery. This "real life" math would prod even math-phobic teens into the exciting world of "real mathematics."

Now students were learning an essentially new language of "sets," numeration in bases, and mathematical reasoning techniques that promised to remove much of the drudgery and fear from studying mathematics. Young teachers, who had been exposed to New Math in undergraduate or graduate preparation courses, essentially promised wary students that math would now become "fun" as abstractions gave way to "real world" use. However, by the early to mid-sixties, cracks were beginning to appear in the SMSG computational universe. First, more senior teachers who had been trained in traditional methods often began passive resistance, either because they thought the new curriculum was basically a fraud or because they did not understand exactly what New Math was expected to accomplish. Quite often, perceptive students tuned into this barely disguised teacher unrest and wondered openly how this schism in math instruction would affect their SAT scores.

In a significant number of cases, veteran teachers who viewed New Math as somewhat of a fraud found new allies in the large number of parents who were increasingly frustrated by their inability to help their children in their math homework assignments or even to understand exactly what their teens were supposed to be learning. Parents who had been happy to receive the aid and support of their own mothers and fathers in navigating the waters of mathematical instruction now felt that they could not substantially assist their own offspring as math instruction had seemingly "gone off the tracks." This vague unease was given a more crystallized stature when author Morris Kline's popular book *Why Johnny Can't Add: The Future of the New Math* assured parents that their instincts had been right: new math was based on a too rapidly expanded terminology that was "often unclear to students, parents and even many teachers; it often took students into remote levels of abstraction, rather than into the real world."

The other "glamour" subject in the post-Sputnik academic universe was science, or more specifically, the individual variations of the "new science," which initially emerged from pilot programs developed by MIT, featuring curriculum packages and textbooks in "new biology," "new chemistry," and "new physics." Promoted enthusiastically by the National Science Foundation, "new science" often seemed to veer between revision of content and method either to attract more students to science careers or to gain at least passive acceptance from students who hated science, had no interest in a scientific career, but who would at least better understand scientific components needed in the contest against the Russians.

This theme, that knowledge of at least some elements of science was a patriotic necessity in an ongoing era of cold war, was reflected in the teaching of increasing numbers of high schools, turning once-voluntary science fair programs and exhibits into almost-mandatory events. Often students with little interest in the science disciplines were dragooned into entering a project in the belief that the mere experience of designing their own experiment would somehow entice boys and girls to gain new insights into and respect for what they saw as alien disciplines. Just as in New Math, the new science revolved around the concept of individual "discovery," which often produced unintended outcomes in which many already math- or science-phobic teens "discovered" that they feared and hated their subjects even more than they had originally realized.

The most positive result of the curricular emphasis on science and mathematics in the early to mid-1960s high schools was that these disciplines did gain considerably more status, and students who were talented in these fields found themselves somewhat less ostracized as "weird," and sometimes even achieved the same status as athletic stars. For example, the Sputnik crisis encouraged new academic opportunities for science- and mathematics-oriented students, such as grants from the American Heart Association and similar organizations to fund Saturday-morning or summer-vacation programs that provided interested students with far more advanced research opportunities than were available in high school courses.

Schools that were wise enough to keep their science fairs strictly voluntary discovered an enormous opportunity for positive publicity with both parents and the broader community by showcasing and rewarding teens who were talented in science in the same way that athletically gifted teens were showcased on playing fields and gymnasiums. For some schools, gifted students named best boy or best girl in externally judged science fairs could be as much of a public relations coup as a league sports championship. This atmosphere of enhanced opportunity or study also began to alter the nature of summer study from what had previously been reserved for either subject-area or behavioral failure to an opportunity to study and discover things that were not readily available in the traditional school year. Remarkably, as the sixties continued, summer school was less and less viewed as a punishment and more often was seen as a reward for good work in conventional academic semesters.

As mathematics and science teachers met at conferences in the celebratory mood of vastly enhanced status now that "we have to beat the Russians," teachers involved in instructing the rest of the curriculum often gathered to determine how to restore relevance to their own disciplines. At least one nonscience, nonmath subject gained in stature from the public outcry over American schools in the wake of Sputnik. A number of educational criteria used the perennial Soviet edge in the space race as a platform to castigate the inequity between the fact that nearly 20 million Soviet children were learning English, but only twenty thousand American students were studying Russian. In a "know thine enemy" moment, a number of American high schools initiated new language programs in Russian, and at least some students and their parents reacted to the lure of both an "exotic" subject that also had "patriotic" overtones. Comparisons between Soviet teens' knowledge of English and the woeful statistics of Americans mastery of Russian gradually escalated into a critique of the general lack of American teens' knowledge of any language but their own. The need for more high school courses in *all* foreign languages was clearly evident in most early sixties high schools, especially in light of the expansion of the National Defense Education Act college and graduate scholarships to include students interested in teaching a foreign language, in addition to the initially denoted math and science fields. Thus, in a somewhat strange expansion of Cold War definitions, high school French teachers were lauded for "doing their part" in keeping America safe, even though France itself was an American ally.

A second nonscience, nonmath subject that discovered rapidly increasing prestige in early sixties high schools gained its new status from a combination of the space race and the lifestyle of the newly installed president. While American critics were already raising unfavorable comparisons between seemingly physically active, physically fit Russian teens and their more inactive, TV-addicted American counterparts, the election of John F. Kennedy was a dream come true for high school physical education instructors. The new president, his numerous siblings, and his equally young advisors and staff members were soon forming a cult of physical fitness from touch football games on the White House lawn to fifty-mile hikes out and back into the Maryland or Virginia countryside. Kennedy and his advisors quickly installed a Presidential Physical Fitness organization that encouraged teens to give up their still-new TV remote control devices and transistor radios in favor of physical activity so the teens could emulate the wildly popular young chief executive. Suddenly, physical education teachers stood considerably taller as gym classes were now repackaged from annoying events in the academic enterprise on the part of less physically gifted students to a neo-Spartan or -Athenian interlude personally endorse by President Kennedy.

If the Sputnik crisis and the space race pushed math, science, foreign languages, and physical education to the positive side of the academic ledger, it was the discipline of history that was most likely to find itself in the negative column. Ironically, in a time in which the sitting president boasted of the value of his Harvard history major experience in his achievement of the highest office in the land, that subject's place in the life of most teens was becoming increasingly endangered. First, by the early to mid-sixties, if virtually everyone knew what basic information biology or chemistry courses actually taught, almost no one could agree what that "other department" down the hall should either teach or even be named. A subject that had already lost luster to math and science was called history in some schools and social studies in others. Some of the teachers in the department were trained historians; some were more interested in geography, economics, or government, and amazingly, nearly a fourth of them were actually certified as physical education teachers. While biographies of Kennedy discussed his notorious appetite for history books as an adolescent, huge numbers of sixties teens routinely rated "history" as boring or irrelevant. To some intelligent teens, this discipline seemed to have all of the characteristics of a really bad TV quiz show, with memorization of irrelevant facts producing very little payback in the rest of their daily experiences. While some teens viewed science or math as beyond their capabilities, they often saw the study of the past as simply boring, with no impact on their lives, laced with memorization of unimportant facts or dates thrown in for good measure.

As the sixties progressed, the traditional history gradually began to give way to "comprehensive social studies," viewed as a six-year junior high–senior high experience, with more substantial elements of geography, government, economics, and even sociology and psychology vying with the traditional history curriculum for predominance. Soon narratives of the American Revolution were vying with units on marriage and the family and budget planning in the more widely defined "social studies" universe.

One of the most hopeful signs for the history/social studies area was the fact that the field seemed particularly amenable to one of the new teaching concepts emerging from the Sputnik crisis. Dr. Francis Keppel, who transitioned from dean of the School of Education at Harvard to commissioner of education under Kennedy, was a strong advocate of the concept of team teaching, which quickly gained substantial financial support from the Ford Foundation. By 1962 pilot programs in a number of high schools were dividing students into classes of widely differing sizes where social studies lessons ranged from small seminar discussions to two-hundred-student experiences in lectures, films, or other audio-visual-dominated venues. A computer based at MIT set up the complex schedule in their "school of the future" programs that seemed, at least initially, like a new adventure for both teachers and students.

However, if parents and school board members complained that they did not understand modern math or modern chemistry, American social studies teachers in this Cold War era often were intimidated by the fact that outsiders knew too much (or at least thought they did) about this field. Academic freedom issues that seldom arose in physics or geometry classes were much more possible in history and social studies classes of that era. For example, in the fall of 1962, a middle-aged social studies teacher in Paradise, California, came under fire when some local American Legion and John Birch Society members accused her of subverting the patriotism of local teens. Virginia Franklin, a winner of a Freedoms Foundation award as an outstanding teacher of "the American credo," enlivened classes with ongoing student debates and encouragement to read material of widely divergent points of view. Yet one student's parents used the emerging new technology of the time to equip their son with a small tape recorder hidden in a hollowed-out section of his class textbook. He carried the recorder almost every day of the 1962–1963 school year until Mrs. Franklin was tipped off by the principal. The community furor over whether the teacher was "subversive" spilled over into the spring 1963 school board election, where pro– and anti–Virginia Franklin slates vied for power while national news magazines ran articles on the school and the election, which ultimately reelected those supporting the teacher, 1,700 to 1,200, while those citizens who had tried to oust Mrs. Franklin vowed to continue the fight.

The ongoing debate about which subjects should be taught and how they should be taught directly affected students in everything from school grading policies to the availability of electives to what the students would be doing from period to period in the typical school day. Yet sometimes even more than home or neighborhood, the American high school was a focal point for friendships, relationships, social successes and failures, and everyday hopes and dreams. A typical coeducational high school was often the gateway to friendship and romance, where boys and girls from often relatively similar social backgrounds living in relative proximity to one another formed a bewildering variety of relationships that, in a society where the single most common age for marriage was eighteen, could often prove, at least technically, permanent.

High school could be enormously competitive. Students vied for coveted spots on socially important sports teams and activities, and vied for the affection of others and the coveted "steady" status. Only one person could be homecoming queen, quarterback of the football team, or editor of the yearbook. There were always finite numbers of "popular" boys and girls, and they hoarded their "steady" availability for the optimal partner. While steady status provided theoretical semipermanence to a relationship, the number of breakups was astronomical, as one or both partners decided to reenter the dating contest to see if they could secure a better draw.

Significant elements of High School, USA, student life during the sixties would seem familiar to teens in the 2010s, yet other aspects would remain unique and special to that select group of boys and girls who experienced their adolescence in that one particular decade. Students who spent most of their high school experience during the first half of the decade were caught between the previous era of relatively relaxed academic demands and relatively minimal overcrowding of the 1950s and moves toward more student rights and freedoms of the later sixties. They enjoyed an adolescent experience in a time when American teens were the envy of young people around the globe, yet they came closer to using their school fallout shelters than any other young people of earlier or later eras.

The first few cohorts of Boomers to attend high school proved to be popular subjects for numerous mass circulation magazines and local and national television specials that attempted to discern why these young people already dressed and spoke so differently than their older siblings of the late fifties and how they reacted to the youth and vigor so evident in the Kennedy White House. There are hints of both the social rebelliousness and the social idealism that would mark their younger brothers and sisters later in the decade, but these attitudes are often at the periphery of greater goals of "I just want high school to be a lot of fun" and "We have to be like everybody else to be accepted."

The denizens of high schools between 1960 and 1964 were portrayed in numerous television series and films, photographed and interviewed for major magazines, analyzed by a burgeoning psychology community, and reincarnated in animated form in *The Jetsons*, set one hundred years in the future. The information on early sixties teens was so voluminous that they could have had their own time capsule in the 1964 New York World's Fair. They said goodbye to Elvis in *Bye Bye Birdie* and welcomed the Beatles. They squeezed their own, often-copied fashion style in an era after the poodle skirt and before the miniskirt. They watched their favorite television characters transform from black and white to "living color," and while still buying millions of 45 rpm singles also became the first mass teen purchasers of LP albums.

Their high school very well might have existed in the previous era of the late fifties and the coming era of the late sixties, but for much of a half decade, it was "theirs" in their own unique yearbooks, science fair projects, teachers, and sports championships. Given the enormous turnover rate of teachers in this era, even their younger brothers and sisters might well experience a very different high school academic experience than these early sixties teens did. High school graduates of 1964 might very well have been welcomed back as college senior visitors in 1968, but how many of "their" teachers were still around to visit? Even for adolescents who feel that high school is miserable, irrelevant, and boring, the high school years fly by, and according to most early sixties surveys, the majority of teens did not believe that their experiences were any of these things.

Photo essays were a very popular media format in the mass-circulation news magazines of this era, and in a time of far fewer privacy laws and less suspicion of authority, many high schools, their teachers, students, and parents were delighted to be singled out for such special attention. One of the most extensive and well researched of these features appeared in *Life* in the autumn of 1963 and focused on a seemingly typical California high school. The students are invariably well groomed yet casual, both sure of themselves but already looking over their shoulder, proud of their parents but just a little rebellious. The mother of a cheerleader is just a little miffed that her daughter seems uninterested in playing golf. One member of a group of girls is temporarily snubbed when she begins dating the president of the student council. Students openly support the existence of cliques, as "the clique is something you can depend on. Maybe you can't depend on any individual friend, but you can on the group." Yet students admit that even in close groups, "You're hardly ever the real you. There's a certain image you want people to have of you."

One obviously caring mother openly wishes that her daughter would choose boyfriends who belong to the family's country club, yet a popular history teacher insists, "These kids can change things some day. Change their attitudes, and you can change the complacency of the middle class." Yet a university sociology professor insists of some kids, "There is nobody better equipped than them to live in a society of all electric kitchens, wall to wall carpets, dishwashers, color T.V.'s, and new cars in the garage." These issues would not even begin to be answered until the second half of the sixties, but meanwhile, these adolescents would choose music, films, fashions, and trends that would define their unique teen experience, a popular-culture world that would begin to change even as they were replaced in those same high schools with their younger siblings, who would dominate the late sixties teen experience.

CHAPTER FOUR

~

Teen Beat

The Twist to the Beatles

Only a little more than four years before the Beatles' iconic appearance on *The Ed Sullivan Show* virtually guaranteed that rock music would be not only the soundtrack of the sixties teen experience but also the most profitable musical genre of the decade, two heavily publicized events very nearly condemned the new musical revolution to the status of a four- or five-year-long fad of the 1950s, an audio equivalent of Davy Crockett caps or hula hoops. To paraphrase the Duke of Wellington concerning Waterloo, the ability of rock and roll music to survive and then prosper into the next decade and more was "a near run thing."

The first of these incidents occurred on a frigid winter night in early February 1959. On this tragic evening, while most adults in Clear Lake, Iowa, watched their favorite television programs, many of the adolescent children packed the Surf Ballroom and ignored the blowing snowstorm to cheer the star acts of the Winter Dance Party caravan. The headliners included radio disc jockey turned recording star the Big Bopper, a New York City teen named Dion DiMucci who was on the cusp of rock stardom, a California teen named Ritchie Valens who had just emerged as rock and roll's first Latino headliner, and a twenty-two-year-old Texan, Buddy Holly, who was now being spoken of with the same level of adulation as Elvis Presley. These four performers, their band members, and their support staff had been touring the Midwest during a particularly cold winter, traveling in a bus that was now suffering from an increasingly inoperative heating system. When the prospect of a long drive in a marginally warm bus to even more frigid Fargo, North

Dakota, began to sink in, an offer by the owner of a small charter plane to fly the foursome to their next venue became increasingly enticing. Only the still-emerging star, Dion Dimucci, balked at the thirty-dollars-a-person tariff, and his three companions were driven by the Surf's manager and his teenage son to a local airport in weather only one step short of whiteout conditions. Just after midnight on February 3, 1959, the charter plane attempted to take off for Fargo, but the craft never left the runway as it spun into a fatal crash.

Ironically, as three members of rock and roll royalty died, the fatal crash launched the future careers of two young teens. When the decimated survivors fronted by Dion took the stage the next evening in North Dakota, a young high school singer named Bobby Vee paired with Holly's group, the Crickets, to pay a musical tribute to the dead stars, while in upstate New York, a twelve-year-old boy pondered the impact of the crash on his own emerging adolescent life. Twelve years later, Don McLean would utilize the musical events of the intervening sixties decade to pen "American Pie," with its subtitle "The Day the Music Died."

Almost eleven months after the crash in Iowa, in the final days of the fifties decade, the man often credited with popularizing the term *rock and roll* tearfully embraced the young teens who had formed the core of his New York–based televised "rock and roll party." While his prime rival for the status of television dance party king, Dick Clark, had divested himself of questionable business interests just before being investigated, Alan Freed was caught in the aftermath of the great television quiz show investigation, as Congress shifted their sights to alleged corruption and payoff in what many adults already believed was a sordid and rebellion-laced rock and roll industry.

The clean-cut and articulate Clark, who tended to consciously tone down the music selections on *American Bandstand*, survived a congressional hearing, but the loudly dressed and less politically astute Freed saw his career disintegrate in the glare of the television cameras as legislators grilled him incessantly. Freed returned to New York with termination notices for both his radio and his television programs, and on a bleak December afternoon introduced a final song, "Shimmy, Shimmy, Ko-Ko Bop" by Little Anthony and the Imperials, as crying girls and obscenity laden boys pushed toward the studio exits. Two years earlier, Danny and the Juniors had scored a huge sequel to "At the Hop" with their paean to "the beat," "Rock and Roll Is Here to Stay." Now, as the fifties ended, if rock and roll was not actually dead, it seemed to be teetering on life support as commentators openly speculated about what musical genre would replace rock and roll in the sixties teen experience.

A few days after Freed's last telecast, *Billboard* magazine published the first Hot 100 chart of pop records for the 1960s. The top-selling single was country and western artist Marty Robbins's rather morbid "gunslinger ballad" "El Paso," narrated by the dying loser of a gunfight over a disputed romance. While emerging teen idols such as Frankie Avalon, Fabian, and Neil Sedaka were represented on the list, a significant number of much more placid songs intended for adult audiences were actually slightly more numerous. Bobby Darin's "Mack the Knife," Andy Williams's "Valley of St. Bernadette," the Browns' "Scarlet Ribbons," Ernie Fields' remake of swing hit "In the Mood," and two platters by jazz vocalist Della Reese hinted that rock and roll was not necessarily the voice of the future.

Only a few weeks into the new year, it seemed that "teen" and "adult contemporary" radio stations were featuring increasingly similar playlists, as Percy Faith's theme from the film *A Summer Place* was followed in quick succession with the themes from *The Apartment*, *The Alamo*, *North to Alaska*, and *Exodus*. By mid-1960 any attempt by radio personalities to maintain a legitimate "Top 40" format meant giving airtime to Mitch Miller and Lawrence Welk, as many fifties rock and roll icons had simply disappeared from the charts. "Dreamy" artists, such as Andy Williams and Steve Lawrence, now competed for top-ten status with jazz vocalists such as Dinah Washington and Sarah Vaughan.

This apparent reversion of teenage-oriented music into a very nearly endangered species at the beginning of the sixties can be relatively easily discerned in both the teen television dance shows and the rankings of best-selling popular songs. For example, an intensive analysis of one of the few teen dance programs from 1960 that still exists in its entirety gives ample evidence of the "endangered" status of real rock and roll at the beginning of the new decade. The *Jack Spector Show* was a one-hour teen dance party broadcast weekly from Providence, Rhode Island. An episode televised in March 1960 displays photogenic, polite teens who enthusiastically applaud a number of relatively second-tier live performers. The most astounding element of this alleged rock and roll program was the almost complete absence of legitimate rock and roll. For example, teens dance to records by popular performers Freddy Cannon and Bobby Darin, but the songs, "Chattanooga Shoe Shine Boy" and "My Darling Clementine," are both basically swing renditions that bobby soxers of twenty years earlier would have found quite familiar. While Cannon would reemerge as a rock performer two years later with "Palisades Park" and a number of subsequent hits, Darin, who had gained huge teen audiences with "Splish Splash," "Queen of the Hop," and "Dream Lover" in the late fifties, had now largely abandoned that genre with his two most recent hits, "Mack the Knife" and "Beyond the Sea," and now seemed to be emerging as the poster boy for some form of neo-swing music that many music critics insisted could make rock and roll largely irrelevant in the coming decade.

The playlist on the Spector program is a fascinating mélange of music styles that have as a common denominator a near absence of what had been called "The Big Beat." The performers include a male quintet of New Yorkers named the Crystals, singing an overchoreographed but insipid pseudo-Doo-wop song; music impresario Bob Crewe, who performs two Andy Williams–type ballads; one of Crewe's "new discoveries," Myrna March, who sings a tune that is very nearly a German march; and most astonishingly, a guest square dance caller who orchestrates bewildered teens in a seemingly unending string of square-dance-oriented tunes. The plucky teens gamely try to dance to this jumbled array of music with couples sometimes nearly knocking into one another as they attempt some form of "rock" dance steps for music not intended for that beat. In a full-hour program, the only fully recognizable rock and roll song is Marv Johnson's "I Love The Way You Love," which became a modest hit, while Spector does live commercials for a local record store featuring a discount on the first volume of a series called "Oldies but Goodies," an album of real rock and roll songs from the now ended 1950s.

The insistence of 1960-era music critics that rock and roll might indeed by replaced by some other, more adult-acceptable genre is graphically supported by the playlists of both local and satellite twenty-first-century "oldies" radio stations that feature an orientation toward the first decade of rock music. A survey of Billboard magazine's "Hot 100" chart of popular music for two years of the sixties decade, 1960 and 1965, reveals a startling reality. A perusal of the top one hundred charted songs for the first week of June 1960 reveals roughly fifteen to twenty records that would normally be featured on 2010 "oldies" play lists; the rest of the chart is composed of movie themes, easy-listening songs, jazz renditions, or simply tunes that carried little interest beyond that time. On the other hand, the list for the first week of June 1965 contains nearly sixty songs that would find regular airplay into the twenty-first century, including almost every one of the top fifty hits of that week. Therefore, suggestions in the first half of 1960 that rock and roll was on its way to cultural irrelevance were not at all exaggerated. Teens still bought records, but a large number of those records were more attuned to adults in the same way that teens watched Gunsmoke or I've Got a Secret, even though those programs, and their commercials, were geared toward an older audience.

Most works on American popular culture during the 1960s place the near-death experience of American rock and roll music almost three years later, in 1963, and insist that it was the Beatles who "saved" this music format from near extinction. The author strongly disagrees with this consensus and hopes to demonstrate that rock music in the last year of the Kennedy administration was vibrant, creative, and merely enhanced, not "saved," by the foursome from Liverpool. The year 1960 seems a much more likely candidate for when the new musical genre came closest to cultural irrelevance, and it was not four British lads but a group of young people of mixed race and gender from Philadelphia row-house neighborhoods who made rock and roll fun once more, while one of them unintentionally became the agent of adult acceptance of at least some forms of "teen music."

On July 25, 1960, a young resident of South Philadelphia achieved a milestone attained earlier by two other young men who resided nearby. The predecessors, Frankie Avalon and Fabian Forte, had already emerged as teen idols, Italian-American demigods worshipped by millions of teen and preteen girls. Ernest Evans was handsome, but as an African American he was not exactly seen as fitting the traditional "teen idol" mode of that time. However, he had recently recorded an upbeat, crisp version of a song originally performed by Hank Ballard, and during the last week of July "The Twist" pushed to the number sixty-one spot on the pop charts and was graced with a star symbol that denoted "great upward progress." Unlike the meteoric rise of the Beatles with "I Want to Hold Your Hand" three-and-a-half years later, Evans, whose stage name was Chubby Checker, spent several weeks trailing Elvis Presley's "It's Now or Never" for the number one record in the nation. Finally, on September 19, when most teens were back in school, "The Twist" took top honors for a single week.

However, contrary to the then-known laws of rock and roll music sales, where most past hits remained permanently in "oldies" status, three rather unique events occurred. First, the record seemed to remain marketable for longer than most songs, with a second run to the top spot the following year. Second, the dance on which the record was based put the jitterbug, the most popular form of teen dancing in the previous decade, on a near-endangered list as adolescents gyrated to the unique form of the twist. Finally, while adults tended to either ridicule or ignore teen dance crazes in the early stages of rock and roll, many of them surreptitiously or openly began twisting in more mature venues. Arthur Murray's dance studios quickly began to offer twist lessons for staid adults who finally had begun to see rock and roll as more fun than teen rebellion. Fashion designers began producing extensive lines of "twist" attire designed to flatter the figures of young and even middle-aged women when they ventured out onto the dance floor.

Movie studios and producers who had caught the beginning of the rock and roll wave four or five years earlier quickly released a series of twist movies with practically the same plots, merely substituting Chubby Checker for Bill Haley and the Comets. For example, impresario Sam Katzman took the basic plotline of his hugely successful *Rock Around the Clock* and remade the film as *Twist Around the Clock*. This film, like several other twist movies, offered an interesting commentary on the evolution of popular music from the fifties into the early sixties. The male lead is a talent agent saddled in the early part of the film with a fading rock combo, complete with black leather jackets and long sideburns. As they play to increasingly miniscule audiences, the agent breaks ties with the group, emphasizing that "rock and roll is dead," with a vow to discover a more profitable "new sound." The unlikely plotline centers on the agent taking a wrong turn into an isolated community that holds a Saturday-night dance whose teens gyrate to an otherwise-unknown dance they cleverly call "the twist." The agent quickly falls in love with the only female member of the band/dance ensemble and introduces the twist to an expectant and grateful wider world.

Katzman's plotline mirrors some of the era's social and music commentators who insisted that original rock and roll was indeed dead and that the twist was actually the initial component of an entirely new genre of teen music, which, unlike the Big Beat, might actually entice adults into the action. In a sense, this is merely a mirror image of other entrepreneurs and critics who hoped and expected to entice teens to what was essentially the adult music of Andy Williams, Steve Lawrence, and an increasingly "grown up" Bobby Darin.

Actually, for the next three years, from late 1960 to late 1963, each of these two apparently contradictory premises would be proven reasonably accurate regarding their impact on teenagers and, to some extent, adult popular culture. During this period, with the single noticeable exception of a newly civilian Elvis Presley, very few of the surviving first-generation rock and roll stars would produce a real hit. A perusal of hit music charts in this era shows virtually no success for Bill Haley, Fats Domino, Jerry Lee Lewis, Little Richard, Chuck Berry, or other early pop icons. Those early sixties stars who had roots in the previous decade—Rick Nelson, Brenda Lee, and the Everly Brothers, for example—were not among the "founders" of the Big Beat and gained much of their success by being viewed as more adult-acceptable singers with a relatively toned-down musical style.

The majority of hit makers in the teen-oriented songs of 1961, 1962, and 1963 were new acts that were taking rock music in new directions, and one of the most prominent centers of this transition was Chubby Checker's home city of Philadelphia.

As "The Twist" emerged as a hugely successful song and dance concept, Dick Clark quickly realized the economic potential of this new trend. Both the song and the singer were promoted vigorously by Clark on *Bandstand*, and the only question was how to turn the single hit into a longer-term teen trend. Only a short distance from the *Bandstand* studios, the owners of "The Twist" label, Bernie Lowe and Kal Mann, developed a plan to turn a song into a franchise. These two middle-aged men, aided substantially by Lowe's high school daughter's hit-picking instincts, developed new dances for Chubby Checker and other new stars for the growing Cameo-Parkway record empire. Lowe and Mann quickly produced a relatively predictable sequel, "Let's Twist Again," for Checker and quickly followed with "Pony Time" and "The Fly." On one level, Checker was then paired off with another South Philadelphian, an Italian American teen named Bobby Rydell, who became Cameo's designated competition to Fabian and Frankie Avalon. Rydell mixed dance songs, such as "The Cha Cha Cha," with an English translation of the Italian hit "Volare" and paeans to teen social life in "Swingin' School" and "Wildwood Days," evoking the best memories of both high school and summer vacations.

While Rydell was matched with Checker in a pairing of white and black teen idols, the new twist king also interacted with a female dance song queen, North Philadelphian Dione LaRue, who was transformed from a church vocalist in a home where dancing was forbidden into Dee Dee Sharp, who at age seventeen released one of the most popular dance records of the sixties, "Mashed Potato Time." Dee Dee and Chubby quickly became the king and queen of teen dance songs and were paired off in both a huge hit, "Slow Twistin'" in early 1962, and a movie reprise in *Don't Knock the Twist*. Soon "Gravy (For My Mashed Potatoes)," "Ride," and "Do the Bird" had Dee Dee Sharp matching Chubby Checker, song for song and dance for dance.

Lowe and Mann, with considerable support from Clark and *Bandstand*, soon found that they had more dance-oriented potential hits than first-tier performers to record them and quickly added two groups to their entourage, the white ensemble the Dovells, fronted by Len Barry, and an African American three-girl, one-boy group, the Orlons. The Dovells' "Bristol Stomp" and "Do the New Continental" and the Orlons' "The Wah-Watusi" and "South Street" evoked the highly choreographed, often very competitive teen dance scene of early 1960s Philadelphia (and many other communities) in much the same way that *Saturday Night Fever* visually chronicled the equally competitive New York disco scene fifteen years later.

Two of Chubby Checker's biggest dance hits, "The Twist" and his 1962 rendition of the limbo, "Limbo Rock," enticed large numbers of adults to view teen music and dancing as nonrebellious. The twist was liberating, in the sense that strict partnering was not required and, to use a slightly later sixties catch phrase, each participant could "do your own thing." In essence, the twist allowed adults entry into a younger world, while also allowing them to show off their particular styles without conforming to a partner's needs (or failings). The dance was "sexy," but without touching, and seemed much more innocent than what fifties teen dances were thought to evoke. The limbo was mildly competitive, in the sense that the limbo bar was gradually dropped lower to the ground so that a decreasing number of participants could continue. On the other hand, the "dance" required no particular dance skills or instruction and could be as easily performed by adults (or little children) as by teens. In this respect, Checker and his dances helped reinvigorate rock and roll by allowing adults to "buy into" teen music, partially making it their own. Twist parties and limbo parties crossed teen, adult, and even child generations, as shown in John Waters's hilarious 1988 satire *Hairspray*.

While the twist era, roughly from late 1960 to late 1963, enticed at least some adults to view teen music from a different prism than the initial generations of rock and roll, that same period also encouraged a new role for the 50 percent of the teens themselves who had been among the most vocal fans but not performers of the Big Beat. The iconic newsreels and television segments that show rock and roll at its inception invariably depict a divided universe. A huge percentage of screaming fans are girls, yet almost all of the performers entertaining them are males.

During the first three or four years of the rock and roll era, period films and teen dance parties, such as *Bandstand*, attempted to portray a more dual-gender performing scene by including at least some female singers in the movie or TV programs. The major problem with this process was that while the male performers were usually actual "rockers," with loud guitars and louder songs, the female performers were almost always singing much "tamer" songs that were more pop than rock. Female singers, such as Georgia Gibbs, Gale Storm, and Gogi Grant, were talented and vivacious, but their styles often belonged to the prerock early fifties. They seldom toured with Buddy Holly or Little Richard, and their songs could be (and were) enjoyed as much by adults as teens. The first real hint of change occurred in 1959 and 1960, when young women or even teen girls, such as Connie Francis, Hayley

Mills, Annette Funicello, and Connie Stevens, essentially combined television, film, and recording careers and used their TV or screen presences as a springboard to music popularity. However, the emergence of female soloists and groups who were primarily singers, not actors, would really begin in the years from the twist to the era of Beatlemania.

The emergence of large numbers of female singers and groups who represented mainstream, teen-oriented, rather than "adult contemporary," formats can be traced back to the very end of 1960 and the first weeks of 1961. In the autumn of 1960, fourteen-year-old high school freshman Kathy Young connected with a vocal group called the Innocents and recorded "A Thousand Stars," in which a male quartet essentially backed up the riveting performance by their younger female soloist. By mid-December, the song had passed every chart record except Elvis Presley's "Are You Lonesome Tonight?" and country singer Floyd Cramer's "Last Date" as the most popular song in the nation. By New Year's Eve, the tune had been joined in the top ten by a similar merger between a high school girl and a male group, Rosie and the Originals' equally stunning "Angel Baby." While the Originals' guitar riffs are often off-key and sound like a novice garage band, Rosie's haunting plea for the return of an absent boyfriend reached three thousand miles across the Atlantic Ocean, as John Lennon acknowledged the impact of the song on his own career.

While neither of these girl-dominated songs could quite reach the number-one position, a group of Passaic, New Jersey, high school girls would accomplish this feat before the first month of 1961 ended. Shirley Owens and her classmates began an unlikely rise to stardom when one of their classmates raved about their musical talent to her mother, a housewife named Florence Greenburg. Mrs. Greenburg was one of many "undercover" middle-aged rock and roll fans, and apparently she also dreamed of starting her own record company. After a short audition, Greenburg signed the group, named the Shirelles, to her equally new record label, Tiara Records. After one or two modest successes by the Shirelles, Greenburg linked up with eighteen-year-old Carole King, a recent high school graduate who was attempting to enter the music business with her boyfriend, and soon-to-be husband, Gerry Goffin. King and Goffin wrote "Will You Still Love Me Tomorrow" for the Shirelles, later gaining local success herself in New York with an "answer" song ("Oh Neil") to fellow Lincoln High graduate Neil Sedaka's huge hit, "Oh! Carol." "Will You Still Love Me Tomorrow" soared to hit status, largely on a combination of a smooth, string-based beat that seemed to be a sixties "answer" to the saxophone rhythms of fifties rock and roll and lyrics that challenged huge numbers of teenage girls—the dilemma of becoming intimate with a boyfriend and then wondering whether he would still care about her the next morning. The Shirelles would quickly become one of John Lennon and Paul McCartney's favorite American groups, and the Beatles' version of a song Burt Bacharach wrote for the Shirelles, "Baby It's You," became one of their most requested album songs on the British side of the Atlantic.

The rise of girl groups in the early 1960s created a fast-opening gateway for young songwriters creating music for teenagers, which, in turn, was often performed by teenagers. For example, the Brill Building at 1619 Broadway in Manhattan attracted young writers to both collaborate and compete with one another to create rock and roll songs that already began to sound quite different than their fifties predecessors and put female performers on a more equal footing with their male counterparts. King and Goffin were joined by two more couples who eventually became musical collaborators, Ellie Greenwich and Jeff Barry and Cynthia Weil and Barry Mann. Their songs were often almost interchangeable for both male and female performers, and, in turn, prompted a number of answer songs from the gender that did not score the original hit. Mann, largely on a dare, wrote top-ten hit "Who Put the Bomp" in less than ten minutes, while King and Goffin, now young parents, asked their babysitter Eva Boyd to record their new song, "The Loco-Motion," while the lyrics were still fresh in their minds. The babysitter soon became hot singer Little Eva, and "The Loco-Motion" reached number one in late summer of 1962.

The initial phase of the girl-group explosion of 1961 to 1963 was largely centered in the New York metropolitan area and tended to be dominated by African American teens, such as the Shirelles, the Cookies, and the Exciters, with a sizeable minority of white teen groups, such as the Angels and Ellie Greenwich's electronically created studio group, the Raindrops. However, by the autumn of 1962, girl groups were expanding both their geographical base and, to some extent, even their definition.

The girl-group sound essentially became bicoastal when young impresario Phil Spector, who was born in the Bronx but moved to Los Angeles as a teen, went from late fifties performer in the Teddy Bears ("To Know Him Is to Love Him") to the innovator of the Wall of Sound recording technique, which featured recording sessions with large multiples of instruments and daring levels of overdubbing. What emerged as the Spector sound featured sometimes-interchangeable, largely teenage, female singers fronting his signature group, the Crystals, while often simultaneously scoring hits as Bob B. Soxx and the Blue Jeans, the Blossoms, and other assorted groups.

Spector scored a top-twenty hit in the early summer of 1962 with the Crystals' "Uptown," a relatively sedate yet socially relevant song that, along with the Drifters' "Up on the Roof" and "On Broadway," gave lucid testimony about what it was like to be young and not particularly well off in a class-conscious and impersonal Gotham. However, almost immediately after this modest success, he largely replaced lead singer Barbara Alston with two teenagers from opposite sides of the country, Darlene Love of Los Angeles and LaLa Brooks from New York. Both of these girls had lives that revolved around high school and church choirs, yet soon their voices, if not always their appearance, became known to almost every teenager during the last year of the Kennedy administration.

Love, who would eventually go on to roles in a number of films, was the lead singer in "He's a Rebel," "Zip-A-Dee-Doo-Dah," "He's Sure the Boy I Love," and "Today I Met the Boy I'm Going to Marry," while Brooks fronted the equally iconic "Da Doo Ron Ron" and "Then He Kissed Me." Yet, as various versions of the Crystals made Spector a millionaire, three more young New York girls would add a new dimension to both the girl group sound and Spector's personal life during the last few weeks of Kennedy's administration. Nedra Talley and her cousins Estelle Bennett and Veronica Bennett, who had gone from sneaking into New York clubs to becoming regulars at the Peppermint Lounge, provided a sound that caused Spector to largely lose interest in his other performers and form the Ronettes, whose "Be My Baby" was perhaps the last superhit before the arrival of the Beatles. Spector's partnership with his new group extended to an often turbulent marriage with Ronnie Bennett Spector, who would actually score much of her most significant success simultaneously with the British Invasion.

While much of the emergence of a significant female component to early 1960s rock and roll music was based around three or four girls singing together with a catchy group name, two suburban high school girls were able to score equally impressive hits on their own. In 1962, as *American Bandstand* approached its fifth anniversary, a fifteen-year-old girl from a suburban Philadelphia Catholic high school pleaded with her mother for permission to attempt to appear on Clark's show as a dancer, a request that was closed for discussion until after her sixteenth birthday. However, her dynamic singing voice soon gained the attention of producers for RCA Victor Records, and on New Year's Day 1963, the young girl, Peggy March, recorded "I Will Follow Him," a cut from a recent Rick Nelson album. The song spent most of that spring as a top-ten hit with three weeks in the number-one position, and the newly emerging star experienced an appearance on *Bandstand* before turning sixteen, but as a performer not a dancer. Juggling a singing career with high school studies, March launched a string of hits, including "I Wish I Were a Princess," which was nearly as successful as her first record, and eventually emerged as German teenagers' favorite American female singer.

At almost the same time that Peggy March's first song began challenging for the top spot in pop music charts, another high school girl was planning her own record debut about ninety miles north of Miss March's Lansdale, Pennsylvania, home. Leslie Gore, the daughter of a Tenafly, New Jersey, swimwear company owner, grew up playing a toy piano and listening to her parents' favorite dance tune records. Soon she was buying dozens of her own 45 rpm singles and lip-syncing the songs word for word. At age fifteen, while enrolled at Dwight School for Girls, she started studying singing under the tutelage of a vocal coach until, by her sixteenth birthday, she was gaining the attention of Mercury Records and their chief music arranger, Quincy Jones, who was destined later to create much of the sound of Michael Jackson.

In late winter 1963, Jones came to the Gore home, weighed down with over two hundred sample records, one of which was to be chosen as Lesley's first single. On March 30, three months after Peggy March's first record session, Leslie Gore recorded "It's My Party," and the song was a major national hit in time for her own seventeenth birthday party, which was most likely much more pleasant for her than the party in the music version. A few weeks later the song was in the top ten in Britain, and the sequel song, "Judy's Turn to Cry," was a top-five song by summer. Lesley's trademark "flip" hairdo made her look like a poised, blond teenage version of First Lady Jackie Kennedy, as Lesley spent her senior year of high school walking away with an armload of record industry awards. Then, somewhere between SAT tests and college application forms, she recorded "You Don't Own Me," a song that many cultural historians consider one of the earliest feminist anthems, and one of the only songs that challenged the Beatles for best-selling record in the wake of Beatlemania.

While the rise of the girl groups gave voice to the longing of many early sixties teen girls for a degree of certainty, compassion, and loyalty in their often emotionally draining relationships with boys, two rather different male-dominated music formats emerged on opposite coasts of the United States during this time period. In the New York and New Jersey area in the early 1960s, as the largely African American Doo-wop music of the fifties was beginning to fade, a large number of white teenage boys, many of them living in Italian neighborhoods, began imitating that sound, filtered through their own ethnic experiences and hopes. Some of these groups essentially became one- or two-hit wonders between 1960 and 1963, including Randy and the Rainbows ("Denise"), the Earls ("Remember Then"), and the Tokens ("The Lion Sleeps Tonight" and "Tonight I Fell in Love"). Many of these songs celebrated the discovery of a new love, the uncertainty whether that love was reciprocated, and the overpowering sadness that accompanied the end of a romance, particularly if the parting was not mutual. However, the New York / New Jersey sound also produced two significantly more successful acts that, in many respects, added an edginess to their songs with more complicated scenarios than the three dilemmas just listed.

On the New York side of the Hudson, a brash Bronx teenage named Dion DiMucci partnered with three other "street corner" enthusiasts to form Dion and the Belmonts, who scored a string of significant late fifties hits with a capstone of "A Teenager in Love," which became a top-ten seller in the summer of 1959. Dion essentially split with the rest of the group and began producing a string of early sixties hits notable for more nuanced, confrontational boy-girl relationships. DiMucci's songs included "The Wanderer," which revels in the freedom granted by the absence of a steady relationship; "Runaround Sue," a caustic account of a relationship-averse girl (who, to be fair, is not more nor less than a female version of the "wanderer"); and a laundry list of failings of the pretentious, shallow "Donna the Prima Donna." Even second-tier hits, such as "Drip Drop" and "Sandy," are hardly romantic ballads, as the former song includes an invitation to a firstfight by an unwanted male visitor, and the latter insists that the fickleness of a former girlfriend has prompted a desire to slap the young lady. If "Teenager in Love" epitomized the inherent confusion of adolescent romance, many of Dion's solo efforts represented a sardonic, male-oriented review of the entire teenage dating scene.

The other superstar New York / New Jersey male act of the early 1960s took its name from a Union, New Jersey, bowling alley, the Four Seasons. A partnership between singers Bob Gaudio and Frankie Valli and producer Bob Crewe emerged when Crewe changed the title of Gaudio's song "Terri" to the name of a prominent New York disc jockey's daughter, Sherry. While this somewhat plaintive invitation from a teen boy to his semi-girlfriend to accompany him to a twist party was a conceptually traditional and hugely successful hit, their next two songs would put them solidly on the road to *Jersey Boys* fame, featuring much more confrontational boy-girl relationships. "Big Girls Don't Cry" features a very sarcastic male rebuttal to a teen girl who has seemingly attempted to adopt a male-oriented laissez-faire attitude toward romantic involvement, while "Walk Like a Man" represents a huge reversal from most earlier teen songs, which stress parental involvement in adolescent romances as almost entirely negative and unwanted by their children. This Four Seasons song places the teen boy's father in the position of sage and advisor, telling his son that "no woman's worth crawlin' on the earth," with a strong hint that his son is so desirable that numerous other young ladies will surely find him attractive in the near future.

While the New York / New Jersey sound of the early 1960s mixed traditional hopes for romance with a certain male bonding over the freedom to be "wanderers" in the crowded streets and bowling alleys of a densely populated metropolis, where walking was still an important activity, songwriters and performers three thousand miles away were scoring equally well with a somewhat different teenage dream. The new sound, focused on a California lifestyle of beaches, cars, and the emerging sport of surfing, presented a somewhat different venue for both male adventure and boy-girl romantic possibilities.

The form of early sixties "teen beat," loosely defined as "the surfing sound," took off from the success of the original *Gidget* film and a pounding "surf beat," initiated by surfer/guitarist Dick Dale. Dale's 1961 hit "Misirlou" featured driving guitars that almost bordered on a Middle Eastern or Israeli folk dance concept. Dale's modest hit tribute to California surfing culture was followed a few months later when a young Hawthorne, California, quintet scored an equally modest vocal hit with the definitive title "Surfing," which peaked at number seventy-five in the Hot 100 in the spring of 1962. However, these five musicians, ranging in age from teens to early twenties, gained national attention by October, when their follow-up song, "Surfing Safari," climbed into the top-twenty lists across the country. Now Brian Wilson, his brothers Carl and Dennis, cousin Mike Love, and neighbor Al Jardine had tapped into many teenagers' secret dreams to simply jettison school and homework and follow the sun and waves indefinitely.

While the Beach Boys scored a moderately successful hit with "Surfing Safari," the full emergence of a musical genre evoking the freedom and pleasure of the surfing culture generally had to wait until the rest of the nation caught up to the warmth and sunshine that California enjoyed year-round. During the spring and summer of 1963, songs celebrating surfing, warm weather, cars, and outdoor activities became ever more noticeable on popular music charts. By Memorial Day, Brian Wilson's group had reached the top three with "Surfing USA," one of the best-selling pop records in the country, and other "surf sounds" were mainstays on top-forty playlists. The Beach Boys were soon engaged in a friendly rivalry with another vocal act, Jan and Dean, who combined pre-med and pre-law courses with hit songs such as "Baby Talk" and "Linda." Brian Wilson gave the duo access to one of his compositions, "Surf City," a male fantasy about surfers who find a beach resort with "two girls for every boy." "Surf City" became the first surfing-oriented song to gain number-one status, much to the chagrin of the Beach Boys' tyrannical, abusive father-manager.

Meanwhile, two bands composed almost entirely of high school students, one of whom was only fourteen, released smash instrumental hits as follow-ups to Dick Dale's "surfer soundtrack." The Chantays' "Pipeline" and the Surfaris' "Wipe Out" became beach party anthems for decades to come, with the former group becoming one of the first rock and roll acts to perform on *The Lawrence Welk Show.*

The Beach Boys and Jan and Dean supplemented their surfing songs with other themes that would appeal to teen imaginations, even when away from the beach. Several of Brian Wilson's productions became two-sided hits, as "Little Deuce Coup," "409," and "Shut Down" appealed to the strong automotive element in teen male culture, while "Be True to Your School" and "In My Room" chronicled both the school spirit and introspective aspects of adolescents of both genders. Jan and Dean's "New Girl in School" addressed the difficulty of teens forced to deal with a whole new set of cliques and unwritten rules in a new school, yet added the pragmatic male view that the new female student might very well appreciate a boy's attentions to mitigate possible ostracism by "mean girls."

By the closing month of 1963, the teen music genre that had seemed nearly extinct only forty months earlier had achieved a sophistication and diversity far beyond anything foreseen during the 1950s. At the same time, the average age of popular performers had dropped significantly, with a far greater percentage of teen singers performing for a teenage audience. Many of the "founders" of rock and roll, Fats Domino, Chuck Berry, Jerry Lee Lewis, and Bill Haley, among others, were considerably older than their fan base in the fifties. By 1963, the new stars, including Stevie Wonder, Hayley Mills, Leslie Gore, and Peggy March, were doing homework and taking final exams just like their fans but combining that with singing careers.

At the same time, during the last year of the Kennedy era, a musical genre rooted in the American experience was beginning to show a notable international flavor. Among the significant hits of 1963, "If You Wanna Be Happy" by Jimmy Soul and "Watermelon Man" by Mongo Santamaría had a strong Caribbean flavor. "Four Strong Winds" by Ian and Sylvia and "Mr. Bass Man" by Johnny Cymbal were Canadian-originated hits, and "Sukiyaki" by Kyo Sakamoto, "Killer Joe" by Rocky Fellers, and "Tie Me Kangaroo Down, Sport" by Rolf Harris were hits imported from Japan, the Philippines, and Australia, respectively. The last top-selling record of the year was "Dominique," a song entirely in French performed by a Belgian nun. Finally, two British groups had managed to establish an English beachhead in its former colonies. The Tornados, a male instrumental group, achieved the first British song to climb to number-one status in America with the somewhat futuristic "electronic" sound of "Telstar," while a young female duo called the Cara-velles ended 1963 with a top-five, very American-sounding song, "You Don't Have to Be a Baby to Cry."

However, behind these small British pop music waves crossing the At-lantic Ocean was a cultural tsunami gathering in that island nation that had marked a turning point in British teen culture in 1963 and would have a similar effect in the United States in 1964. The usually staid, adult-oriented *Time* magazine gave fair warning of this cultural upheaval in its issue dated exactly one week before the assassination of John F. Kennedy. In a true rarity for this periodical, there were actually two major features on teen music as a transatlantic phenomenon. The "Show Business" segment relayed a gener-ally positive narrative of current teen "idol" Sister Luc-Gabrielle, the "round faced, bespectacled" thirty-year-old Belgian nun who, armed with her trusty guitar, had sung a musical narrative of her religious order's patron saint and founder, St. Dominic. Quickly packaged as "Soeur Sourire" (Sister Smile), the Singing Nun sold four hundred thousand singles of "Dominique" in only three weeks, with album sales already topping three hundred thousand. The *Time* columnist issued a faintly bemused "just us adults" surprise that Ameri-can teens had made a bespectacled nun, who normally wore a gray apron as she cleaned sugar beets on the convent farm, a "princess" of rock and roll.

However, that same issue's "Music" segment crossed the English Channel with a report on Britain's "new madness" surrounding four Liverpool lads aged twenty to twenty-three who seemed to be mesmerizing Britons from school girls to the Queen Mother. The correspondent introduced American readers to "four boys who look like shaggy Peter Pans with mushroom hair-cuts and high white shirt collars, who sing songs that consist mainly of 'Yeh! Yeh! Yeh!'" An interview with Brian Epstein revealed a feeling of shock and wonder as the impresario insisted, "I dropped in at a smoky, squalid cellar, and there were these four youths. Their act was ragged, their clothes were a mess, and yet, I sensed at once that there was something here."

That "something" had already created a near riot at a concert in Carlisle; four thousand fans standing all night in Newcastle, "faces pinched and grim in a drenching rain," waiting for the wail of sirens that would bring the Beatles to their town; and finally, in a hint that "Beatlemania, as Britons call the new madness, is really striking everywhere," a command performance for the Queen Mother at London's Prince of Wales Theater. The Beatles had breached the final moat of British class distinctions when, as Queen Eliza-beth's mother beamed, John Lennon yelled to the audience, "Those in the cheaper seats, clap. The rest of you, rattle your jewelry."

A horrible tragedy would confront Americans only a week after this article appeared, as a young acting, yet middle-aged president made his fateful trip to Dallas. One season of innocence had now ended, and in some respects, America and its teens would never be quite the same. Yet ten weeks after the tragedy in Texas, the four young men who caused the "British madness" would land at a New York airport newly renamed for the martyred president, and for most teens and at least some adults, a new form of innocent magic would return. Beatlemania would prove to be a highly transferable madness, and a teenage music scene that had progressively expanded since Chubby Checker's new dance would now soar into a new phase that would sometimes enter popular cultural mythology.

CHAPTER FIVE

~

Teens on Screen

It is more than a slight possibility that many Elizabethan-era adolescents who emerged from the Globe Theater after viewing *Romeo and Juliet* could see some portion of their own experiences in this romantic, yet tragic, tale. Shakespeare's tale of a family feud gone viral at least tacitly admitted the existence of some life experiences between childhood and full adulthood, while, in turn, it is probable that a large number of early seventeenth-century proto-teens had a more emotional attachment to this play than *Henry V* or *Julius Caesar*.

As the entertainment universe expanded in the twentieth century to include film, and then television, visualizing the adolescent experience became one of the staples of Hollywood production activities. The Roaring Twenties motion picture provided a steady stream of silent, yet often suggestive, images of the escapades and challenges of a young generation centered on a "Flaming Youth" mindset that featured flappers, vamps, and collegians as models for a new generation that seemed to be successfully challenging adult Victorian, largely small-town values. The early years of the Great Depression temporarily pushed everyday adolescent experiences to the background, as "child star" movies featuring Shirley Temple and gangster films featuring postadolescent James Cagney squeezed the teen experience from the silver screen for a short time. However, by the very late thirties, patrons flocked to movie theaters to see a teenager, Dorothy Gale, befriend a scarecrow and battle green witches, while the Andy Hardy and Nancy Drew series focused on "typical," if often overly comic or overly adventurous, teenagers of the swing era.

The American entry into World War II after the Japanese attack on Pearl Harbor encouraged a string of films focusing on adolescent confusion over shortages, dislocation, and danger to either family members or love interests stationed overseas, perhaps best portrayed in producer David O. Selznick's *Since You Went Away*, featuring teens played by Jennifer Jones and Shirley Temple confronting an emotional roller coaster made barely tolerable by the tenacity of parent Claudette Colbert. However, the late war years and early postwar era saw a film boomlet in depicting the now increasingly labeled "teen-age" experience in the seemingly more innocent times of the first two or three decades of the century. Those films often centered around talented actresses such as Judy Garland and Jeanne Crain in period dramas or comedies from the St. Louis World Fair of 1904 to the Roaring Twenties, including *Meet Me in St. Louis*, *Margie*, and *Cheaper By the Dozen*. *Margie*, which depicts the Roaring Twenties high school experience from two decades later through the reminiscences of a student (Jeanne Crain) and her male French teacher (Glenn Langan) is probably the first "technically advanced" (sound and color) film depicting a typical high school atmosphere that would in some respects still be recognizable to sixties teens, although the student-teacher relationship that results in their eventual marriage might have been grounds for dismissal in that later decade.

By the mid-1950s, the trend in historically oriented teen character films had begun to give way to "contemporary issue" films that were increasingly labeled "teen pics." Almost immediately after James Dean's explosive starring film debut in John Steinbeck's 1916-era *East of Eden* (1955), most teen-oriented movies of the late fifties were set in the present, with the main variation being the topic of the feature. Teen pics ranged from teen alienation and delinquency (*Rebel Without a Cause*, *Blackboard Jungle*) to romantic comedy (*Tammy and the Bachelor*, *April Love*). Emerging subgenres included teen-focused horror films (*I Was a Teenage Werewolf*), showcases for emerging rock and roll stars (*Rock Around the Clock*), and films on controversial topics like high school pregnancy (*Blue Denim*).

In a society where nearly half of the population was under twenty-one and the other half were increasingly fascinated (or apprehensive) about the emerging teen lifestyle, it was fairly predictable that teen-oriented films were not going to disappear with the end of the fifties decade. However, as the sixties began, even relatively recent fifties teen pics, such as *Blackboard Jungle* and *High School Confidential*, began to seem a bit outdated in the supercharged, changing atmosphere of teen culture. Three of the most iconic early 1960s films, all released within the first eighteen months of the new decade, were beginning to depict a rather different teen experience than their very recent fifties predecessors.

During the first year and a half of the 1960s, large numbers of adults thrilled to award-winning films such as *The Apartment*, *Spartacus*, and *Exodus*. Yet a trio of much lower-budgeted, teen-oriented films not only established the careers of a number of young actors but also offered a hint that the image of this new decade's teenagers might be quite different than the already fondly discussed Fabulous Fifties. The first of this teen-oriented trio was initially recognized mainly for the fact that it represented a new medium for the recognized Pied Piper of teendom, Dick Clark.

Clark, who could never be accused of indolence, juggled a daily dance party in Philadelphia, a Saturday-night showcase in New York, and both producing and acting duties in California to complete *Because They're Young*. Adapted from John Farris's book *Harrison High*, the film offered a multidimensional foray into a "typical" American high school from the perspective of the faculty (centered on history teacher Clark), the school's "in crowd," and those who existed on the margins, including at least one character about to graduate from minor juvenile delinquency to full-fledged adult crime.

The subplots of the film ran the gamut from Clark's running duel with a by-the-book principal and his roller-coaster romance with a school secretary who doesn't trust teachers, to the struggle of transfer students to gain acceptance in a school where all of the cliques seem to have already been filled by the incumbents.

In a major break from the *Blackboard Jungle* genre of the fifties, Harrison High is depicted as a solidly middle-class school where the most significant crises are generated by external factors, ranging from the disparaging remarks of a (never seen) alcoholic mother concerning one girl's social life and career goals, the sexual escapades of a male student's single-parent mother, and the threatened intrusions into a closed school dance by a pack of delinquents from a neighboring "vo tech" school. Unlike the menace oozing from Vic Morrow and his henchmen in Glenn Ford's *Blackboard Jungle* class, Clark's students adore him, seek his advice, and babysit for his young nephew. The switchblades and black leather jackets still appear, but there is a hint that they are hopelessly out-of-date and come from rowdies who are not enrolled at Harrison.

Although it is difficult to maintain the tension of the plot when there is neither one really horrendous teacher nor one real juvenile delinquent within Harrison High's precincts, this journey into the teen image of the early 1960s does offer two major merits that made it popular for that era's teens and a valuable window into sixties high school experience today.

First, in a casting decision that continues to affect teen films and televi-sion in the 2010s, Clark decided to forgo the use of more mature actors in several key parts and utilized real teens. Unlike twenty-first-century hits such as *Glee* and *The Vampire Diaries*, which often feature actors in their midtwenties attempting to portray adolescents, *Because They're Young* has a more realistic teenage feel. For example, the two female leads, Roberta Shore and Tuesday Weld, were both real-live seventeen-year-olds who appear just as young (and slightly nervous).

Second, most of the major characters in the film present a realistic mix of positive and negative attributes, including Clark's sometimes grouchy demeanor toward his nine-year-old orphaned nephew. Harrison sports hero, Doug McLure, at times swaggers with self importance, calling less-celebrated students by their last names. Mickey Callan lurches between good behav-ior and actual criminality. Roberta Shore is often a spoiled princess who alternately entices and rejects McClure's advances. *Because They're Young* featured far less action than its fifties teen-pic predecessors, but it is likely that a much larger percentage of its teen audience could fully identify with this emerging early sixties high school environment.

A year after Dick Clark pushed fifties-style juvenile delinquents to the fringes of his Harrison High community, director Buzz Kulik dispensed with delinquent characters' services entirely in *The Explosive Generation*. At first glance, Kulik's Madison High School could be a few miles down the freeway from Harrison High in its solidly middle-class, suburban Los Angeles setting. Yet this film has a more documentary-type edge to it with far more tension between the students and most of the adults than with each other. The lone consistently sympathetic adult character is English teacher William Shatner, who unlike Clark has no romantic activities or nephew to guide and, instead, very nearly gets fired for his insistence on students' rights to freedom of speech. The four principal teen characters in the film, played by Lee Kinsolv-ing, Billy Gray, Patty McCormack, and Beau Bridges, are the only obvious professional actors at Madison, while most of the remaining cast seems as if they might actually attend this school in real life, as the director failed to excise a number of gaffes, including one teen girl almost falling over a chair as she backs away from Shatner's desk. Even a number of Shatner's teaching colleagues have the feel and look of veteran teachers coping with the low pay and overcrowded classrooms of the early sixties.

The only mention of teen crime in *The Explosive Generation* is when Gray laughingly challenges young lovers Kinsolving and McCormack that the last one to reach the ocean from Gray's father's beach house will be a juvenile delinquent. The plotline of the film centers around a very sixties-relevant topic, as Shatner gives students in his Senior Problems course permission to draw up questions concerning sexual relations that will be discussed during the next class. As hugely exaggerated accounts of this alleged sex survey drift from school to parents, McCormack's PTA-president mother and other outraged parents set in motion a chain of events that leads to Shatner's dismissal. In an evocative prediction of future events in the coming decade, the students retaliate with a huge protest rally that is met with a police threat to open up with fire hoses unless the pupils return to class, with the police chief instructing the teens to remember that they should only be seen, not heard.

The students' response, largely developed by Kinsolving, is to take this command in its most literal sense and refuse to speak at all during the school day, which very nearly gets the student leaders expelled. In an almost eerie prognostication of the difference between the fifties and upcoming sixties teen experience, Shatner peers out of the principal's window at the student protestors, as principal Ed Platt threatens to use force if Shatner refuses to convince the pupils to return to class. Shatner's response is that while young people in other nations have already gone into the streets to secure their rights and demands, "In this nation we have had only silence. Now this silence may be ending!" However, a 1961 film is not an actual school of 1968, and in the end, the PTA president, the principal, and the other parents relent, and the final scene shows Shatner reading the student questions to a newly empowered band of teenagers.

While *Because They're Young* and *The Explosive Generation* focused on early sixties teen experience in high school, director Henry Levin's *Where the Boys Are* makes the jump to the first year of college and its mixed menu of social freedom and repression. This lush widescreen Cinemascope-Technicolor production has much less of a documentary feel than the two other films, and there are a number of slapstick comic elements in the plot, but there is virtually no safety net for these adolescents as, for better or worse, the parental figures in the Clark and Kulick films become nonexistent in this feature.

The film focuses on four female college freshmen attending a "large Midwestern university" that seems to be permanently entombed in snow. The girls—brainy but rebellious Dolores Hart, budding beauty queen Yvette Mimieux, field hockey star Connie Francis, and tall, marriage-fixated Paula Prentiss—have spent much of their freshman year in failed romances and nearly failing grades, with former high school valedictorian Hart threatened with expulsion if her grades do not improve substantially after spring break. The immediate response to their predicament is a road trip to Fort Lauderdale, with Hart promising herself that she will improve her failing grades by studying on the Florida beach.

Once the quartet reaches Florida, the film divides into a number of concurrent plotlines, which veer from visual comedy to near tragedy, as each young lady seeks romance in the sunshine, buoyed by an innocent optimism that is not an unreasonable trait for teen collegians of either the sixties or the 2010s.

Hart, who is the female lead in the film, is promptly caught between the need to study in order to avoid embarrassing her parents by flunking out and her chance encounter with fabulously wealthy Brown University senior George Hamilton, who in an early sixties context presents a real possibility of making her academic challenges a moot point. Once aboard Hamilton's yacht, the prospect of becoming "Mrs. Rider Smith" with a bevy of servants almost makes her upcoming Russian exam seem ludicrous, yet Hart successfully fends off her suitor's most blatant advances.

On the other hand, as the second lead, Mimieux is virtually obsessed with finding and marrying an "Ivy Leaguer" who will far transcend the status and money of any "state U" counterparts and quickly gets at least part of her wish fulfilled as she "falls in love" with several predatory upperclassmen who allegedly fulfill her institutional qualifications. Yet, in a series of one-night stands, she finds herself passed from one rake to the next, ends up abandoned in a seedy motel, staggering into a near-fatal encounter with an auto on a crowded highway, until she is rescued by Hart and Hamilton. As Mimieux partially regains consciousness in the intensive care unit, she confesses to Hart that her allegedly Ivy League pedigreed "boyfriend" "isn't even a Yalie."

While Prentiss and Francis gain some measure of success in their own romantic quests, as the pair drives back to school with a weirdly dressed Jim Hutton and extremely nearsighted college jazz musician, Frank Gorshin, in tow, the outcome for Mimieux and Hart is barely within the parameters of traditional romantic comedies. Mimieux leaves Fort Lauderdale physically injured, emotionally scarred, and keenly aware of her lost innocence with little to look forward to except rigorous exams for which she has not studied. Hart, who like Mimeiux was a real-life teen playing a teen, nearly breaks up with Hamilton, who in turn vaguely invites her to attend his Brown graduation with no clear indication as to whether an engagement ring will be in her future or whether she will be expelled from her college.

While *Where the Boys Are* is generally considered to be the prototypical "beach" or "spring fling" movie, the film deals with far more serious issues than its successors and provides an excellent window into the early sixties dilemma for teens in college, especially females, as to whether the college experience is intended primarily for finding a suitable husband or whether it might unlock the portal to a more exciting, yet more daunting experience attempting to combine career and homemaking, either sequentially or in tandem.

None of these three motion pictures discussed was in any great danger of appearing on adult "must see" lists during the early 1960s. Yet each gives interested individuals in twenty-first-century America a reasonably good window into the world inhabited by teens in the early 1960s and hints at a sometimes conscious and sometimes unconscious feeling among the huge cohort of newly adolescent Baby Boomers that "their" decade as teens might be a quite different experience than the fifties of their older siblings.

This trio of films evokes very little of the adolescent rage of *Blackboard Jungle* or the alienation in *Rebel Without a Cause*. In these early sixties films, the protagonists generally have a clear sense of purpose, from securing freedom of speech in class in *The Explosive Generation* to securing suitable "husbands in training" in *Where the Boys Are*. These early sixties teen pics not only broke substantially from the previous decade's plotlines, they also set a template for a number of video images for the next several years, ranging from the dynamic, concerned young teacher of television's *Mr. Novak* to the teen beach vacation romp of the *Beach Party* series and its many competitors.

One of the most definitive film images of teen lifestyle during the first half of the 1960s was a group of adolescents cavorting along the beach in an apparently endless summer of surfboards, guitars, and picnic bonfires. Whether or not most teens could actually surf or play guitar was immaterial; sixties teens were filmed doing things that most adults did not do, and they were often visualized doing these things with few, if any, adults in sight. Two films, one each on either side of the fifties/sixties divide, set the stage for this largely adult-free, teen-dominated tropical paradise. The first was the previously mentioned *Where the Boys Are*, which once it abandons deans and professors in the Midwestern snow, leaves the rest of the film almost entirely to the young people. The other film, released in the waning days of the 1950s, gives the adults a tiny bit more authority but also introduces those surfboards and guitars so necessary to teen beach existence.

The slightly earlier companion film to Dolores Hart's collegiate beach adventures was based on a real female teenager's attempts to enter the then-male-dominated pursuit of surfing. In 1959 director Paul Wendkos adapted Frederick Kohner's novel about his daughter's adventures as a diminutive apprentice surfer called Gidget, a combination of *girl* and *midget*. Wendkos developed his film script around the young lady who was the most recognizable female teen movie star of the period, Sandra Dee, and paired her with two contenders for her affection: teen singing idol James Darren as Moondoggie, her more-or-less faithful age mate, and Cliff Robertson as adult surfing star

Big Kahuna. Dee proved her enormous talent as she spent this last year of the 1950s shuttling between the steamy embraces of Troy Donahue in *A Summer Place* and her more adolescent role in *Gidget*, and became a romantic fantasy for many early sixties teen boys and a poster girl for even mildly assertive girls as they watched her compete against males in the surf and then twirl them around her little finger on land.

Gidget was so successful that it morphed into a trilogy that essentially spanned beachfronts from Hawaii to Europe, but without Dee carrying the surfboard as Deborah Walley fronted *Gidget Goes Hawaiian* in 1961 and Cindy Carol starred in *Gidget Goes to Rome* two years later. The sequels turned the features into a sixties franchise. Yet just as the *Gidget* series wound down, director William Asher pulled the surfing scene back to California with *Beach Party*. While the plotline of the *Gidget* films alternated between the heroine's surfing adventures and her membership in a family, Asher cast his still basically adolescent surfers in an environment where parents are virtually never mentioned, let alone seen.

The strongest adult presence in any of the extended series of "beach" movies came in inaugural *Beach Party* in 1963, which cast Bob Cummings, who had previously played a rather lecherous bachelor photographer on the *Love That Bob* television series, as a similarly inclined college professor in the film. Cummings, armed with ample telephoto camera equipment, studies teen beach culture as an anthropology experiment, largely focusing on the off-again, on-again romance of Annette Funicello and Frankie Avalon to prove the "wild" behavior of that era's adolescents. The film soon becomes a double-ended romantic comedy as Cummings pursues fellow adult Dorothy Malone while snooping on the teen surfing and beach parties, with all Los Angeles adult beach lovers seemingly permanently banned from the seaside.

Beach Party proved far more popular among teens than the now fast-slipping *Gidget* movie franchise, and Asher spent the next two years alternating between directing his wife, Elizabeth Montgomery, as Samantha Stevens on the hit television program *Bewitched* and churning out *Beach Party* sequels, such as *Bikini Beach*, *Beach Blanket Bingo*, and two or three other similarly plotted efforts. One plotline that clearly labels the films as sixties endeavors is Asher's use of a comic conflict between Frankie and Annette and their occasional stand-in stars and comic actor Harvey Lembeck, who is cast as motorcycle gang leader Eric von Zipper, a buffoonish relic from the previous decade. Lembeck and his even more moronic followers are outfitted in classic fifties biker fashion and are constantly bested in "combat" by the hipper, smarter, and better looking sixties surfers in a slapstick form of generational conflict.

While Asher limited the generational conflict to "sixties" teens and vaguely young-adult "fifties" bikers, director Don Weis took the comic aspect of an increasingly perceived generation gap a step further in his 1965 gender-issue comedy *Billie*. Weis snagged multimedia superstar Patty Duke during her television show hiatus and in between recording sessions for her new rock music album to play an athletically gifted track competitor who attends a high school with no girls track team.

The diminutive Duke, who is very noticeably a teenager playing someone her own age, is paired off against mayoral candidate and father Jim Backus, on hiatus from *Gilligan's Island*, who is campaigning on a "keep women at home" platform, an outdated theme by the midsixties. The recurring "girl power" theme is hammered home as Duke sings, dances, and runs her way to both romance and track championships, changing her father into a proto-feminist at the very moment she quits the boys team to concentrate on solidifying her newfound dating relationship.

One of the main distinctions between the numerous teen-oriented films produced in Hollywood in the second half of the 1950s and the industry's equally generous number of adolescent-themed movies in the early to mid-sixties was a noticeable shift from juvenile delinquency themes to either more nuanced dramas or beach-oriented comedies. On the other hand, the rival television industry, far less attuned to niche audiences, considered itself daring to air even three prime-time, primarily adolescent-themed programs in the first half of the sixties, which was exactly three more than during the previous five years.

Between late 1959 and the autumn of 1963, the television networks debuted three fairly successful programs that focused on, respectively, a teenage boy's high school experience, an adolescent girl's adventures, and a young English teacher in a typical high school. These three programs, *The Many Loves of Dobie Gillis*, *The Patty Duke Show*, and *Mr. Novak*, provided a both comedic and dramatic tapestry of the high school and broader adolescent experience during the first half of the sixties decade.

Dobie Gillis, which debuted a few weeks before the onset of the sixties, revolved around characters developed by author Max Shulman, who had followed a popular book and film comedy about a small town coping with the Cold War in *Rally Round the Flag, Boys!* with his teen satire. The male and female teen leads in *Rally Round the Flag*, Dwayne Hickman and Tuesday Weld, were brought in as the leads in the new television show, which veered significantly away from most contemporary family situation comedies.

First, the centerpiece of family comedy interaction, the suburban single home, was eliminated as Dobie lives over his family's store. Most of the action is centered on four locales, the town high school, the local malt shop, the Gillis family grocery store, and a small park where Dobie sits on a bench in front of a statue of "The Thinker" and interprets the plotline for the television audience. Unlike most situation comedies, the teen-parent dialogue does not occur in a living room, kitchen, or study but in the grocery store, as the ill-tempered, overly critical Herbert Gillis alternates between stacking cans of peas and criticizing Dobie as lazy and useless, a confrontation softened only by the interventions of mother/wife Winnie, who attempts to remind her husband of the complexities of his own adolescent years.

While the first part of the series title, *The Many Loves . . .* , implies a new romance each episode, most of Dobie's social life veers back and forth between his heart's desire, Thalia (Weld) and Zelda, an annoying, smart, much-less-attractive classmate who is determined to marry Dobie and turn him from a dreamer to a hardworking success. On the surface, the handsome Dobie and the enormously attractive Thalia are a potentially ideal couple, but Thalia's latent feelings are trumped by the practicality of being in a relatively impoverished household, which often fixates her attention on rich but totally self-centered classmates.

The *Dobie Gillis* program represents somewhat of a sea change for traditional, family-oriented situation comedies, as the dialogue contains far more biting satire than most television comedy of that era. Dobie's hometown is neither Mayberry nor an attractive suburb; it is depicted, within the limits of Hollywood filming, as a not particularly affluent or attractive small city located in a region that would begin to emerge as the "rust belt" a decade later. The teachers in Dobie's high school are clearly overworked and underpaid, and in some episodes are on the verge of quitting for more lucrative careers. It is clear from the beginning that Dobie has little chance to win the affection of Thalia, or most other really desirable female classmates, who all seem to vie for the limited supply of well-to-do boys. In turn, the teachers are so badly paid by the tightwad school board that even the parsimonious Herbert Gillis occasionally slips Dobie's teachers free food, and the lead male instructor, Mr. Pomfrit, eventually quits to teach in a community college, where, as he tells Dobie, "They pay something called a living wage."

Dobie Gillis also entered new territory in chronicling early sixties teen culture in the character development of Dobie's closest friend, Maynard G. Krebs. Maynard, played by future *Gilligan's Island* star, Bob Denver, represents the emerging counterculture of the era, as he is a teenaged beatnik, complete with torn T-shirt, beret, goatee, and bongo drums. The writers were never able to fully reconcile Maynard's regalia with high school dress codes of the era, but in many respects Krebs is the real hero of the show, a person truly without malice or selfishness who will never betray Dobie and accepts his friend's fixation on girls instead of his one true friend with remarkable grace.

In many respects, using the cover that teens are inherently impossible to understand by adults, the *Dobie Gillis* writers created a program that challenged the status quo on a variety of levels where more mainstream "family" or "adult" shows would not dare to go. There is just a hint in the show that, while the juvenile delinquency threat to adult power structure has largely dissipated, there just might be some new form of teen counterculture shocking their elders before the new decade is over.

While *Dobie Gillis* finished its CBS run in the late spring of 1963, the ABC network quickly filled the adolescent-centered comedy void only a few months later with a new female high school "heroine." The network was anxious to utilize the talents of diminutive teen Academy Award–winning actress Patty Duke, who shifted from the intensely dramatic world of Helen Keller in *The Miracle Worker* to a comedy about identical twin cousins in a Brooklyn Heights high school.

Sidney Sheldon, who had won his own Oscar for Best Original Screenplay in the 1947 film *The Bachelor and the Bobby-Soxer*, signed the sixteen-year-old actress as the first young star to have a television show named after her, while establishing a certain continuity with the recently ended *Dobie Gillis* by signing the two main teachers in the series, William Schallert and Jean Byron, to be the parents of the wild and carefree Patty Lane and her improbable Scottish identical cousin, Cathy Lane, a shy, well-travelled intellectual who spends much of her time repairing Patty's social and educational disasters.

Sheldon broke from the domination of television filming in Hollywood by producing the show in New York, partially because that state's child labor laws were more liberal than California's, allowing Duke to work more hours per day, at least until she reached eighteen, and later episodes could be generated out west. Thus, just as Dobie Gillis's high school experience was slightly outside the emerging demographic mainstream, being set in a small city, Patty and Cathy Lane's Brooklyn Heights High offered a somewhat more big-city feel than most traditional family situation comedies.

The Patty Duke Show is at the same time less caustic and more optimistic than *Dobie Gillis*. While Dobie pursues his quixotic relationship with Thalia, Patty has her steady boyfriend, Richard, wrapped around her little finger, even as she flirts outrageously with most of the male population of her high school. However, Sheldon, who not only produced but wrote the majority of episode scripts, had a keen eye for the teen experience and their relationships with adults and younger siblings. Notable plotlines include a hilarious episode in which Patty's intelligence is tested by an educational computer;

the often clueless heroine manages almost by accident to reprogram the typical sixties behemoth of steel and flashing lights, called a "computing machine," which certifies her as a genius. In a mild poke at post-Sputnik fascination with an easy fix to allegedly inferior American teen intelligence, everyone from the principal and the computer designer to faculty, siblings, and parents virtually worships her with everything from awards to breakfast in bed while discovery of a design flaw sends her crashing back to academic mediocrity. A second signature episode places Cathy and then Patty in the role of substitute instructor for an absent teacher and offers a commentary on the loneliness of actual teachers, who are often ignored by lackadaisical students, yet not supported by principals when they attempt to crack down. Finally, a third episode unites the usually feuding Patty and Cathy in support of preteen brother Ross, who has been invited to his first boy-girl dance by a young lady and is tempted to leave the security of childhood for the uncertainty and emotional roller coaster of very early adolescence. The plotlines not only transcend particularly sixties teen affairs for larger adolescent issues still relevant in the twenty-first century, but the presence of a very real and very young-looking adolescent in the lead role(s) is a refreshing variant on the tendency of many youth-oriented programs of the 2010s, utilizing "teen" characters often played by actors nearly ten years older than their screen age.

The third major teen-centered television program of the early to mid-1960s was a drama, not a comedy, and viewed the adolescent experience through the eyes of a young, idealistic teacher who has made these young people the centerpiece of his own universe. In the autumn of 1963, as ABC was debuting *Patty Duke*, the National Broadcasting Company took on the daunting prospect of countering ABC's hit series *Combat!* and CBS's iconic *Gunsmoke* with a dramatic series in which twenty-nine-year-old Yale graduate James Franciscus took on overcrowded high school English classes for $5,842 as *Mr. Novak*. This idealistic young instructor was eager to "wage war five days a week against ignorance, intolerance and injustice" in a network resume that gave Novak virtually superhero status.

Despite the fact that the students were generally better dressed, more photogenic, and more articulate than their more mundane actual counterparts, the series quickly gained plaudits everywhere from the National Education Association to *Time* magazine. The producers made sure that teachers across the country got to see scripts before the airdates in order to add numerous realistic touches to the final product. *Time* ran an extensive feature on the new program, applauding its realism based on extensive research at fifty real high schools and its willingness to tackle such still-novel social issues as racial prejudice, cheating, and rebellious young teachers who felt shackled by a bloated and unresponsive educational bureaucracy. As the news magazine insisted, "Mr. Novak might not keep all teen boys from watching Combat," but if the program could hold some boys and most of the girls, "it will graduate with honors."

Mr. Novak made a major break from 1950s television programs that centered on high school teachers. During that previous decade, teachers had been portrayed as either simpletons, as in Mr. Peepers, or as man-hungry single women, as in the title character of Our Miss Brooks, who would often forsake interest in teaching to pursue "dreamboat" biology teacher Mr. Boynton. Mr. Novak is handsome, smart, and enormously focused on the welfare of his students, to the point of breaking or at least seemingly bending the rules for their welfare. The program emerged as a composite of an anthology drama and a regular casted series, in the sense that much of Franciscus's student population seemed to change from week to week as a new student's issue emerged. Yet several of the fellow teachers, counselors, and administrators remained constant, with first-rate actors such as Dean Jagger and Burgess Meredith providing mentoring for the young instructor. If 1950s teachers winced every week at Miss Brooks and Mr. Peepers, their sixties counterparts perhaps viewed Mr. Novak as a more glamorous but realistic version of themselves, much the way World War II veterans viewed actors Vic Morrow and Rich Jason, as their platoon weekly battled the Wehrmacht on the competing Tuesday-night hit, Combat!

Dobie Gillis, Patty Duke, and Mr. Novak defined much of the television version of the high school experience during the first half of the sixties decade. However, the continued strong presence of a number of iconic family programs, often erroneously called fifties sitcoms, provided adults, teens, and preteens with a view of what the teenage experience was at least supposed to look like from network scriptwriters, especially outside the high school classroom.

A recurring topic of interest in both popular and more academic studies of American postwar popular culture has been the impact of the hugely popular family-centered situation comedies that filled much of the network primetime schedule from roughly the mid-1950s into the first part of the 1960s. Some of the most prominent and frequently analyzed examples of this genre were Father Knows Best, Ozzie and Harriet, The Donna Reed Show, Leave It to Beaver, and My Three Sons. However, while these programs are frequently described in the context of fifties popular culture and television, a careful perusal of network television grids from this era reveal that more episodes of these five series were telecast in the 1960s than the more commonly depicted 1950s.

Among these five programs, only *Father Knows Best* had a rather limited presence in the sixties, as it ran from 1955 to 1962, while *Leave It to Beaver* almost straddled the two decades, running from 1957 to 1963. The extremely long-running *Ozzie and Harriet* was a significant presence in both decades in its 1952 to 1966 run, while *The Donna Reed Show* (1958 to 1966) and *My Three Sons* (1960 to 1970) were minimal presences in the earlier decade. All of these programs had very broad-based audiences of which teens constituted a relatively small, yet still demographically important, segment. Yet each of these programs featured one or more teen regulars who formed a significant plotline in at least some, or even the majority, of episodes.

The Nelsons were the "oldest" (and also the most authentic) family of the group as the sixties began. Ozzie and Harriet were now in late middle age, and David, who was actually now heavily involved in production, was depicted as a student in college and then law school. On the other hand, Ricky, who was actually a late teen at the beginning of the sixties, played slightly younger roles in deference to his status as one of the most prominent teen idols of the early sixties. Between 1960 and 1963, when Ricky married teenager Kristin Harmon and had a baby, much of the plotline in the Nelson household revolved around Rick's teen high jinks, usually designed to set the stage for the obligatory song late in the episode. The plotlines still contained enough domestic banter among Ozzie, Harriet, and their assorted neighbors and friends to keep the huge adult audience relatively content, but Ozzie's insistence that his show would be the only television outlet for Ricky's long string of hit songs guaranteed substantial subplots or even entire programs geared toward teen audiences, especially his huge adolescent female fan base.

While Rick Nelson's late teen experience seemed to include little need or opportunity for serious parental intervention or advice, *Father Knows Best* spent the relatively brief 1960s portion of its run with Robert Young and Jane Wyatt dealing with three children in very distinct periods of the teen experience. Betty (Elinor Donahue) had spent most of her high school years in the late 1950s and by the dawn of the new decade was cast as a late teen navigating the world of college and part-time jobs, interspersed with "serious" romances expected of a "princess" who was soon destined for marriage. On the other hand, Bud (Billy Gray) was at the peak of high school adolescence in the early sixties, moonlighting during hiatus periods in feature-length teen-oriented films. Plotlines clearly show Bud at least partially listening to the Wyatt/Young advice on offer, yet just rebellious enough to carry relatively comic crises to their somewhat predictable resolutions. As the program entered its final (sixties) phase, Kitten (Lauren Chapin) and her activities became a popular role model for American girls making a transition from preteen to full adolescence, equipped with a certain sense of humor and cuteness but facing the same lack of glamour that complicated Kitten's TV transition from junior high school to senior high.

The major rival to the boy-girl sibling rivalry among the Anderson children was the only other mixed-gender teen household of the five programs, *The Donna Reed Show*. The program revolved around parents just a bit younger than the Andersons, consisting of Dr. Alex Stone, a highly empathetic physician, and Donna Stone, an equally sympathetic housewife and mother. Donna Reed was a relatively high-profile screen actress but not a comedian, so most of the "comic" aspect of the program revolved around teenager Mary (Shelley Fabares) and slightly younger brother, Jeff (Paul Peterson). By the 1962–1963 period, the original cast and siblings were more and more often the focal point of programs, and they were able to use their popularity among preteens and teen audiences to secure major recording contracts, including top-ten hits "Johnny Angel," sung by Fabares, and "My Dad" by Peterson. The shift in direction from parents to children is quite noticeable in a 1962 episode centering around Mary practicing for a school variety show in which she just happens to sing "Johnny Angel." As Mary sings with accompanying guitarists and backup singers, Donna Reed looks on with a mixture of awe and perhaps sadness at her daughter's new level of independence, with her sole remaining authority being her ability to hush Mary's boyfriend as he is about to make a comment to Mrs. Stone midsong.

While *Father Knows Best* frequently depicted middle child Billy Gray as caught between his older and younger sisters, with quite different interactions between the two girls, *The Donna Reed Show* entered one aspect of that plotline when Shelly Fabares left the show to do films, forcing Mary to go away to college. The program producers concocted a clever alternative, with the Stones effectively adopting a younger sibling for Jeff, who in real life was his sister Patty Peterson. Thus, plotlines based on the tension between older sister and younger brother quickly underwent a sea change into a far less contentious relationship between the two real siblings.

The sparks that fly between sibling rivals Jeff and Mary on *The Donna Reed Show* are far less evident on the generally better remembered and more frequently discussed (and parodied) *Leave It to Beaver*. Both of these programs hit the peak of their popularity in the early 1960s, but while the former program retooled characters and plots to survive until 1966, the latter show ended production in 1963, with Beaver clearly headed into full adolescence. *Leave It to Beaver* differed somewhat from the three previously discussed programs in that from the start to the finish of the series most of the plotlines focus on the distinct, yet interlocking, worlds of two boys, Theodore (Beaver) and

Wally, with parents Ward and June serving as advisors, mentors, and even referees. Unlike *Ozzie and Harriet*, we know far more about the children's friends than those of the parents. Eddie Haskell, Lumpy Rutherford, and Larry Mondello are all major elements in the narrative, with Ward and June often called upon to sort out the crises created more often by these flawed children and teens than the Cleavers' own sons. While a two-child family is on the lower end of the sixties spectrum, the shared bedroom of two boys not extremely close in age was often representative of larger, mixed-gender real families. On a relatively innocent level, Beaver and Wally use that room to plot strategies to navigate the shoals of their separate journeys through childhood and adolescence, even if those voyages were mostly less fraught with perils than real sixties preteens and teens. However, even if issues were a little too easily solved, *everybody* knew a real-life Eddie Haskell, a two-faced operator with virtually no redeeming qualities. Beaver Cleaver, the adorable fifties child, transformed into an extremely likable adolescent in the sixties, and his older brother never fully abandoned him for either male companions or girlfriends during those final seasons. This relationship would prove more permanent than many situation comedies, as the show continued into future decades in both rerun and sequel format. *Leave It to Beaver* represented the "typical" middle-class late fifties to early sixties family in almost every category, other than its relatively small size and lack of female children, yet the only one of this situation comedy quintet to be telecast entirely in the 1960s prospered with a plotline decidedly unusual for a typical sixties household.

My Three Sons, which had the distinction of airing from 1960 to 1970, created the opportunity for new teen-experience plotlines with its scenario of creating a family with three motherless boys being raised by two unrelated men. The ABC network had not entered totally uncharted territory in this genre, as rival NBC had featured John Forsythe as a rich playboy uncle to a teenage niece in the fairly successful *Bachelor Father*. Much of the comedy of this program emerged from the general cluelessness of "Uncle Bentley" to the responsibility of raising any sort of adolescent and especially a teenage girl, even if he did have a live-in houseboy to ease the crises.

My Three Sons was a bit more relevant, in the sense that the program paired successful screen actor Fred MacMurray with *I Love Lucy* alumnus William Frawley as a widower and his acerbic father-in-law and simplified their task by making all of the children boys. Many sixties child and teen viewers were fascinated by the interaction of characters in a family of apparently well-adjusted, normal people in a household that was quite exotic at that time and place. Children and even adolescents would discuss the complexities of living in a family where the substitute for the mother figure was that often gruff, sarcastic, if caring, Bub, who was a bit like having a somewhat salty chief petty officer or sergeant in charge of a household, a far cry from Donna Stone or June Cleaver, even if Fred MacMurray could hold his own with Carl Betz or Hugh Beaumont in the caring and advice-giving father category. As a preteen and teen in a "traditional" two-parent, two-boy, two-girl sixties family, I personally found My Three Sons to be a sort of exotic adventure into a realm quite a bit different from myself or my friends. Decades later, more than any other sixties television program or film, this show would, unfortunately, enter my real world, as I was thrust into the Fred MacMurray role in my own life. However, ironically, no sixties set of plotline challenges seemed so easily met when I compared the relatively mature Douglas children to my own three sons, who consisted of an infant, a toddler, and an elementary school child, with no William Frawley character in sight.

However, in all fairness, My Three Sons should not be evaluated in its relationship to real-life single parentage of much younger children several decades later, but in the program's rather intriguing ability to convey the image of rather specially circumstanced preteens and teens of the 1960s. The trio of Mike, Robbie, and Chip Douglas add an additional dimension to the Wally and Beaver Cleaver alliance, as Mike's relative maturity often makes him a junior partner in authority with his father and grandfather almost as often as he slips back into simply the older brother persona. More than the four previously mentioned series, My Three Sons represented a sort of "alternative universe" to sixties teens who lived in two-parent households, yet the program became a template for more common nontraditional family situation comedies in later decades, from Punky Brewster to Full House. Ironically, as the later sixties brought increasing hints that American family structure was about to become less easily defined, the producers of My Three Sons did a plotline about-face and gave Fred MacMurray a wife, daughter, and family structure closer to its early sixties competitors. The primarily teen-oriented programs, such as Dobie Gillis and Patty Duke and the more family-inclined Donna Reed and Leave It to Beaver all presented the teenage experience through the prism of fictional characters and families, most of whom still tended to be more self-assured and telegenic than the average adolescent watching on a flickering twenty-one-inch screen. However, that same screen brought real teenagers into the living room in a sort of early version of reality television called the teen dance party.

The teen dance party was essentially a 1950s concept that continued to flourish and even expand for much of the following decade. By the 1960s, relatively small cities, such as Providence, Rhode Island; Syracuse, New

York; and Allentown, Pennsylvania, were home to either weekly afternoon, Saturday-afternoon, or early evening dance shows. Some programs tapped into special features to gain regional or even national syndication. For example, the Detroit program *Teen Time* was able to tap into the exploding Motown music incubator to feature major stars such as the Supremes and Stevie Wonder, while the California-based *Lloyd Thaxton Show* offered the innovation of featuring underclassmen from a different local college each day both to dance and to engage in music-driven game competition.

However, for much of the first half of the 1960s, the most widely recognizable image of American teens was the primarily, but not exclusively, Philadelphia-based adolescent dancing around the WFIL TV Channel 6 studios under the watchful eye of their impresario, Dick Clark. In the same way that many iconic family sitcoms are referred to as fifties programs, Clark's *American Bandstand*, if frequently presented in a 1950s context, actually ran 60 percent of its Philadelphia-based daily programming in the sixties. By the early 1960s, Clark and his producers had solidified a profitable and well-publicized program format that was a fascinating combination of predictability and innovation. *Bandstand* was divided into four or five half-hour segments, so that while Philadelphia teens had access to a program that ran as long as a major sporting event, stations in other markets could tap into as many or as few segments as they wished, depending on the popularity of alternative local programs. Thus, on days when two or even three guest artists were scheduled to appear on *Bandstand*, lesser-known acts were penciled into the smaller audience program blocs, while more recognizable established acts appeared in the most heavily viewed segments.

A fairly wide spectrum of guest artists appeared on the program to lip-sync a new song that needed to be plugged or to perform a past hit, if the artist's career was in a temporary dry spell or a permanent decline. While the heavily female audience was truly ecstatic when teen heartthrobs such as Fabian appeared, the emotional level dropped down to "correctly polite" when less teen-oriented acts somehow found their way into the studio. One of the few surviving complete episodes shows an almost painful interaction between the polite but obviously bored teen audience and pre–rock and roll guest artist Georgia Gibbs, who thanks to a poorly chosen wardrobe, appears nearly fifty and regales the squirming adolescents with tales of remodeling her apartment in Danish Modern furniture. While some lucky teens did get to see relatively well-known artists perform, the length and daily format of the program ensured that infrequent or one-time teen visitors had a better chance to view a second- or third-tier performer and receive a "celebrity" autograph that would produce only shrugs in the high school cafeteria.

Bandstand's on-screen teens, viewed and often envied by the rest of America's adolescent population, actually consisted of a hodgepodge of three different constituencies. One group of teens was present in order to ensure that *Bandstand* was really *American Bandstand*. Television viewers from across the nation were invited to write in for tickets to be in the live audience, and a lucky few would even get to participate in dance contests with an introduction, including the ABC affiliate on which they viewed the program. These lucky teens had tickets that guaranteed admission, which was not the case for the second category of eager young adolescents.

While tickets were most often distributed to young viewers who lived outside of the Philadelphia area in order to "nationalize" what in some respects was merely a local dance party, entry was always allowed to a second group of fans who attended local high schools. Instead of arriving with tickets, these teens knew that successful entry was possible by simply being early enough to secure a space in ever-lengthening lines snaking out from the WFIL TV studios. Since *Bandstand* went on the air soon after most high schools closed for the day, the highest probability of admission went to teens who attended schools near the station. This favored status was most apparent to students of two schools within a short walk to the television station, West Catholic High School for Girls and West Catholic High School for Boys, both Gothic-looking structures that towered over the endless brick row houses in which their students resided. A second tier of schools was located a short subway, elevated train, bus, or trolley car ride away and extended from other parts of the city of Philadelphia to its inner-ring suburbs. Given the right transit connections, these slightly less-favored teens could still secure a place before the studio door opened. On the other hand, enterprising students who lived too far away from *Bandstand* to arrive on time for the program sometimes merely cut their final school period or managed to schedule a study hall or nonrequired elective from which they might occasionally negotiate an early dismissal. This pool of teens was much too large to ensure daily entrance to the program, but these boys and girls usually managed to secure entry just often enough that they were somewhat recognizable to the huge national audience.

The third group of *Bandstand* teens constituted a form of royalty that was recognized all across America. These teens were denoted as "regulars," and their faces showed up on camera day after day. They were often just a little more attractive, a little more poised, and a little more skilled dancers than most other teens around them. By the early 1960s, most of the "original" fifties regulars had moved on toward adulthood, and new faces appeared as the twist replaced the stroll. These teens paid somewhat of a price for their "regular" status, as Clark monitored their behavior more than he did infrequent or onetime visitors. Regulars had to be full-time high school students between fourteen and eighteen years of age, and each marking period Clark perused their report cards, exiling low achievers until their grades improved. However, the almost parental scrutiny brought a huge return in the form of fan clubs, tremendous amounts of fan mail, and near teen idol status in the surging number of teen magazines. In a cross between an adult soap opera and a twenty-first-century reality show, these royal couples sizzled the cameras with romantic slow dances, and then shocked their myriad fans by splitting up and finding new partners. While adolescent girls were far more open about their interest in these surrogate romances, many teen boys admitted more privately that they had a crush on a regular who they would most likely never meet in real life. Also, like a reality show, Clark and his producers spiced up the action by occasionally moving the locale from the studio to an outdoor venue in which the usually stringent dress regulations were relaxed, and sometimes new partners were found at an amusement park, rodeo, or haunted house. In turn, ratings almost always rose even higher on these "special" days, which vicariously pulled in teens nationwide.

As American teenagers relaxed in movie theaters or their living rooms to watch young people like them experience the wonders and problems of adolescence in a compressed time span, ordinary boys and girls sometimes reflected on the accelerating pace of their own high school careers. Soon after the sweet sixteen parties and the anxiety of the first (or second or third) driver's examination were over, many teens watched students only one year older than themselves sign their yearbook a final time and collect their caps and gowns in home room. On the last day of eleventh grade, there might very well be a final assembly in which the front rows in the school auditorium might be vacant as the seniors had already graduated. Yet less than three months later, these juniors would sit in those same seats and begin the first part of a great transition that, for more and more sixties teens, would result in facing the ultimate academic challenge, enrollment in a college in which adolescence and adulthood coexisted on an often-confusing common ground.

CHAPTER SIX

~

Teens in Transition

Home Room to Dorm Room

Anyone who has ever attended a high school graduation ceremony as an adult usually encounters a pageantlike atmosphere as impossibly young-looking capped and gowned teenagers progress to a stage and receive stirring promises of the exciting prospects that await them in speeches from administrators, faculty, and student leaders. A time traveler journeying forward from the 1960s or a contemporary counterpart traveling back to that era would notice some differences in fashion and hairstyles, but the ceremony itself would look remarkably familiar as this special day almost always celebrates past accomplishment, present recognition, and future possibilities. However, while the ceremony itself would look very similar in either period, this moment of transition would be perceived rather differently by a substantial number of graduates from the two eras.

First, most of the 2010s graduates would be peering out at an audience that contained parents who were about as likely to hold a high school diploma as the students on the stage; parents would, of course, be proud and excited, but at some point in the ceremony they would very likely think of their own version of this day a generation earlier. On the other hand, a substantial percentage of 1960s graduates would be accomplishing something that their parents had not experienced. While over 75 percent of early sixties teens would graduate from high school, and this number would push another ten to twelve points higher before the decade's end, only 38 percent of 1940 eighteen-year-olds finished high school. Something like half of the parents in the audience were watching their teenage child participate in an academic milestone that they had never experienced themselves.

A second and even more noteworthy difference between the otherwise similar 1960 and 2010 high school graduation is the fact that before the sixties were over, proportionally more than four times as many of those eager young graduates would be proceeding to another level of education than their parents. On the eve of Pearl Harbor, only 13 percent of teens would even enter college; on the eve of Woodstock, half of their children would experience some form of campus life. However, that spectacular growth would come at an enormous psychological cost. Due to a continuation of enormously heightened educational expectations and the sheer growth in teen numbers due to the Baby Boom, the period between the eve of twelfth grade and the end of freshman year of college would become a two-year emotional roller coaster of transition that would often turn senior year of high school and the initial year of higher education into a succession of challenges that ended as often in tearful defeat as heady victory.

High school seniors of the 2010s who plan on continuing their education most often face two significant challenges on their road to the college experience: gaining entrance to an institution at or near the top of their list of preferred schools, and meeting the skyrocketing cost of attending many universities. This process can be emotionally draining, but since there are generally more openings in the nation's more than four thousand colleges than there are total number of high school graduates interested in attending those colleges, the most common adult question to twenty-first-century high school seniors is, "Where are you going to college?" rather than "Did you get *into* college?" Contemporary teens are very emotional about securing acceptance into at least one of their favorite schools, but they usually have at least a vague realization that they are protected by an academic safety net of numerous colleges actively soliciting their application, as indicated by scores of colorful glossy brochures sent to high school seniors entering the academic shopping spree. In fact, it might be fairly stated that the most intense pressure in the contemporary college admissions process is on often-harried parents who must somehow cobble together the funding needed to send their child to the "college of his or her choice" in an environment where the cost of higher education far outpaces salary gains and an increasing number of children have discovered that the only experience better than four years in college is to extend their stay an extra year or two.

If modern "teens in transition" experience at least some emotional trepidation in navigating academic waters where the existence of more college seats than total applicants significantly lessens total failure in that quest, the parents of young scholars in the sixties faced more daunting challenges.

This great transition, the emotional roller coaster of the sixties collegiate admissions contest, was often a kind of academic boot camp, where just as in the military service new terms and acronyms emerged with almost numbing rapidity. Terms such as PSAT, SAT, ACT, GPA, WX, achievement test, academic probation, dean's list, and academic dismissal were set against a backdrop of anxiety and near-magic anticipation that began to set in as eleventh graders watched seniors close their lockers with a final clang and perhaps a final twist of the number-coded wheel that protected their small personal space in what was now their alma mater.

Now, on a hot June day, these sixteen- or seventeen-year-old juniors were either formally or informally recognized as the new seniors and students a year younger slipped into their still relatively coveted "second from the top" status. For many of those teens, this summer approached with spectacular promise; many of them now had drivers' licenses and either their own car or access to one at least some of the time. The following fall would bring the prospect of more electives, being treated a lot more like adults by their teachers, and the beginning of a clear-cut direction for their future lives. By the midpoint of the decade, there were about three million boys and girls ready to enjoy their last full high school summer, and more than half of them had at least some interest in continuing their education beyond high school. Yet lying just outside the summer tableaux of beaches, pools, sleeping late, and enjoying freedom from homework was the grim reality that their elders had not yet constructed enough colleges to handle all who wished to attend, and securing one of those limited spaces would require more than a little effort and anxiety.

The first flicker of anxiety, or sometimes confidence, had most likely occurred before these teens had assumed their coveted new senior status. Sometime during eleventh grade, many of these boys and girls had taken the PSAT, which seemed a sort of academic version of spring training in baseball or the preseason games in the National Football League. Tests were taken using no. 2 pencils, and scores were sent to homes with the emphasis that this test officially "didn't count" as part of the formal college admission process. However, each test taker was given a percentile score and information on how to translate that number into something approximate to the real SAT equivalent. Then, just as summer loomed on the horizon, many eleventh graders sat for their first real Scholastic Aptitude Test. Sometime during the summer, official-looking envelopes arrived in home mailboxes, and students, their friends, and parents entered a strange mathematical universe where a "perfect" score counted as an 800 and a student who had somehow failed to answer a single question correctly still received a 200. A tiny number of students nationwide hit the double perfection of 800 on both the Math and Verbal sections, and this magic 1600 not only released these lucky few from the need to utilize subsequent test dates but virtually guaranteed admission to at least some college.

Almost any score under perfection virtually assured further Saturday-morning appointments with proctors, no. 2 pencils, and multiple-choice examinations that British students interested in the American university experience so quaintly called "bubble tests," referring to the rows of small black ovals that allowed no room for interpretation or divergent ideas. These two main scores, often combined with the initial round of aptitude tests, based on specific subject areas, often prodded some rising seniors to spend the summer thinking or rethinking potential college majors, while more than a few others began to rethink their interest in continuing the quest for college altogether.

Then, just as summer heat and unstructured days seemed like they would last forever, these sixties teens entered familiar brick or stone buildings for the last "back to school day" they would share with this particular group of peers. If our now increasingly experienced twenty-first-century time traveler returned to a particular September day in the 1960s mainly to concentrate on shadowing a representative group of new seniors, he or she might insist upon returning that the sixties teens looked a bit older than their modern counterparts, as their hair styles and fashions somehow made them appear just a bit more "adult" than 2010s teens. Yet as these same sixties twelfth graders shifted into their classrooms to meet their final coterie of high school teachers, those instructors might have spent a moment to wistfully remember when they themselves looked that young.

Now, as seniors opened their new textbooks, appraised the classroom "chemistry" that may or may not have changed appreciably since junior year, and tried to gauge the level of work expected by their instructors, they began to peruse school calendars that increasingly contained the word *senior* before key events. Seniors prepared to attend their last homecoming event, as students and members of their class would now be elected as king and queen and members of the court. Some seniors might spend part of that event's football game talking with recent graduates now at college, who would regale the seniors with tales of college life with varying degrees of accuracy.

Sixties teens shared an anticipation for a seminal social event both remarkably similar yet tantalizingly different with their 2010s counterparts. For adolescents of that earlier time, this major event was called *the prom*, an event that in future decades became the somewhat less definitive "going to prom," almost as if there were a large number of these events on offer. Yet if sixties high school seniors made more of this event's distinctiveness, they (or their parents) also tended to spend far less money on the experience than their future counterparts. The sixties version of this special dance somehow had a need for fewer limousines, less ornate tuxedos, and more inexpensive prom dresses combined with more adult supervision and more opportunity for some statement of commitment, from steady status to engagement ring.

Sometime between homecoming weekend and prom night, work would begin in earnest of the narrative of that particular group of seniors. While test papers would be soon jettisoned, honors and certificates stowed in drawers, and school newspapers stashed and forgotten or merely disposed of, the yearbook would place this particular group of seniors forever as a distinct unit, always the "Class of 1964" or "Class of 1967," with members of that group permanently placing members of the first class below them as juniors and students two years younger as sophomores, as if they would never advance further in this unique universe, just as the class preceding them always saw *them* as permanent juniors in their world of 1963 or 1966. The yearbook was special because, while all school events of that year were somehow included, they were always narrated from the perspective of the seniors. In many schools, underclassmen could play superstar roles, even editor of the school newspaper, but in most schools, the yearbook staff consisted only of seniors. While students in lower grades were depicted individually in very small pictures or no picture at all, seniors were far more prominently displayed as permanent eighteen-year-olds who, at least in that book, would never age further.

The seniors who served as yearbook staff members dispensed an interesting combination of generosity and selfishness, truth and fiction, throughout the pages of their volume. For instance, while all seniors were displayed in the same-size senior portrait, in the rest of the book it was clear that some graduates were more equal than others. Seniors who had joined few activities or had not particularly impressed anyone could graduate with that single portrait as the only testament that they even existed. Yet others who were cuter, more athletic, or more versatile became virtual regulars, as they appeared over and over throughout the pages. In this context, the yearbook was also the primary forum for the famous "most likely to . . ." segment, allegedly based on a poll of all seniors but often suspected to have been cooked up by some inner circle who had few issues with subjective judgment. This was the world of the high school royalty, the "Who's Who" of seniors that somehow were expected to take their special powers into the world beyond school. They were the best dressed, most musical, class flirts, best looking, most responsible, best personality, most artistic, most athletic, class clowns, and most importantly, either most popular or most likely to succeed. Some school officials or faculty advisors allowed students only one or two categories of distinction; others allowed near monopolies, where somehow the class clown and most responsible were the same person. Sometimes the prognostications looked amazingly prescient three or four decades later; other times the "royals" were reduced to mere mortals in adult life.

Yet if a perusal of most sixties high school yearbooks often evokes little of the egalitarianism that was thought to be in the air during the decade, the boys and girls charged with developing the captions accompanying the senior portraits often displayed a charity and compassion that spoke well of their preparation for adulthood. These teens seemed able to put a positive spin on an individual's undistinguished high school career and accentuate character traits that most other classmates never noticed.

The same generous prose that summarized the high school career of seniors who were graduating from schools small enough to provide commentary above name and address appears in most yearbook accounts of school activities during the course of the year. Dances are often described as "magical," even if many students did not remember much magic that evening. School classes taught by boring teachers and endured by fidgety students somehow emerged as exciting seminars in yearbook photos and prose. Some yearbook sports editors (including this author) had to put a positive spin on teams that lost twice as often as they won by emphasizing each team's spirit and character rather than athletic prowess.

Most 1960s yearbook descriptions of students and school life would seem quite contemporary to modern readers able to get past bouffant hairdos, more formal school wear, and particularly unflattering eyeglasses. However, some of the similarities between the two eras begin to break down when under the glare of some substantial differences in perceptions of post–high school life in the two generations of teens. A larger number of sixties teens faced a much more rapid entry into the realities of the adult world due to a combination of early average age of marriage, a stronger possibility of failure to win admission to any college, and the reality of male military conscription, which rose steadily during the decade.

First, sixties teens lived in a society in which, for much of the decade, the two most common ages for girls to be married were eighteen and nineteen, and boys were only marginally older. The going-steady concept in high school had many aspects of a trial marriage, and for many teens the formal wear of the senior prom was merely a dress rehearsal for a relatively imminent marriage. Couples who were steadies in their senior year of high school were routinely discussing marriage, and breakups became less and less common as graduation approached. A steady relationship that survived until graduation had already essentially been vetted by significant relatives in both families, and failure to actively attempt to break up the couple was tacit admission by parents that the relationship was acceptable and, in some cases, even highly desirable. A comparison of 1960s and contemporary issues of magazines, such as *Seventeen* and *Glamour* reveal much more specific articles and advertisement treatment of impending marriage during the earlier decade. Seventeen-year-old girls of the sixties seem to be expected to be aware of what type of silverware, dishes, furniture, and other home furnishings they would prefer in an obviously not-too-distant married world. At the same time, women's and general readership magazines carried a significant number of articles and advertisements that depicted married teenage or very early twenties mothers as very common and normal aspects of womanhood, and in some respects complemented the information provided by the teen magazines, with a message that either college or marriage and motherhood (and sometimes both) would be exciting reasons to find it good to be female in the 1960s.

While teen males were certainly an integral part of this seemingly logical outcome of high school steady relationships, a major potential distraction for post–high school males was the existence of a gradually escalating demand from the American military for conscripted servicemen. While twenty-first-century teen boys see military service as one among several post–high school options, all physically fit sixties American males were liable to serve in the armed forces sometime between eighteen and thirty-five. Ironically, due to the lower birth rate of pre-Boomer males, a graduating high school boy of the more peaceful first third of that decade had a higher probability of seeing military service than the late sixties Vietnam War–dominated period, especially if the young man remained single past his early twenties. However, at any point in the decade, a national "sorting machine" loomed over every male high school graduate, in which at different times the age at which he was married, his ability to enter college and receive good grades, and the job or career in which he was employed would determine whether he was exempt from service, deferred from service, or spent anywhere from two to four years in uniform.

The final distinction between the post–high school experience of 1960s and 2010s teens is the simple fact that, during the earlier period, it was quite possible to plan a college career and then discover that no institution offered you an acceptance. Every agency from the federal government to local counties was engaged in plans to rapidly expand the nation's higher education system to meet the needs of both the vastly expanded teen population and the explosion of what was generally called the "knowledge industry," which was producing a seemingly insatiable need for well-educated workers. These plans and programs would substantially raise the number of college seats available to high school graduates each year during the sixties decade, and a combination of completed buildings and a drop in the birth rate would shift entrance to a buyer's market by the 1970s and 1980s. Some stopgap solutions were in place to partially ease the crisis in the sixties. Colleges located in or near cities opened evening schools that featured relatively more relaxed admissions standards for working people who would attend part-time. Some four-year schools offered branch campuses, largely for full-time commuters, who might or might not be recent high school graduates. However, there was not yet room for anywhere near all of the high school graduate teens who wished to pursue a "traditional" course of study in what came to be defined as "the college experience." While large numbers of hopeful teens were not even permitted to make the transition to this experience, even the millions of adolescents who had gotten past the first line of gatekeepers and secured acceptance would find their experience as college freshmen often rather different than either that of their modern counterparts or their own expectations.

Roughly three months after their principal shook their hand and presented them with a diploma, roughly one-third to one-half of those teens would make the transition from being high school boys and girls to college men and women. Student enrollment in American colleges was rising so rapidly during this decade that in each successive year of the sixties a larger percentage of teens was trading the high school home room for the collegiate dorm room, even if that room often held three or four students, though it had been designed for only two. These teens were invited to participate in a rough-and-ready environment of overcrowding and unanticipated challenges that was part of the collegiate experience of the often-married GI Bill veterans immediately after World War II. Like those adult war veterans, many sixties teens began their college experience against a backdrop that seemed closer to a Wild West frontier boomtown than a placid, ivy-covered parkland. Professors and lecturers competed with jackhammers and steam shovels, buildings in varied states of construction loomed over campus landmarks, and more than a few collegiate teens attended class, ate their meals, and slept in prefabricated surplus military buildings that had once held the GIs, sailors, Marines, and airmen who had relatively recently crushed the Axis powers.

Even before the sixties freshmen attended their first class, these newly arrived teenaged men and women were operating in a rather different collegiate reality than their counterparts of the twenty-first-century. The sixties teens were part of a collegiate seller's market, and they knew it. Virtually every freshman knew at least some, and perhaps many, other teens who had received the dreaded thin envelopes that signified rejection of admission to every institution on his or her application list. The lucky students who had received at least one thick envelope that included affirmation of acceptance padded with numerous registration forms were told by teachers, parents, friends, and the college itself that they were enormously fortunate to receive this offer, with a provision that if they did not quickly confirm their acceptance, the prized slot in the next freshman class would be passed on to someone else on the huge waiting list. College officials believed they had a responsibility to put a roof over a student's head, even if that roof was over a dorm room that was too hot or too cold, or crowded with more beds than it was designed for; provide enough food to ensure adequate nutrition, even if it was boring and nearly tasteless; and provide institutional facilities that were at least physically safe. This reality is almost a world apart from the contemporary student's buyer's market, in which huge numbers of institutions are vying to ensure that their new freshman class will be large enough to meet the academic budget. Modern students often base their choice of several admission offers on the ability of the chosen institution to provide onsite health care, physical fitness and recreation facilities, adequate communication and entertainment infrastructure, a pleasant living environment with dining halls that feature a wide variety of dishes with unlimited refills, and a general physical ambience that ensures that the chosen institution still looks like a real college.

The 1960s version of the collegiate residential experience tended to offer fewer amenities, more restrictions, and less privacy that its twenty-first-century counterpart. First, while American colleges varied widely in their rules and provisions for electronic entertainment, a very large number of institutions tended to prohibit underclassmen from having either television sets or telephones in their rooms. Ironically, while sixties teens were just beginning to gain some access to these devices in their rooms at home, thanks to the rapid expansion of cheap, portable televisions, "princess" phones, and more competitive pricing for the addition of extra phone lines, these two keys to the outside world were often communally shared devices in many colleges. Freshmen television viewing centered around either floor or dormitory-wide lounges or recreation rooms in which some vague calculus of earliness of arrival, democratic vote, or even playful intimidation determined which of the three network programs on offer were to be viewed by the audience. A teen who developed a fondness for *Mr. Novak*, *The Avengers*, or *The Mod Squad* in high school might find that either a majority or a minority of more assertive young men or women set the channel selector on *Combat!*, *The Man from U.N.C.L.E.*, or *Bonanza* and those personal favorites would remain unviewed until the end of term or summer. Also, even when a favorite or even tolerable program was airing, many of the other viewers tended to keep up a somewhat satirical commentary so that the dialogue was lost in an adolescent cacophony.

If the dormitory lounge became a less-than-ideal venue for video entertainment, many sixties underclassmen faced even more grief when they attempted to use the archetypal telephone on the dorm hall wall. The ubiquitous black pay phones were the primary conduit to family at home, romantic partners on another campus, or even friends separated by the expanse of a large university setting. Phone conversations on these devices offered the ambience of a constantly repeated operator demand for more coins, the smirks or commentary of loitering hall mates, and the icy glares of the queue of residents who wanted to use the coveted device. In a true irony, just as American teens were achieving a certain progress in acquiring these two major appliances for their personal use at home, they were once again relinquishing them as they became nominally adult college men and women. One of the possible reasons for the enormous student interest in the music of that era may be at least partially attributable to the absence of regular access to televisions and telephones. Dorm room portable radio and record players were the only routinely available, personalized form of entertainment.

The Spartan-like administrative ban on personal televisions and telephones frequently extended to a similar prohibition on underclassman access to private automobiles. While sixties teens might have had access to a personal or at least a parental car during the last years of high school, in many cases college teens entered a no-drive zone where they reverted back to early teenage status regarding freedom of movement.

The second social reality for teen college underclassmen was an encounter with lifestyle restrictions that could often rival, or even surpass, parental interference. Much of underclass social life operated in the shadow of "parietals," a set of curfews and restrictions that varied somewhat from college to college. Relatively liberal institutions were beginning to experiment with some levels of mixed-gender housing, with some schools featuring at least a few large dormitories where men and women shared lounges and dining facilities but slept in separate wings in which the girls' side was locked off from the boys' side after a certain time of night. A few daring institutions even toyed with the idea of coed dorms by floor, although this tended to be offered to upperclassmen much more often than freshmen. Most residential facilities in typical American colleges tended to have minimal gender mixing until the very late 1960s at the earliest. Much of the campus social life between young students took place in the shadow of a variety of curfews that tended to be stricter on weeknights than weekends and more rigidly enforced toward females than males.

Teen collegians who groused about curfews in their coeducational schools would have received little sympathy from high school classmates who were newly enrolled at the hundreds of single-sex colleges that were still an integral part of the higher education landscape throughout the sixties. Colleges that permit the enrollment of only one gender have become extremely rare during the twenty-first-century, as even boys and girls who attended and possibly enjoyed single-sex high schools generally show little enthusiasm for continuing that format into higher education. Yet throughout most of the sixties, many prominent private colleges and even some major state universities enforced some level of gender separation in enrollment. Until the last months of that decade, six of the eight Ivy League colleges were either all male on the undergraduate level or only allowed females to enroll in coordinate women's colleges (e.g., Radcliffe at Harvard and Barnard at Columbia); one school, Pennsylvania, was in effect coeducational but still required female arts and sciences majors to at least register separately, and only Cornell was emphatically coeducational. Major Catholic universities such as Notre Dame and Georgetown were still primarily male institutions for most of the sixties, while significant Southern schools, such as Duke and Tulane, featured coordinated men's and women's undergraduate colleges.

These largely male bastions were balanced by more than two hundred women's colleges that stretched from the Atlantic to the Pacific, with locations that sometimes virtually adjoined a men's school while at other times maintaining a significant distance from any male collegians. Many of these single-sex schools featured special weekends, dances, dinners, and mixed-gender theater productions to encourage some form of dating opportunities, and teen-oriented magazines frequently ran opinion columns about the relative merits of "on campus" and "separate campus" relationships, each of which had strong supporters and detractors. The August 1961 issue of *Seventeen* included an extensive feature on a nineteen-year-old male Yale student's weekend with a Smith girl. The feature was subtitled "a boy who is used to playing it cool reports on the danger of courting a pretty girl on her home territory." Barry Lydgate compared himself to a "knight on a crusade" as he made his way to the dormitory of his weekend date, admitting he was thinking "condescending Big College Man thoughts" until the emergence of competition at a Saturday-night dance turned him into the supplicant's role, and he was "hooked" by the end of the visit.

A *Seventeen* article four years later, "A Boy's Point of View," featuring teen contributor Jimmy Wescott, also focused on the complications of relatively distant underclass relationships, due to either single-sex schools or high school romances that continued to blossom in college. In the general absence of a car for either person, he noted, "The rule is that you plan and pay for your own travel, but the minute you arrive, if you're a girl, he must take care of all expenses." Noting the somewhat peculiar ambience of a geographically all-male college, "You'll find out right away that everybody will be a little bit crazy. Some level headed fellows you have learned to count on can suddenly turn into unpredictable zanies under the excitement of big weekends." The worst shock for girls who had become close friends with a boy in high school was that soon after starting his college career, "He may suddenly emerge as a boor and a bore and an unspeakable oaf besides." That will call into play the question of whether "you are bound, within reasonable limits, to be loyal to him."

Students who resided at coeducational or single-sex colleges faced somewhat different impediments to fulfilling their goals for enjoying themselves and, in many cases, discovering a partner for life. Students living on the same campus dealt with problems ranging from annoying displays of "substitute parent" controls on the part of administrators to the potential boredom of familiarity. Long-distance relationships, often based on the lack of students of the opposite gender at the teen's institution, provided much less opportunity for boredom and more intense use of limited time together but were marred by the difficulty in communication in an age before laptops, cell phones, and text messages, complicated even further by a general lack of availability of automobiles in underclass life.

However, a common point among teen colleges in these varied academic venues was the very much enhanced possibility of academic failure and dismissal compared to 2010 counterparts. Most academic officials and educational historians tend to agree that a combination of creeping grade inflation, enhanced academic support facilities, and the more commonplace intervention of parents into their children's academic experience has created an environment in which, although college continues to be a more significantly academic world than the high school experience, the sanction of absolute dismissal with no possibility of future reenrollment is far less common than during the 1960s.

Well before student unrest on college campus became a national debate, national magazines and local newspapers began carrying major features on the increasing difficulty of successfully navigating the transition from high school to college. Articles with titles such as "The Freshman Blues" and "Crack up on Campus" suggested that the placid and seemingly easy college academic experience of the 1950s had halted abruptly by the middle of the

1960s. As Boomers surged into only partially prepared colleges, academic deans shook new students with grim stories of huge flunk-out rates, and professors matter-of-factly bragged about their high number of low grades. When *Life* magazine shadowed a Yale freshman during his first semester of college, the subject of the feature, Tim Thompson, revealed a grim schedule of nights of four to six hours of sleep interspersed with all-night study sessions, which produced barely passing grades and an insistence that "sometimes I get the 'what am I doing here' feeling." Even at this prestigious university, freshmen slept and studied in overcrowded rooms with threadbare carpets and Spartan furnishings and encountered sleep deprivation week after week, as, according to one academic counselor, "They run into pressure far beyond anything they dream of in high school and beyond anything they would have felt 10 years ago." While college presidents routinely told teens and their parents at freshman orientation that "this is a competitive school, but it is a competition which rewards all of its participants," news magazines ran photo essays of tearful freshmen embracing now-former roommates as they faced the even greater terror of coping with parents who wonder, either vocally or silently, how their star high school child could be banished from the collegiate world.

In January of 1965, another *Life* columnist, Donald Jackson, visited numerous college campuses and focused on the increasingly difficult transitions of teens from high school to college. Noting the obvious signs of sleep deprivation and fatalistic approaches to future low grades, Jackson insisted that "there seems now to be no end to a pressure that starts early for today's youth and keeps building steadily and inexorably" as they enter college. Jackson quoted a wry comment from Harold Taylor, the former president of Saint Lawrence College that, "If we continue the way we are going, the nursery school will be a kind of advanced placement for three and four year olds going to Harvard."

Critics of the seemingly unrelenting pressure placed on sixties teens as they attempted to cope with parental and other adult expectations in this period of transition noted that students were increasingly asked to do more than was physically possible with overwhelming workloads and both high schools and colleges that seemed to grade more strictly than ten years earlier. They were being told to better organize their time and become more efficient people, but frustrated by failure, nearly one teen collegian in four was seeking major psychological help at many universities. They faced both parents and teachers who always told them, "You are capable of doing better," seemingly no matter how well the teens did.

Yet whether they were in college or high school or even junior high school, at the same time that they were being told by adults that hard work counted for more than pleasure, they were also living in an affluent society in which television, radio, and magazine ads offered them an invitation to enter another world, a world where they would be seen as valuable as adults and where their expectations and dreams and even fantasies would be catered to. Sixties teens were not only students faced with academic challenges and choices, they were also consumers, fought over by companies and often envied by their counterparts outside the shores of the American nation.

~

CHAPTER SEVEN

Teen Consumers and Adolescent Ambassadors

During the last few weeks of the 1950s, American television networks and mass-circulation magazines ran numerous features on the possible social, cultural, and economic changes that the upcoming sixties decade might bring. Yet at least one major article in *Life* magazine focused its view of the near future exclusively on the nation's exploding population of adolescents. An essay titled "A New $10 Billion Power: The U.S. Teenage Consumer" insisted that companies that could meet the purchasing demands of young people would discover opportunities for enormous business success. A profile of an American family with multiple teenage children showed parents beaming with delight as their daughters showered them with kisses as they tried on extensive new wardrobes that the correspondent gravely insisted was but one example of "how modern teenagers are spoiled to death," while hinting at many more similar scenes in the new decade.

Momentary judgmental chiding quickly gave way to effusive optimism at the "growing number of businessmen who realize that American teenagers have emerged as big time consumers in the U.S. economy. They are multiplying rapidly in number. They spend more and have more spent on them. And they have minds of their own about what they want. The time is past when a boy's chief possession was a bike, and a girl's wardrobe consisted of one fancy dress worn with a string of dime store pearls. What Depression bred parents may still think of as luxuries are looked on as necessities by their offspring."

The combination of ample funds from generous allowances and part-time jobs, a rapidly expanding segment of the consumer market, and relatively gullible, inexperienced financial sense was irresistible to advertisers and manufacturers. Teen consumers were expected to be a major component in sixties prosperity, a reality that no media outlet could ignore. For example, one acerbic *New Yorker* writer insisted that "merchants now eye teenagers the way stockmen eye cattle." Journalists marveled at how upper-middle-class parents, living in an era where an average American family budgeted expenses on a $7,000 annual income, might spend $4,000 a year to "keep" a single teenage daughter in the state expected of her modestly affluent lifestyle of ample wardrobe, regular beauty parlor excursions, private phone line, room furnishing, and regular additions to her hope chest. Where her mother made do with two swim suits, she viewed seven as minimally acceptable. Even families with much tighter budgets were now faced with the reality that their teens were part of an age group that ate 20 percent more food than adults, consumed 145 million gallons of ice cream per year, drank 3.5 billion quarts of milk annually, and far more than the twenty-first-century teen, dominated the consumption of American soft drinks.

Marketing executives of the 1950s had already perceived the enormous potential of teen consumers who had relatively few necessities to pay for and, thus, were at liberty to buy mainly discretionary products. Journalists interviewing adolescents on their spending habits were often met with cheerful admissions that much of the fun was simply being able to spend on anything that looked "neat" or "cool" at that particular moment and that much of what they bought was usually related to a desire to either "fit in" or "be popular." However, by the early to mid-1960s, experts on teen sociology and psychology were informing business and advertising executives that the current decade was developing a new consumer profile rather different than the fifties.

Researchers, such as Yale University scholar Louise Bates-Ames and Grace and Fred Hechinger, authors of *Teenage Tyranny*, began to discover that sixties fifteen-year-olds were effectively acting like eighteen-year-old consumers from the previous decade. Thirteen-year-old girls were now using significant amounts of makeup; fourteen-year-old boys and girls were vetoing parental choices in wardrobe; sixteen-year-olds increasingly limited adult choice in their wardrobe to paying the bills for them. Scholars noted an increased exaggeration of what teens believed to be "absolutely necessary" to their social existence, which turned their natural inclination for exaggeration into a purchasing "arms race" that seemed to have very high ceilings required for satisfaction. In 2010s terminology, many sixties teen consumers were fifties teens on steroids, a condition that baffled parents and enticed advertising executives to seemingly work around the clock to take advantage of this emerging condition.

On a superficial level, the primary media outlets for advertising to teenagers were the same in the 1960s as the previous decade: mainly radio commercials, television commercials, and print ads. However, a teenager in 1966 lived in a very different advertising and consuming universe than his or her counterpart ten years earlier. First, the number of radio stations carrying teen-friendly rock music was substantially higher in the sixties than in the fifties. In 1956 stations carrying popular music were largely attempting to focus on dual audiences, young-to-middle-aged adults tuned in to hear pop music hits, and teenagers waiting to listen to the still far-less-numerous rock and roll songs they generally preferred. Sponsors still focused primarily on the older of the two audiences, so there were proportionately fewer acne cream ads than coffee commercials to entice purchasers. By 1966 pop music found most of its audience on adult contemporary, easy listening, or "middle of the road" stations largely ignored by teens, who now tuned into a burgeoning number of both AM and FM rock stations packaged as "The Music Explosion" or some similar catch phrase that effectively meant that no Perry Como or Doris Day fans need tune in. The AM rock stations carried a heavy load of commercials, often inserting advertisements after every second or third record in an attempt to peddle everything from soft drinks to local amusement park admissions to teens who, on average, were blasting their transistor radios four or more hours a day.

On the other hand, while there were no "Music Explosion" television channels in 1966, the medium itself looked dramatically changed since a decade earlier. First, compared to 1956, there were far more channels to choose from, in turn permitting more teen-oriented programming. By the mid-1960s, many smaller communities who ten years ago had either no television or access to one fuzzy station were now served by cable companies who offered at least twelve or thirteen channels, with the promise of significantly more outlets in the near future. In turn, larger cities, which by FCC regulations were not yet permitted to have cable service, had substantially expanded their services through the emergence of hundreds of higher-band ultra-high-frequency channels, which could be accessed by tuning the dial to numbers greater than 13. For example, Philadelphia, which had three very-high-frequency stations (2 to 13 on the dial) in 1960 had expanded to seven stations by 1966, with a concurrent major surge in teen-oriented programming in the process. Finally, to the utter delight of the advertising industry, all of the networks had shifted to complete color telecasting of all prime-time programs by fall 1966. Now, for the first time, television, including the commercials, was a riot of color with many ads developed specifically to utilize this new dimension in advertising.

Teens could now view the exciting new fashions, cosmetics, and other products of the new "mod" era in "living color," which made the products seem even more intriguing and worthwhile. Almost like the moment when Dorothy Gale's world changes from Kansas black and white to the bright colors of Oz, many of the products of the teen world now appeared even more enticing.

Finally, while substantial numbers of print ads were already appearing in color during the 1950s, teen consumers of the sixties were exposed to a massive increase in the numbers of magazines devoted almost exclusively to their age group. While the significant teen-oriented magazines of the fifties—*Seventeen, 16, Teen, American Girl,* and *Boy's Life*—all added readers during the next decade, new outlets such as *Teen Screen, Teen Time,* and *Teen Age* were in direct competition by 1966, while the at least partially teen-oriented *Rolling Stone* magazine would join the foray a year later. Many of the sixties versions of these periodicals attempted to maximize the validity of their articles and advertisements by hiring more teenage writers and staff members, using slogans such as "the magazine *for* teens *by* teens," supplemented by photos of youthful staff.

At an initial glance, the dominance of teen magazines that were published predominantly with a female audience in mind suggests that girls were the main target of sixties youth advertising. However, on closer inspection, it seems that this was not entirely the case. First, many ads for teen boys ran in periodicals that included adolescent readers as part of a wider age continuum. Comic books, auto magazines, and sports magazines ran numerous advertisements for bodybuilding courses, personal grooming, hair care, and other items of teen interest, even though many of their readers were either younger or older than the teen population.

Second, there appeared to be a noticeable trend in technically girl-oriented magazines to at least modestly diversify both articles and advertisements to a slightly more gender-neutral segment. For example, the middle of the decade *Seventeen* magazine's film reviews included *The Russians Are Coming*, a political satire, *The Agony and the Ecstasy*, a Renaissance-era spectacular, and *Winning*, a film centered on auto racing, all of which would attract at least as many male teens as females. *Teen Age* regularly included full lyrics to popular songs as an aid to amateur rock bands and singers, and *Teen* magazine's editor, rock music columnist, and movie and television editor were all young men writing features that would appear to assume some male readership. While it is reasonable to assume that few teenage boys would purchase *Teen Screen* in lieu of *Spiderman* comic books or a football preview magazine, the reality of large numbers of American households featuring teenagers of both genders may very well have persuaded both magazine publishers and advertisers to include at least some features and ads that might entice the thousands of boys who leafed through coffee-table magazines purchased by their sisters or girlfriends.

One of the most fascinating ways to gain a sense of teen consumer trends during the 1960s is to peruse the advertisements carried in major teen-oriented magazines of the period and view commercials on television programs popular with adolescent viewers during the period. Gaining access to the former source is relatively easy, if somewhat time consuming, as a representative selection of most teen magazines can be obtained from online vendors from every year of the decade. However many teen-oriented television programs of the era are available as DVD sets, very few include original commercials. Fortunately, a few websites offer complete episodes with advertising, but they are primarily limited to one national teen program, *Shindig!*, which ran from 1964 to 1966, and occasional episodes of teen-oriented shows produced by local stations throughout the decade.

A perusal of print ads in dozens of teen magazines spanning the decade reveals a generally predictable emphasis on fashion, personal grooming, and entertainment while graphically demonstrating how some aspects of the teen environment underwent significant attention during the course of the decade. Teens of the modern era have always lived in a fast-changing adolescent world, but the teen consumer of 1969 functioned in a vastly different environment than his or her 1960 counterpart, while, paradoxically, being prompted to purchase products based on the same desire for popularity, acceptance, and enjoyment.

For example, a 1961 issue of *Seventeen* magazine featured a Cutex lipstick ad featuring a teen model with a "Jackie Kennedy flip" hairdo and advertising a "revolutionary new principle" in lipstick, a case designed to look like a "jeweler's original," while costing less than a dollar. Eight years later, the same magazine featured an ad with a very modish teen with long straight hair and far more eye makeup announcing an "evolutionary new lipstick" designed "to wear to the moon," a product that is the "lipstick of tomorrow."

In that same vein, an early sixties deodorant advertisement for Mum, a cream deodorant for girls, featuring a teenage girl hand in hand with what is most likely her future husband, comfortable with the assurance that "now, you're naturally sweet," because the product stops odor without stopping up pores. Eight years later, the deodorant scene shifts to two couples who are members of a wedding party with one young lady afraid to wave at the newlyweds due to wetness under her arms. The prescribed remedy is Right Guard, a spray deodorant for both genders, in a far more space-age container than its predecessor yet still essentially accomplishing the same task.

The rapid pace of change among teen consumers as to what was "cool" or "uncool" must have been a major challenge for adult advertising executives and, perhaps, the teenagers themselves during that tumultuous decade. Every sixties magazine carried numerous ads for the still relatively new contact lenses. One advertisement congratulates teens "who are among the lucky people who can wear contact lenses," hinting quite correctly that a substantial minority of teens could not adapt to wearing "those tiny discs that prevent you from changing your normal youthful looks. You remain as your friends know you and like you." Yet by the end of the decade, when contact lenses became less expensive and could successfully be worn by more teens, magazine fashion ads and features are full of young people who have eagerly adapted to wearing hippie- or mod-style spectacles, sometimes made with clear lenses for teens with good vision and a high sense of the latest fashion.

Two advertising genres provide a microcosm of changing teen consumer devices during the 1960s. First, teen magazine fashion ads during the first third of the decade feature models wearing dresses at about twice the rate that they wear slacks, yet during the final three years of the era, the ratio is generally reversed. During the early sixties, ads imply that pants are socially acceptable in very informal settings, such as playing ping-pong in a recreation room, attending a football pep rally, or riding a bicycle. On the other hand, by 1968 or 1969 pants are now featured in classroom scenes, dance clubs, and obvious dating situations, with jeans now creeping into the more informal settings. In turn, in the majority of date scenarios in early sixties advertisements, most boys are depicted wearing either a blazer or sport coat and tie or a dressy sweater and dress shirt at almost everything except beach or sports settings, while by the end of the decade shirts and ties are obviously reserved for very special occasions.

A similar cultural transformation can be observed in the American music industry's concept of how to sell records to the teen generation. Sixties teen magazines regularly featured extensive advertising from competing record companies enticing young people to join their record club, which offered an initial purchase of several long-play albums for a very low price, provided the customer purchased additional records every month at the full price for the next year or two. For example, a two-page ad in a 1961 issue of *Seventeen* offered subscribers five albums for $1.99 in return for monthly purchases of records for $3.99 during the following year of each month's club selection, "chosen by the Club's staff of music experts." Yet in the same month that the twist craze was sweeping the nation and rock and roll was reestablishing itself as the primary music genre for teens, of the sixty-four albums on offer, only four records, those by the Everly Brothers, Roy Hamilton, the Platters, and Johnny Horton could be considered teen music. Most of the remaining selections are relatively evenly divided among show tunes, such as *Camelot* and *The King and I*, adult pop artists, such as Mitch Miller and Patti Page, jazz albums, and classical albums, with a smaller sprinkling of comedy, such as Bob Newhart and Shelley Berman.

It is readily apparent that this ad was simply the same one that was concurrently running in adult magazines such as *Time*, *Life*, and *TV Guide*, and Columbia Records advertising executives were convinced that either a number of *Seventeen* readers were in college and had graduated from rock and roll to more mature tastes or that a number of high school students had more eclectic music tastes than adults suspected.

Eight years later, the same record company ran a two-page ad in *Seventeen* that, at first glance, has an amazingly similar format. Yet closer examination reveals a huge cultural shift in concepts of teen consumer trends. Now the introductory offer has been substantially improved; a subscriber would receive twelve albums for $3.98 in return for buying ten additional records at $3.98 each over the next year. As an additional incentive, each new customer will receive that most essential musical accessory for any sixties teen, a free transistor radio. The double-page ad still features show tunes, classical music, adult pop, and comedy, but while the total selection has been nearly doubled to 120 albums, fewer than thirty are in all of these categories combined. The remaining selections include a dozen country and western albums and nearly eighty rock albums from Iron Butterfly and the Zombies to Junior Walker and the All Stars and the Rolling Stones. Music fans who disliked the rock genre might still find a dozen albums they would enjoy, but it is clear that teenage musical tastes are far more on the mind of Columbia executives than they were several years earlier, especially since teens were now purchasing nearly 60 percent of all records.

The limited availability of sixties television series DVDs that include period commercials makes a decadelong analysis of television marketing for teens less comprehensive. However, the perusal of the nearly one hundred episodes of one major teen-oriented program that still includes original advertising gives some clues of teen consumer interest in the middle of the decade. *Shindig!* was aired by ABC from 1964 to 1966 and did so well in the ratings that during its last several months the program was aired twice a week. Unlike the later MTV era when the profusion of television stations allowed networks to air programs and commercials almost exclusively designed to target teen audiences, *Shindig!* was a prime-time program in an era of only three networks, which meant that even though it was teen oriented, a substantial portion of its audience would be younger than thirteen and older than nineteen. The program carried far more teen-oriented commercials using teen actors than a more adult program, such as *Gunsmoke* or *What's My Line?*, and the advertising segments are loaded with male and female grooming products from Dippity-Do hair gel for girls to Score hair gel for boys, while Listerine ads invariably featured a teen boy or girl who has been somehow ostracized until an adult mentor reminds them of bad breath and Listerine. While NBC's rival rock show *Hullaballo* featured Clearasil as a major sponsor, *Shindig!* countered with rapidly emerging competitor Stridex, ads that were relatively original in the sense that each show featured (a usually very handsome or attractive) boy or girl selected from the audience to come onstage and wash their face as host Jimmy O'Neill discussed the extra cleaning power of medicated pads that would always display the "hidden" dirt after the teen washed. Another interesting dimension of *Shindig!* advertising was that its primary beverage sponsor was the American Milk Board, which alternated between commercials of teen heartthrob Bobby Sherman drinking milk after a song and filmed commercials of teens achieving adolescent dreams as senators or newspaper editors after drinking several glasses of milk a day as young people.

On the other hand, the reality of a large postteen audience that advertising executives assumed included numerous housewives meant that teen-oriented commercials alternated with ads for laundry cleaners, storage bags, pasta sauce, and cookies, which demonstrated the ability of smart wives to make husband and children clean, well fed, and happy.

The photogenic boys and girls who obligingly swabbed their faces with Stridex pads for Jimmy O'Neill were in many respects as much adolescent ambassadors as teen consumers. These kids were not professional models and could realistically be pictured sitting next to a potential acne medication customer in their high school home room. However, these young people were ambassadors in the sense that they tended to be the teen leaders in their schools. On camera, they appear far more attractive than average teens of the era, and ironically, either due to very diligent skin care or very lucky genes, have virtually no sign of acne issues themselves. These were the teens who were in the homecoming court, were on student council, and represented their high school in statewide model legislatures or mock political conventions. Other kids used their new slang words and paid careful attention to their grooming choices and fashion styles. It was little wonder that companies with products to entice teen consumers would search out envied ambassadors to be models for the rest of the "crowd."

Two decades earlier, local department stores began recruiting particularly attractive university coeds to become members of their "college board," who were initially glorified sales personnel who offered fashion advice and modeled clothes in between manning the cash register. Eventually, most leading department stores opened "college shops," and even *Mademoiselle* magazine selected eager coed readers to function as junior fashion consultants with an opportunity to become a guest editor for the magazine's annual back-to-college issue.

By the 1960s it was becoming readily apparent that even junior high school girls were beginning to overrule their mothers in fashion choices, and since teen girls between thirteen and eighteen were now spending over four billion dollars a year on clothes, it was time to move the advisory-board age limit noticeably lower. For example, by 1965 virtually every Macy's department store in the nation had replaced or altered the now seemingly snobby college shop with a Hi-Set Center featuring "Fashion a Go-Go" that could put plastic boots, fishnet stockings, and jockey caps on eleven-year-olds. Since only a minority of girls went to college and everyone went to high school, the age limits to be selected for the advisory board plunged rapidly. Most of these girls no longer manned cash tills but, in essence, traded their time, expertise, and "teen leader" status in return for fashionable wardrobes. These girls were no longer glorified shopgirls but "roving ambassadors" who modeled fashions at school or social gatherings. Soon some stores turned the advisory boards into coed ventures as sixties boys began to far outstrip their predecessors as fashion-conscious kids in a teen world that was in ever-accelerating levels of change. Boys and girls were officially chosen on the basis of their school- and community-leadership skills, their academic standing, and their fashion interest, but their most important characteristic was ambassadorial status derived from being recognized as a teen leader by their peers.

On Wednesday, July 11, 1962, as teens listened to Dee Dee Sharp ask for gravy for her mashed potatoes and Freddy Cannon evoked every teen's joy of summer freedom in "Palisades Park," an American rocket blasted off from its launch pad and joined the ever-increasing flotilla of spacecraft that had joined Sputnik in orbital success. On this hot summer day, the United States took a massive lead in a key aspect of the space race, as the craft on the top of the rocket was Telstar, the first communications satellite.

Soon after achieving orbit, one of the last barriers between America and Europe was smashed as President Kennedy gave a live address to the people of Britain while Queen Elizabeth reciprocated for the British nation. A few days later, many Britons scratched their heads as they watched the perplexing action unfolding in a Phillies-Cubs baseball game, live from

Wrigley Field, Chicago, while Americans suffered the same quandary, viewing a cricket match from the far side of the Atlantic. In turn, the launch of Telstar became an unofficial launching pad for a new CBS prime-time fall series titled *Fair Exchange* that featured American and British teenage girls crossing the ocean to stay with the families of two men who had formed a lifelong friendship during World War II. Each obtained an obnoxious early teen surrogate brother who acted even more incomprehensibly than their real siblings. *Fair Exchange* was, at its best, a modest, one-season phenomenon, but it established a transatlantic video bridge that would one day allow American teens to view *American Idol* one evening, fly across the Atlantic, and watch an almost identical *Pop Idol* the next night, hosted by the same celebrity host.

Shortly before the launch of Telstar, the weekly newsmagazine *U.S. News and World Report* ran an extended feature titled "Is the World Going American? How the US Is Being Imitated Abroad" that viewed much of the "Americanization" of Europe and Asia from the prism of foreign fascination with American youth culture. The article noted how Britain's first commercial television channel was already showing a teenage rock and roll program, *Oh Boy!*, which largely featured British acts singing American rock and roll songs. Ironically, the program's producer, Jack Goode, would use *Oh Boy!*'s frenetic format as the basis of an almost exact duplicate called *Shindig!* two years after Telstar.

The article noted how French teens were increasingly jettisoning traditional cuisine for hamburgers, hot dogs, and soft drinks; Italian couples packed new drive-in theaters; and a large German department store chain was opening specialized teenage shops where boys and girls could stock up on American records and clothes. Other sure signs of Americanization of foreign youth included Norwegian high school English textbooks dropping *honour*, *favour*, and *tyre* for American spellings, and the emergence of blue jeans as the informal uniform of casual wear all over Europe. As one correspondent noted with a combination of enthusiasm and adult sarcasm, "You can hear rock and roll from a jukebox from Sicily to Scotland, and the 'beat' competes for teen entertainment popularity with American pinball machines, which French kids call 'Le Tilt.'" George Allen, the very adult director of the United States Information Agency, insisted that while the American government was not officially pushing American youth culture as part of Cold War strategy, it was clear that American teen lifestyles were regarded as the wave of the future, "and the wave seems to be gathering in force and strength."

While Allen was probably accurate in his sense of foreign youth and American teen culture, the 1960s represent a sometimes paradoxical bridge between the decade immediately preceding it and the level of cultural contact in the twenty-first century. Since jet passenger travel was initiated only months before the onset of the sixties, that decade can accurately be described as the genesis of jet-age culture. The novelty of rapid passenger air travel is a frequent theme of the decade's romantic comedies, and European and American actors and musicians regularly crisscrossed the Atlantic for films and concerts. A combination of high jet fares and relatively limited international flights meant that much of the American culture seeping into other youth cultures was more through films, television, music, and clothes than long café discussions between large numbers of American and host-country teens. Both collegiate and high school exchange and foreign-study programs were a small fraction of twenty-first-century counterparts, and most American teens did not hold a passport.

Yet despite these obvious logistical barriers, teens in a surprisingly large number of foreign nations, including some with minimal freedom of information, were successful in discovering the special lure of American sixties teen culture. First, the 1960s brought an ever-expanding volume of teen-oriented dance parties across the globe. Britain's *Oh Boy!* and *Ready Steady Go*, German programs such as *Beat Club* and *Beat, Beat, Beat,* and Australian television's *Six O'clock Rock* and *Australian Bandstand* featured both cover versions of American rock songs and American artists attempting to widen their sales appeal. For example, one episode of the Bremen-based *Beat Club* featured live performances by Sonny and Cher, Polish star Helena Miliski singing a Jerry Butler hit in Polish, a mixed American-British group called the Washington D.C.'s, a German group named the Country Stars singing a medley of Johnny Cash hits, and British female singer Carol Friday singing Motown hit "Heat Wave." The scene of this action was a set decorated as a mock American frontier town with rustic display signs, such as Idaho, Montana, and Dakota, adding an additional "authentic" touch.

Second, a perusal of dozens of sixties teen magazines suggests that a rather large number of foreign teens who could read at least some English were avid readers of American adolescent periodicals. For example, the "Penny for Your Thoughts" write-in section of one 1961 issue of *American Girl* included letters from readers in Renfrenshire, Scotland; Dundee, Scotland; Trondheim, Norway; Caracas, Venezuela; and Sydney, Australia, among the first dozen letters; a representative 1963 issue of *Teen Screen*'s "The Problem Clinic" included correspondence from London, England; Munich, Germany; and Kitz, Germany, in the first ten queries. A surprisingly large proportion of the websites I utilized to acquire period magazines were outside North

America, and many of the issues had prices in foreign currency stamped over the American denomination.

On the other hand, even before the onset of Beatlemania in the United States, a surprisingly large number of American teenagers were already developing an interest in youth culture beyond the shores of their own nation. For example, a four-page fashion spread in an issue of *Seventeen* published while the Beatles were still performing in smoky Liverpool dives was titled "Meet the Chelsea Girl." The girl in question was described as "the smartest girl this side of 20 and that side of 14. She's from London's colorful old Chelsea section, home of Angry Young Men and exciting young women. She started The Chelsea Look, a smashing idea in fashion, slightly zany, intellectual and real news." Models were photographed with "coffee house" pants, low-cut leather boots, and "free form" dresses with long, straight hair and far more eye makeup than American fashion of the era would probably tolerate, an exotic alternative to "all American" fashions of the era.

At the same time that British fashion was gaining at least a small bridgehead in American department stores, teenage or very young adult British performers were provoking interest from American adolescents as very adult music and film impresarios. Pre-Beatles American pop music charts were increasingly peppered with foreign, especially British, hits that never seriously challenged Chubby Checker or the Beach Boys but still made it clear to American teens that rock and roll was going international. Laurie London's "He's Got the Whole World in His Hands," the Dusty Springfield–fronted Springfield's "Silver Threads and Golden Needles," Frank Ifield's "I Remember You," and Cliff Richard's "Lucky Lips" were all substantial hits in the United States, and somewhat symbolically, the first British song to hit number one on American charts was the Tornados' aptly titled "Telstar" in the autumn of 1962.

The September 1963 issue of *Teen* magazine had sixteen-year-old British teenager Wendy Turner on its cover, and an extensive article insisted that this "bundle of wit and charm whose personality may win her stardom" was essentially the new rival in the Disney studios to fellow Brit Hayley Mills, with whom she would costar in the film *Summer Magic*. The article featured "candid" shots of Turner and Mills clowning together in their studio school classroom, while both insisted that despite their "natural" British reserve, they were not actually snobs. Yet in a startling frankness for a reading audience composed primarily of American teen girls, Turner suggested that even though teens in the former colonies were "happy go lucky," British girls had better complexions, "while English boys, even the controversial 'teddy Boys,' were far better dressed than their 'sloppy' American counterparts."

Miss Turner would never seriously challenge Hayley Mills's huge popularity among American teens, from *The Parent Trap* to *The Trouble with Angels*, but the fact that she continued to be featured in teen magazines along with other rising young British Hollywood stars, such as Michael Anderson and Judy Carne, hints that teen "ambassadors" of adolescent culture were not exclusively American, even before the emergence of the Beatles.

On the other hand, a perusal of what American teens read, watched, and listened to in the 1960s reveals a huge uptick in international peer culture awareness after the Beatles' arrival in New York on that cold February afternoon in 1964. Even at the beginning of the decade, many American teens were at least moderately aware that there was a certain commonality of adolescent experience in many parts of the world, but the American-centric elements of this belief were singularly challenged by four young men from a fading British port city.

The musical aspects of Beatlemania will be discussed in a later chapter, but in a cultural sense the arrival of John, George, Paul, and Ringo in the United States created a sense of teen universality in America that would continue long after the initial near hysteria subsided. For example, huge numbers of teen boys who had grown up with extremely short hair, jeans, chinos, and sneakers were now demanding that their barbers fashion some form of Beatles-oriented hair style, while comparing notes on the availability of collarless suit jackets and heeled low boots, a look that would very likely have attracted jeers or even physical assault only a few months earlier. In turn, fairly levelheaded, conservative American girls became fascinated by the exotic, "raccoon eyed" makeup of Dusty Springfield and the long, straight, parted-in-the-middle hair of Sandie Shaw and Marianne Faithful, while for both genders an all-expenses-paid trip to Carnaby Street in London or the Cavern in Liverpool might become a dreamed-of pilgrimage to trump Disneyland or Rockefeller Center, venues that, ironically, remained dream destinations for many foreign adolescents.

American kids of the fifties always had too many immigrant grandparents, mothers who were European war brides, or fathers who had served overseas to view their experience in a totally closed universe. However, on February 9, 1964, as the Fab Four sang "All My Loving" as their first number on *The Ed Sullivan Show*, the teens of the United States would in some ways become the most internationally curious citizens of the republic, a process that would be repeated seventeen years later when on August 1, 1981, another British group, the Buggles, performed "Video Killed the Radio Star" on the newly launched MTV network.

The onset of Beatlemania in the United States, followed by the subsequent British Invasion of numerous male and female bands and singers, heightened the awareness among American teenagers that adolescence was a global experience that fashioned unique bonds between young people living thousands of miles from one another that were not shared by parents watching television only a floor below them. Even before most American teens knew who the Beatles were, there was a growing fascination with how teens in other societies lived, as reflected in regular features, such as "Teen Life in Denmark" or "Teen Life in Israel," which were sprinkled throughout most teen-oriented magazines of the early sixties. However, it appears that even after the first tremors of Beatlemania had subsided, the generally young staff members of teen magazines sensed that their readers craved more extensive treatment of global teen society, and more emphasis was placed on features focusing on the experiences of foreign students who lived or studied in the United States for extended periods. Later in the decade, this was expanded to an increasingly critical analysis of the whole American teen society by international peers who increasingly pulled no punches in what they sometimes saw as the dark side of the United States and its adolescents.

A fairly typical example of what one might call the "exchange teen" experience is an article in a 1966 issue of *Seventeen* magazine titled "A Year of Seven New Words," written by a young lady from Rimini, Italy, who spent a year in a Nebraska high school. She had left Europe determined to show her American hosts that "Italians do more than eat pizzas, sing arias, and for guys, court foreign girls," while admitting, "I had a million questions and doubts about the large, rich young country I'm going to live in. I feel fear, as well as joy, in English, I was bewildered. An Italian discovered America in 1492, and I'm going to discover it now."

Marina Ciccioni visited state fairs, cheered at basketball games, and clarified American teens' misconception that Italy had no television and little knowledge of the Beatles, while writing to her Italian classmates that Chicago was not still the home of Prohibition and there were no more cattle drives across the Midwest plains. She watched American teens sleeping in study halls, noted the pride with which boys wore their letter sweaters and the equal pride of the girls holding their hands, and danced in basement rec rooms full of empty Coke bottles, bags of potato chips, and blasting record players. The America she saw was one of "hundreds of backyard equipped ranch houses, too many cars, too much noise, and yet wonderfully welcoming." As a teen ambassador, Marina was determined to learn the slang words used by her fellow adolescents, which could then be relayed to her peers in

Italy. The representative words she chose were "slumber party," "gee whiz," "treat," "clobber," "nickname," "neat," and "had a riot," and she wondered whether American adults actually understood this form of "teen English."

Articles in teen magazines about exchange students such as Miss Ciccioni represented comparisons of American and foreign teen life by young people living a relatively assimilated lifestyle in an American home for a finite amount of time. An alternative tactic used by an increasing number of teen magazines in the midsixties was to hold roundtable discussions about American adolescent society attended by foreign teens, who enrolled in school in America but still lived with their diplomat parent families.

An extensive article in *Teen Age* magazine included a number of quite positive views of American teen culture among students attending the United Nations International School in New York City. A sixteen-year-old boy from England insisted, "I feel very much at home in America. My crowd treats me as an equal, and they're all American born. We like to hang out in the neighborhood pizzaria in the afternoons." Yet he noted how many of his American peers now thought that Europe "is the source of new styles in clothes and shoes."

On the other hand, the forum included students from Russia and its "eastern Bloc" allies, who tended to have far more mixed feelings about American teens and their culture. The author of the article, Edward Douglass, noted that "all of these students have a wide knowledge of history, sociology and psychology, and this is often evident in their interaction," a situation which brought a frankness that Douglass admitted "produced a sometimes disturbing commentary on American life."

A fifteen-year-old Polish girl sensed a level of self-delusion among American teens that the teens themselves seldom noted. "I think it is sometimes difficult to see the forest for the trees, and I suppose that we at the U.N. School, not really part of that forest, can look objectively at the trees. I am referring, of course, to American teenagers." She admitted, "I do not always feel accepted in this country. Perhaps it is because I do not conform to what others are doing."

A sixteen-year-old girl from Yugoslavia, an officially neutral but Marxist nation, was even more specific in her criticism of American teenage girls. "This past summer in my Long Island neighborhood, I met a group of girls who I understand are typical American teenagers. All they did, day after day, was to go to the corner candy store and talk about boys, hair styles and who they wanted to date. The girls were actually bored to death—they never tired of saying so. I think that's terrible. Kids in America have too much freedom—it makes them grow up too quickly."

Even the British panelist, who admitted his delight in acquiring so many American friends, saw a dark side to too much Americanization of global youth culture. "I think wealth is at the root of the teen conformity problem. American kids now have the money to do and buy what they want. They can afford to compete—for the sharpest clothes, the latest records and the nicest cars. Businessmen, I suspect, are very aware of this and exploit it."

As sixties teens grew up in an American culture that was both increasingly affluent and yet seen as too materialist and conformist by both domestic and foreign critics, young people often veered between determination to be accepted as adults as quickly as possible and a desire to postpone entry into that world by maintaining a separate universe in everything from music tastes to fashions. As the decade wore on, this distinction began to be called the generation gap and would emerge as one of the distinctive elements of the culture of the 1960s.

CHAPTER EIGHT

~

Coping with the Generation Gap

Early in the final summer of the presidency of John Fitzgerald Kennedy, Columbia Pictures released the film version of a Broadway musical comedy that was eagerly anticipated by both teenagers and their parents. *Bye Bye Birdie* had emerged as a huge stage success in the very first months of the new decade as a satire of the conflicting lifestyles of modern parents and their adolescent children, wrapped around a plotline featuring the final days of civilian life for newly drafted rock and roll star Conrad Birdie, a very thinly disguised stand-in for Elvis Presley.

Bye Bye Birdie was the last major media event before the arrival of the Beatles roughly eight months later, and it garnered two cover stories by *Life* magazine as well as dozens of articles and advertisements in the teen-oriented press. The reality of two distinct age group audiences was reflected in the *Life* covers, which featured successively the lead adult female actress, Janet Leigh, and the lead adolescent female actress, Ann-Margaret. Leigh, who was coming to the film from already-demanding roles in relatively recent hits such as *The Vikings* and *Psycho*, was lauded as "a new Janet Leigh, who is marveled for her transformation and her courage" as she emerged as "an astonishing acrobatic dancer who vaulted and tumbled and risked her neck in roof raising numbers that would tax an experienced stunt girl." Two months of rehearsals and filming produced a concussion, scarred shins, and twelve pounds lost from her famous figure "as the most physically active adult on the set." On the other hand, her younger counterpart, Ann-Margaret, only two years after her first screen test, had graduated from $500-an-appearance television singing sultry ballads to $50,000 for her *Birdie* role, as "she just about runs away from the picture with a subdeb's freshness and a spitfire fervor as her torrid dancing and singing almost replaces central heating in the movie theater." Ann-Margaret was lauded for her ability to "project the moony moods of a lovelorn teenager. As everybody knows, teenagers and soda fountains go together. She makes both as seductive as a double malted."

Bye Bye Birdie was a smash hit in a still rather innocent New Frontier era because it followed an essentially two-tiered plotline in which adults and teens gently poke fun at each other's lifestyles with a still less-than-malicious satire. Generational lines were clearly drawn but could still be safely crossed on occasion as the plot centers around Kim McAfee's (Ann-Margaret) selection at random by public relations secretary Rosie (Leigh) to bestow a final kiss on national television for rock idol Conrad Birdie on the eve of his army induction. While Kim, her boyfriend Hugo Peabody (rock crooner Bobby Rydell), and their myriad friends at Sweet Apple High School fall in and out of love at a breathtaking pace, Rosie uses her equally noticeable smiles and energy to snag full-time chemist and part-time song writer Albert (Dick Van Dyke) by securing rights for him to pen the "goodbye anthem," "One Last Kiss," which will presumably vault the couple to marriage and suburbia.

The film readily acknowledges the reality of a generational divide but then segues seamlessly from rock songs to more standard show-tune fare, as it pokes equal fun at the rituals of teen dating and adult social clubs. Whether it is Conrad Birdie's binge drinking away from his teen fans or some parents' equal overindulgence in alcohol, out of sight of their teen children, none of these activities seems to have a very serious side to it. In the end, teens and adults learn to cope with the other group's sometimes-unthinking stereotyping, and it is clear that teen couple Hugo and Kim and adult couple Albert and Rosie have much more in common than initially implied, even if they view their early sixties world from very different generational prisms.

At about the same time that *Bye Bye Birdie* was putting generational differences on screen, publisher William Gaines's satirical *Mad* magazine used this gap for much of its print narrative on sixties society. Two of the magazine's most hilarious articles, "What Would Happen If Teens Ran the Country" and "Tomorrow's Parents," feature alternate or future societies in which the surge of teens in the sixties wreaks havoc with parent-adolescent relationships. The first article begins in pseudo-newsmagazine style, soberly informing readers that "today more manufacturers and entertainers are gearing their products for the teen market. Which means that more and more, teenagers are taking over our way of life." This announcement is followed by a pictorial essay about a "near future" society where teens had, indeed, used their swelling numbers to "take over" key aspects of American society. The first frame depicts a confident teen couple handing supplicant parents money as they go out the door with the caption, "Parents would be given a reasonable allowance (75 cents a month) and given occasional privileges like using the family car if they have finished their housework." Another frame shows teen boys and girls walking confidently down a street with USA decals on their jackets. The caption notes, "All taxes would be eliminated; instead every teenager in the country would become a member of the USA club and be require to pay dues of 50 cents a week. Social Security would start at 20, and all adults over 19 would have to be in bed at 10:00 o'clock." The final box shows middle-aged adults of both genders engaged in a brawl during the performance of a symphony orchestra, hurling chairs and breaking furniture, as "Someday adults will begin to rebel against teen authority, spurred on by their wild and riotous music."

The emergence of the huge sixties teen generation as arbiters of society was developed once again several months later in a feature called "Tomorrow's Parents." The introduction notes that, "Much has been written about the teenager of today—but in every article we've seen, one important fact has been overlooked or ignored: namely that the teenager of today is the parent of tomorrow! Yes, frightening as it may seem, we cannot escape the fact that the rebellious adolescent of the present will someday become the mother symbol and father image for the rebellious adolescent of the future. So, with this horrible thought in mind, we sneak a peek into the future for a glimpse of what it will be like when today's teenagers become parents."

The artwork begins with a full-page rendition of an unkempt recreation room with a May 1981 wall calendar and portraits of gray-haired teen idols on the wall, floor and end tables covered with used soda bottles, cigarette butts, and overflowing ashtrays, while a middle-aged man in a leather jacket and jeans plays bongos and his wife sprawls across a sofa talking on the phone. All of this is against a background of a blaring rock concert on television and records dropping onto a turntable while two immaculately groomed and well-dressed teenage children stand on the stairs watching their parents, arms folded in disgust. The backstory to this picture emerges as frames showing the parents in the 1970s spoiling their children with unlimited supplies of records, sodas, and cigarettes and then watching in terror as their children ignore all of those "advantages," as the son and daughter insist on "keeping their rooms neat and clean, read books, drink milk, watch only Educational T.V. and don't go steady even though they are well past twelve." Later, the parents watch sadly as their children go on to become a physicist and surgeon, only to recover in the twenty-first century when, as aging grandparents, they see rebellious young versions of themselves running to embrace them as they welcome their "real swinging grandcats" in a futuristic home complete with a helicopter pad in the yard.

Both *Bye Bye Birdie* and *Mad* magazine provided a humorous spin to the generational divide that had spilled over from the 1950s into the early and middle years of the new decade. While the term *generation gap* did not become commonly used until the second half of the sixties, both adult- and teen-oriented magazines and books monitored concerns that each age group confronted regarding the attitudes and behavior of the people on the other side of an often poorly defined age divide, even if both groups tacitly admitted that not everyone on the other side of that boundary behaved with equal levels of exasperating actions.

As American adults and teens segued from the 1950s into the new decade, unresolved or only partially resolved generational issues from the previous decade began to appear in somewhat altered versions as the first half of the sixties progressed. For example, adult concerns with teenage steady relationships and adolescent gang-induced juvenile delinquency of the fifties morphed somewhat into concern with *preteen* steady relationships and *suburban, middle-class* delinquency, while teenagers expressed increasing dissatisfaction with significantly expanded school workloads and more stringent grading policies that had been debated immediately after Sputnik but were actually implemented mostly in the early years of the sixties.

By the early sixties, adult disapproval with the institutionalization of steady relationships between high school couples had not officially disappeared, but many parents tacitly admitted that there was little they could do to dissolve their own sixteen- or seventeen-year-old child's relationship when the concept of going steady had become informally institutionalized in most high schools. Therefore, the media outlets gradually shifted their attention to the "crisis" that seemed to be emerging as preteens, or "subteens," often appropriated their older brothers' and sisters' relationships for their own social lives. Now newspaper and magazine headlines warned of the consequences of junior high and middle school partnerships in titles such as "Boys and Girls Too Old, Too Soon," and "Too Many Subteens Grow Up Too Soon and Too Fast."

In the summer of 1962, *Life* magazine ran an extensive photo essay focusing on a "typical" preteen girl, "a pocket femme fatale who can wind a boy around her little finger" and worked hard at "interesting male suitors who were becoming 'miniature adults,'" as they lined up to compete for the favors of their "sub-teen damsel." The article depicted the emergence of steady dating among ten- to thirteen-year-old "attractive children of a generation whose jumble of innocence and worldly wisdom is unnaturally precocious and alarming. Without knowing what they are doing, or why, they are rushing and being rushed into growing up too soon."

Magazines geared toward middle-class parents carried photo essays on eleven- and twelve-year-old girls who "turned themselves out in mascara, pancake makeup and 'adult' hairdos to impress male 'party hounds' in pursuit," as part of an endless round of campaigns to capture or be captured, with the ultimate goal being steady status, something roundly condemned for seventeen-year-olds only a few years earlier. Some child psychologists insisted that, while these preteen boys and girls engaged in exploring the physical symbols of a steady relationship—rings, necking, close dancing—too many adults stood by and winked at this behavior as "cute." One article quoted a concerned but generally resigned mother as saying, "You can't stop your child. Everybody is doing it. Makeup and lipstick starts at ten. If you deprive them of it, it becomes more attractive, and they just devise other ways to do it. Going steady's a habit, a convenience. It takes some getting used to by parents, even if they're partying too much and dancing too early." More than a few mothers of preteens blamed at least part of the problem on print advertisements that touted preteen wigs, makeup, and fashions that promised, "Now you can be as glamorous as your mother."

Journalists covering the great preteen steady debate found little difficulty in finding parents who admitted, "It's so cute to see a couple of 12 year old sweethearts acting like grownups," or mothers and fathers who admitted that because they suffered from unpopularity when they were young, they felt that the danger of early relationships was a reasonable price to pay for offspring who would be well adjusted and popular. The explosion of preteen charm schools and dance classes allowed these parents to have vicarious success in their children's ability to become poised and popular and to jettison the awkwardness that had once plagued those mothers and fathers.

On the other hand, the numerous parents who found nothing cute about premature dabbling in adult relationships received significant support from child and adolescent psychologists and counselors of the era. For example, Sylvia Bauman, a child therapist at Albert Einstein College of Medicine in New York, insisted to a *Life* magazine journalist that "tacit parental acceptance" of preteen dating was a huge mistake, as "Many children would secretly welcome being told 'no' by their parents. As the parents let themselves be stampeded into accepting this pairing off, many of the children would prefer to be either alone or in larger groups." Bauman noted that "an eleven year old girl should have another little girl as her best friend, not a miniature husband."

Dr. Francis Ilg, director of the Gesell Institute of Child Development, noted that the mixed feelings of parents toward preteen relationships were simultaneously accelerating and short-circuiting the transition from childhood to young adulthood, as these participants in "Tom Thumb marriages" "never learn about the world or other people because their interests are restricted to themselves and the response of the other boy or girl to themselves. These emotional relationships demand a much greater degree of maturity than the youngsters possess."

While preteens nervously mimicked adult romantic relationships as though they were trying out a game they didn't really know how to play, their older siblings of high school age were increasingly making headlines in media outlets with a related, but often more disturbing, mimicry of adult "cocktail parties," which sometimes resulted in destruction and violence. Just as fifties-era big-city "rumbles" and gang wars of *West Side Story* fame began to at least temporarily diminish, suburban adolescents seemed to be increasingly attracted to a less organized form of antisocial behavior in turning seemingly innocent teen parties into orgies of vandalism.

Typical of the local and national media attention to suburban teen "crashers," a July 1963 *Life* magazine article by staff writer Robert Wallace chronicled an alleged demolition of adolescent social norms in which "even teens who are seemingly supplied with all of the necessities and most of the luxuries of life commit acts of violence that often exceeds that of their delinquent cousins in the slums." As one article noted, "From Connecticut to California, stories emerge of even small teen parties being 'invaded' by large numbers of gate crashers where homes are looted, girls are raped, and sometimes, teenagers have died."

During the summer of 1963, national magazines carried random samples of suburban teen violence that frequently occurred in the most fashionable, affluent communities of the era. In Grosse Point, Michigan, a small, invitation-only party turned into a near riot with over one hundred crashers smashing the kitchen furniture, overturning the stove and refrigerator, and breaking all the kitchen windows before they dispersed. Teens asked to leave a party in the Wilshire section of Los Angeles blasted the house with gunfire from rifles and shotguns pulled from their cars. A fashionable suburb of Dallas was the site of a pool party gone wild, as scores of crashers demolished nearly all the patio furniture, smashed scores of liquor bottles, and caused $10,000 in property damage, as almost all of the forty-nine teens arrested by police were described as "from the better families of the city."

From the adult side of the generation gap, it appeared that if preteens were somehow growing up too soon in their premature steady relationships, high school teens were responding to the historic prosperity and comfort provided by their parents with acts of rebellion that simply proved that many contemporary teens were thoroughly spoiled. Books such as *Teenage Tyranny* and *Suburbia's Coddled Kids* resonated with large numbers of adults, who viewed sixties teens as a spoiled generation that received too many material benefits and not enough discipline. Robert Wallace's interviews of teenagers revealed a disturbing increase in the cleavage between adults and adolescent identities and the tendency of teens to consistently use "us" of themselves and "them" in reference to their elders. Even as early as 1963, the sixties teen identity seemed to be based on the premise that "teens wonder why they should be committed to a world that they see as a sorry mess" and ask "what's so good about the adult world."

If adult-oriented media was clearly describing a generation gap before the term itself was actually used, teen-oriented magazine articles showed that the more peaceful first half of the sixties was hardly an age of adolescent joy at adult behavior. Almost every teen magazine had some form of "Teen Forum," "Speak Out," or "Young Living" column that allowed their readers to express their opinions, not only on the teen experience but also on their relationship with the adult world. From teen perspectives, well before "don't trust anyone over thirty" became a battle cry, it was clear that many adolescents felt that a combination of materialism, arbitrary and capricious house rules, and escalating school achievement and grade expectations were making the teen experience a less-than-enviable prospect.

The first issue—the highly publicized debate over the merits and limits of the emerging "acquisitive society" of a prosperous, increasingly suburbanized America—hardly escaped the attention of teens. One adult newsmagazine, critical of the spoiled attitudes of contemporary adolescents, also noted their significant levels of moral indignation over what at least some believed was a pointless fixation on wealth and status by their parents. A number of national surveys of teens found that many adolescents felt that their personal lives had been deeply affected either by the frequent absence of fathers who were either working extraordinarily long hours at the office or frequently away from home on business trips or by the constant corporate transfers of parents from community to community, which created a rootless, insecure existence for the many teens who were perennial "new kids in the class" at numerous stages of their academic experiences. Teens also believed (with some possible accuracy) that parents willingly accepted these transfers in order to gain both improved status and more upscale homes and furnishings in a never-ending "keep up with the Joneses" treadmill that proved much more advantageous for adults than adolescents, who in essence reclimbed the teen social pyramid at each successive location and in each successive school. While some television programs and films (such as *Meet Me in St. Louis*) featured plotlines where parents canceled transfers after consultation with their children, the real world of the corporate merry-go-round seemed to include minimal consideration of adolescent needs.

While even national newsmagazines carried features on the psychological impact on adolescents being forced to repeatedly initiate new relationships in frequent parental career relocations, most teen magazine "Sounding Board" features during the first half of the sixties continued to be dominated by complaints about more traditional generational issues, such as lack of privacy and adult failure to understand adolescent feelings.

One representative sample, the June 1963 *Seventeen* magazine segment "Young Living," featured fairly predictable complaints to feature writer Abigail Wood. One sixteen-year-old girl insisted, "My inability to confide in my mother, especially about dating problems, brings grief to both of us. When I broke up with my boyfriend, my Mom was very angry because I called my girlfriend first and then told me that my boyfriend was 'lousy' anyway. She also said that because I didn't confide in her, there would be no more drive-in movies and no long dress for the prom. If I wanted a dress, my girlfriend should buy it."

A second complaint centered around a common issue in a culture in which there were generally still more potential users of telephones than there were instruments available. This young lady insisted that every time she was engaged in phone conversations, her mother would routinely listen in on the other phone, and when confronted with that practice, the mother countered, "It's my telephone, I pay the bill." This fifteen-year-old also dealt with physical privacy issues as a closed door in her bedroom seemed to be an invitation for her mother to barge in.

The most common journalist response in these seemingly ubiquitous features in most of the era's teen magazines was a general sympathy for the letter writer combined with an extensive analysis of why adults acted the way they did, with a suggestion that the teens should perhaps meet their elders more than halfway in the generational divide. The fifteen-year-old honor student dealing with her mother's deficiencies in phone etiquette was supported in her right to privacy but told that "Sometimes a girl simply has to ride out a situation that can't be changed. But learning to do that as peaceably as possible is also part of growing up."

A teen magazine article in 1965, "Why Your Parents Don't Understand You," cites five points of contention between adults and high schoolers: parental refusal to accept teen maturity; interference in choice of friends or dates; lack of appreciation for the need for privacy; underestimation of teen decision-making abilities; and lack of understanding of the natural idealism of adolescents. Yet the article is generally very supportive of the sacrifices that parents were making to provide a "good life" for their teens and insists that "the role of parent to teenager is as challenging and confusing as being a teenager—they are always adjusting to a 'new you.'" This article was one of many teen advice features during the sixties that emphasized the economic and cultural differences between contemporary society and a generation earlier. "Your parents very likely grew up in the Depression of the Thirties and were teenagers during World War II when money was short, goods scarce, travel limited, and most people less sophisticated than people now. They grew up before television, nuclear physics, the United Nations—a much simpler world. Going by *their* generation's standards of frugality and relative provincialism, they might see you and your friends as extravagant, fast and overly sophisticated."

While both adult and teen magazines frequently chided sixties teens for not fully appreciating how much more opportunity they enjoyed to fulfill their dreams than their parents encountered, more than a few adolescents implied that the route to those dreams was through an increasingly rigorous educational system that placed far more pressure on them than had been the experience of either their parents or even their older siblings of the 1950s.

A combination of fear that American high schools were lagging even further behind their Soviet counterparts in academic achievement and a surge in teen high school graduates before the already-overburdened colleges were fully expanded to receive them placed teens of the first half of the sixties in a more competitive environment than either immediately before or after them. Principals, counselors, and teachers were often remarkably frank in their admission that course requirements and grading policies had been tightened, especially for the growing number of teens interested in some form of higher education. For example, numerous high schools raised the numerical equivalents for letter grades to 93–100 instead of 90–100 for an A, and 85–92 instead of 80–90 for B grades, and so on, to show their commitment to rigor and raising the bar of student achievement. Even the level of failure was lowered to new depths in many academically rigorous schools. Traditional grade point equivalents where an A was worth a 4, B a 3, and so on down to an F being a zero could now become an F-1 for grades below 65 or an F-2 for grades below 60, which actually subtracted from "positive" number to produce potentially unbelievably low grade point averages. Yet this draconian system was in operation at a point where overcrowded colleges were becoming ever more choosey in their selection of acceptable candidates.

Meanwhile, as assignments and grading grew more stringent in high schools, guidance counselors and principals increasingly discouraged "academic" students from taking study halls or even less-demanding courses so they could more fully participate in the academic arms race to gain college admission.

The increasing fixation of school officials on raising the academic bar to increasingly daunting levels gradually percolated into teen forums in adolescent-oriented media. One of *Seventeen* magazines's regular features, "Colleges and Careers," began to shift from relatively straightforward information on college acceptance and jobs opportunities into teen reader critiques of current grading, testing, and curricular issues. For example, in one forum titled "What's Bugging You about School" a New Hampshire teen insisted, "At my school, a student with high national test scores is expected to pursue a program in agreement with his 'level' of intelligence. This always means an abundance of math, languages and sciences, with no time left over for other kinds of courses. This often leads to a stereotyped program that's seldom altered to meet the individual's needs and desires. Since schools strive to turn out well rounded students, it seems ironic that they so seldom allow individuals to study in many areas. I think that a bright student could make just as good an artist or home economist as she could a math teacher or nuclear scientist."

Subsequent columns about school issues included teen essays on the overuse of multiple choice tests, the increasing difficulty in achieving good grades due to heightened numerical thresholds, and the rampant censoring of reading materials and discussion topics in many high schools.

Most of the adult concerns with preteen steady relationships, teen binge drinking and party crashing, and teen concerns with frequent family relocation and more stringent academic expectations would continue to evoke some emotional responses as the first half of the sixties segued into the middle and later years. Yet by 1965 or 1966, new issues were beginning to emerge as points of contention, and the term *generation gap* was beginning to emerge. By early 1966 both ABC and NBC were airing prime-time specials titled *The Teen Revolution*, with the "Peacock Network" promising "to reveal what the 4,000 young people of Lexington, Massachusetts, are up to," as the teen would be told, "Don't look now, that's a T.V. camera over your shoulder."

The newly emerging elements of this generation gap were actually largely dominated by the now famous cliché of generational dispute in the sixties: sex, drugs, and rock and roll, especially if the first term included fashion and related culture. The first two issues will be discussed in the remainder of this chapter; the third will be part of the chronicle in the next chapter. All three of these generational points of contention are quite real, but as will be seen they are complicated by lack of agreement on the dividing line between "kid" and "adult" membership and the reality that neither group was in any case a unified entity in any real or imagined "confrontation" or "gap."

The sex part of the generation gap triumvirate actually began more as a conflict over fashion statements than over the specific sexual activities of sixties teens. During the first four years of the 1960s, as the greaser look of many fifties male teens gave way to a newly dominant short-haired style, many adolescents and adult males shared a very similar look that was in many respects an affirmation of the World War II "combat crop" adopted by sixties teens' fathers during the 1940s. Then, soon after the first Beatles television performances, a growing number of young men, in more than a few cases encouraged by teen girls, began adopting a more shaggy appearance that was, in turn, reinforced by successive waves of newly emerging British and American male performers and bands.

Soon, a significant number of American teen boys who previously spent almost no time on hair care were taking photos of their favorite performers to willing barbers and asking for a look that entailed far more than a buzz cut. In turn, these boys were now receiving negative or sarcastic comments from older males, ranging from fathers to parents of actual or potential girlfriends to semistrangers making comments from park benches and beach umbrellas. Much of the commentary was both sexually related and yet enormously contradictory, as more than a few longer-haired boys were alternately derided as "looking like a girl" yet warned away from girls as sexually loose or predatory. Somehow, the long, powdered wigs of American Continental Army soldiers or the shoulder-length tresses of many Civil War combatants were forgotten by many male adults who saw long-haired boys as a clear and present danger to the security of the Republic, while, in turn, some of the teens (often supported by their girlfriends) grew their hair even longer just to prove their defiance. Now traditional gatekeepers, employers of part-time jobs, parents of potential girlfriends, and teachers might be viewing adolescent boys through the prism of hair length or style before any other factor was considered, while boys who had initially been rather neutral regarding hair style now saw hair length as a statement of possible independence, rebellion, or even sexual identity.

If hair length differences between adult men and teen boys were provoking generational skirmishes during the sixties, skirt length differences between female adults and adolescents were soon providing a new front in the generational war. Whatever differences 1950s mothers and daughters may have had over social and sexual mores, the poodle skirt and related fifties fashion statements were hardly viewed as sexually provocative. However, by the mid-1960s, the go-go and swinging fashions for young people were increasingly revolving around very short skirts that were made even more daring by vinyl plastic boots, sensuous makeup, and alluring hairstyles that made the teen girl fashions of only a decade earlier now seen virtually matronly.

Just as British rock groups such as the Beatles spurred American boys to wear longer hair, London fashion designer Mary Quant's interpretation of "anything goes" sixties fashions enticed girls to much shorter skirts. As a fashion, the miniskirt was now worn most effectively by the very young. Teamed up with geometric black and white op art patterns, the mini became an essential part of the developing mod girl image and quickly spread to America, supported by the new British supermodels, such as Twiggy and Jean Shrimpton. As old ideas about fashion were being turned upside down, many adults were initially shocked by skirts cut eight or nine inches above the knee, while many teen girls saw the mini as a sign of greater freedom and relaxation in dress. Thus the miniskirt for girls, much as long hair for boys, wavered somewhere between fashion statement and sexual suggestiveness for both young admirers and older critics.

Paradoxically, while conflicts over hair length between teen boys and mainly adult males were frequently featured in print and visual media of the era and chronicled in popular music by Sonny and Cher in "I Got You Babe" and Sonny alone in "Laugh at Me," miniskirts on teenage girls evoked far less generational hostility outside the halls of high schools. While skirt length did become a contentious point in an increasing number of sixties high schools, adult reaction in noneducational environments seemed relatively muted, at least in comparison to the great "hair controversy," as skirt length for adult women simply shrank at a less accelerated pace than for their teen daughters.

More specific discussions of relationships and sexuality beyond popular culture and fashion also frequently proved to be less generationally confrontational than the popular images of the decade would suggest. As the sixties progressed, the sexual component of teen magazine relationship segments became mildly more explicit but would have provided few shocks to any adult readers. For example, the July 1964 issue of *Seventeen* magazine escalated the usual bland dating dos and don'ts of most teen magazines with a more open discussion of expectations on the part of six male high school students. Most of the boys insisted that parents and other adult role models had been influential in their moral foundations but far less valuable in interpreting the physical aspect of romantic relationships, which was often left to more experienced teen peers or print and film sources.

The *Seventeen* article provided its primarily female audience with contradictory information that while "among guys, everybody's just about ready to go pretty far with girls these days," it's also true that "boys want a girl to go out with for yourself, not necessarily for sex." The panelists generally agreed that girls were more thoughtful and mature because they were also vulnerable with "a lot more to lose," but were somewhat vague on how this might affect their own actions.

On the other hand, the generally adult female readership of *McCall's* magazine could open up an issue of that journal to find an article titled "A New View of College Sex," which produced far more explicit outcomes for older adolescents who were attending college in 1966. In an article much more clinical in tone than the *Seventeen* forum, author and researcher Vance Packard informed adults that "there has been a crumbling of traditional controls over the sexual awakening and maturity of young people. Parental control has clearly declined. Parents are often confused and helpless." Yet the responses of more than two thousand students produced the bewildering reality that while 60 percent more girls were sexually active than a generation earlier, their male counterparts were behaving no differently than late adolescents of 1940.

If the sex aspect of the kids-adult generational conflict was at best an uncertain trumpet for battle, the drugs portion of the equation could perhaps offer more promise for differentiating adults from teens. In a *Life* article, "A Town in Trouble," the magazine zeroed in on drug use by high school students in the town of Fort Bragg, California, depicting a "contemporary sickness, a plague of the Sixties," as much of the student body "sits listless and drab," as students seemed dazed and exhausted after rampant weekend drug use, with one teacher complaining, "I'm the only one alive in the classroom, it's spooky." Where more fortunate high schools had "bright dresses and bustle," at this school "lethargic students sit like wounded sparrows, stirring only to beg money from one another in a student body where the majority of the students appeared to be on speed, LSD or Demerol."

Yet even in this school, where an estimated 75 percent of the 550 students were regularly using some illegal substance and some drugs were seeping down to sixth graders, it was made apparent that conditions were gradually improving when previously uninvolved parents and energetic school officials and drug counselors finally bonded together. The storyline revealed a relatively happy ending: "Students are brightly dressed once more, youthful energy courses through their lunch hours, miniskirts and long hair are once again contentious issues." Yet the authors hinted that a possible reason for parental inability to discern a massive youth drug problem was the "easy tolerance to liquor in town," in which much of the social life included "washing the family car and getting drunk," as their teens were shooting speed at the same time and not far away.

While the term *generation gap* had achieved cover-story status by the last third of the sixties decade, the debate between adults and "the kids" often took paths other than the standard issues of sex, drugs, and rock and roll. For example, an article in *Seventeen* in early 1969 was a satire on the new movie ratings system written by two teen girls who turned the tables on adult oversight of films appropriate for young people in an article titled "What Parents Should See." The two young ladies insisted, tongue-in-cheek, that teens "must consider the individual parent. Some adults are more mature or more set in their ways and are rarely influenced by anything. Others, on the other hand, are willing to accept radical ideas in an effort to stay young. The real problem with movies today is that they are filled with symbolism and are often difficult to understand. A parent viewing such a film may come home and ask you some surprisingly pointed questions which you may find difficult to answer or feel should not be answered at that particular time." This humorous role reversal between parent and teen ended with a satirical tip to adolescents "struggling" to keep recalcitrant parents "in line" in their entertainment choices. If adults insisted on attending films meant particularly for a teen audience, "if your parents should come home shocked or bewildered by what they have seen in the neighborhood movie, be patient, answer their questions, put them on a steady diet of the 'good old movies' on T.V.'s late show."

While the sixties generational debate could sometimes unleash unexpected humor, it could also generate surprisingly mature response from many teens on national policies that affected their lives. High schoolers and teen college underclassmen were often notable elements of protests against the Vietnam war military conscription, especially as they chanted about adult hypocrisy at "being old enough to fight but not old enough to vote." Yet when presidential aspirant Robert Kennedy and advisors to Republican President Richard Nixon called for universal service in return for lowering the voting age to eighteen, a surprisingly high percentage of teenage girls insisted that their gender should serve as well if they expected to be treated as equals. A 1969 coast-to-coast poll of adolescent girls by *Seventeen* magazine found that nearly two-thirds of the respondents felt that young men should have a choice of national service or military duty, while this group of thirteen- to nineteen-year-old females included a majority response that *everyone* should be expected to serve his or her country between high school and college, with the promise that "only by making it compulsory can we assure the rewards and opportunities of national service. A national service in which *all* participated would make a tremendous contribution to our country and encourage the realization of the benefits of our society." Even among the minority, who were far less enthusiastic about the idea, a frequent observation by girls was, "I don't believe in the draft, but if it's required for men, it should be required for women."

Like the Vietnam War that spawned at least part of the furor, the generational conflict that became an integral part of sixties teen life splashed over into the 1970s. However, by the autumn of 1969, the number of American troops serving in Vietnam had begun an irreversible decline, the capricious Selective Service System had been turned into a more predictable lottery, and both the end of conscription and the eighteen-year-old vote were almost certain to be realities by the early seventies. Teens in high school still marched against wars and banded together in a number of ways to encourage their school leaders to modernize policies on dress, speech, and deportment. Adult response was almost always mixed, but change was already in the air, and an informality of dress and speech that would have been shocking to a 1960 teen transported to the future was clearly in place in more than a few schools. One of the best teen-oriented articles in *Life* magazine during the sixties was titled "The Happy Protest in High School Fashion," and the authors hinted that in this context at least the kids were clearly scenting victory.

> The latest rule in girls' high school fashion is that there isn't any. Custom, which once upon a time demanded letter sweaters and saddle shoes, now insists "wear your own thing." This freaky new freedom makes the very idea of school-imposed dress codes seem hopelessly old fashioned. Many principals now just relax and enjoy the scene—now Pucci tights, bell bottomed jump suits, buckskins, Bermuda overalls and tapestried shirts. Now fashion diversity rules in many high schools—some mod, some straight—all different. Kids shop at strange places—anything from boutiques to thrift shops and dime stores, and sew old brocade curtains into flaming coats and madras bedspreads into saris.

By the late 1960s, much of the generation gap was as likely *intra*generational as *inter*generational. Teens had successfully appropriated much of the underpinning of popular culture from their elders, and if high school fashion was a riot of styles, late teen music was a riot of genres, where the villagelike shared experience from Elvis Presley to the Beach Boys had transformed into a smorgasbord of sounds in a genre that had morphed from rock and roll to just rock music.

~

CHAPTER NINE

The Teen Music Explosion, 1964–1969

Myth and Reality

As the Beatles flew eastward across the Atlantic at the conclusion of their first triumphant "invasion" of the New World, a music form until recently seen by the adult world as a somewhat bizarre soundtrack to the ritual of teen social life began to be parsed and analyzed by social scientists, psychologists, and business experts as one of the major aspects of the whole sixties cultural experience. While the Elvis Presley phenomenon had burst upon mature Americans as a form of musical Roman candle, then settled back into a niche teen story as other stories and crises emerged, Beatlemania largely turned what was routinely called teen music into the coin of the realm for the whole recording industry for both the remainder of the 1960s and far into the next century.

Yet the British Invasion and its related international and American aftershocks not only turned rock and roll or rock music into the dominant audio entertainment form, it also initiated a series of myths and actualities that are often difficult to separate from each other, as the gap between what journalists and scholars thought was happening in the teen music world and the actual events have sometimes been hopelessly blurred. The teen "music explosion" of 1964 to 1969, roughly from Beatlemania to Woodstock, has so often been hijacked by individuals with particular social, cultural, and political agendas that the narrative of what sixties preteens and teens *really* listened to and cared about has become hostage to a number of cultural conflicts that remain supercharged four or five decades after the events. Perhaps the best place to begin to separate myth and reality is to return to 1964 and through popular music charts, teen and adult magazine features, and music program videos suggest some revision to what was thought to have happened in the wake of the Beatles' conquering of American adolescent culture.

The first assertion that can be challenged about the Beatles' impact on American teen culture is that the arrival of the Fab Four essentially ended much of the American-dominated music scene of the previous year or two. A number of both American and British popular music documentaries on the sixties assert that the arrival of the British Invasion was something akin to a musical Norman Conquest of American teen culture, which swept away the rules of early sixties American pop. For example, one comprehensive film documentary, *The British Invasion: The First Wave*, narrated by British actor Michael York, loftily intones the conventional wisdom that American teen music in 1963 was "little more than novelty tunes" and, thus, an empty pasture just waiting for musical cultivation from the other side of the Atlantic. Yet this "barren soil" saw the emergence that year of Bob Dylan, the Beach Boys, Stevie Wonder, Martha and the Vandellas, and the Four Seasons— hardly an insignificant cast. A companion corollary is that American music was in such a creative slump that the arrival of the British groups essentially annihilated homegrown pop and rock acts. Again, a summary of *Billboard* magazine and similar "hot 100" or "top 40" lists reveals a far more complex outcome.

One of the realities of the emergence of the rock and roll genre in 1955 or 1956 was the pace of rise to stardom and fall to nonentity was much more frenetic than in the Big Band era of the forties and the adult pop sound of much of the fifties. Performers such as Frank Sinatra, Perry Como, Doris Day, and Patti Page released numerous hits from one decade to another and retained fan loyalty from young adulthood all the way to old age. The much more adolescent-based rock audience was far more fickle, and even top stars who did not die in plane crashes or car wrecks saw their popularity diminish in an amazingly brief time frame. Thus many of the most successful artists during the summer of 1961 had almost totally disappeared by the summer of 1963, months before the Beatles were on American pop charts. Bobby Lewis, with number-one hit "Tossin' and Turnin'," the Regents with "Barbara Ann," Curtis Lee with "Pretty Little Angel Eyes," and Linda Scott with "Don't Bet Money Honey" had essentially disappeared from the playlists two years later, while others, such as Sam Cooke, Rick Nelson, the Drifters, and Brenda Lee were still significant teen music stars.

Then, as the British Invasion surged into America beginning in 1964, the zero-sum game of popular music ensured that at least some American artists' careers would edge downward, and there was no rhyme or reason as to which artists were substantially affected and which emerged rather unscathed. For example, Rick Nelson, Bobby Rydell, the Essex, and the Shirelles would now enter a lengthy, sometimes permanent, exile from the charts, yet the Four Seasons, the Beach Boys, the Miracles, and Gene Pitney were even more popular in 1964 (and beyond) than they were in 1963.

The reality of Beatlemania and the British Invasion, in fact, seems to be one of a rising tide raising all (or at least many) boats. The arrival of musical acts from across the Atlantic enormously enhanced the impact of the relatively new rock and roll genre on a variety of age groups in American society. First, the arrival of the Beatles, and their friendly competitors from Newcastle to London, dramatically extended the range of teen music from adolescents to young adults and sometimes even further. After the initial Elvis Presley media frenzy, the adult-oriented media, as opposed to teen magazines, largely ignored "kid music" until John, Paul, George, and Ringo arrived. Up until 1964, *teens* certainly knew their favorite recording stars, and those teens *did* buy the vast majority of 45 rpm singles. Yet beginning with the Beatles, the adult media quickly jumped on what had been a teen bandwagon and helped turn what was then advertised as teen music into rock music, which had no absolute age ceiling. One of the most important contributions of the Beatles in turning teen music into a far less age-limited cultural phenomenon is that they brought numerous British friends with them, and Americans from a surprisingly wide spectrum of age groups were quickly enchanted by one or more of those entertainers.

Suddenly, everything British was that much smarter and more "in," not only for high school girls but also for their older sisters in college or in careers. Singers from twentysomething Dusty Springfield to seventeen-year-old Marianne Faithful to fourteen-year-old Lulu appeared on American television screens with heavy eye makeup, short skirts, and leather boots that emphasized a European sophistication that tempted a wide age range of female Americans to reconsider their style options, while in turn stirring romantic fantasies in equally wide-eyed American males. Anglo-Caribbean teen Millie Small added the extra spice of ska music in "My Boy Lollipop," while redheaded Cilla Black specialized in sophisticated ballads generated by Italian pop songwriters.

The male elements of the British Invasion washed up on American shores in serial fashion that allowed young listeners to appreciate their uniqueness before choosing which acts would gain their favor and their sales. Again, contrary to later conventional wisdom, the main initial competition to the Beatles was not the Rolling Stones but another London-based group, the Dave Clark Five. The purveyors of the "Tottenham Sound" would never quite project the telegenic quirkiness and individuality of the Beatles, but they appealed to girls as generally more handsome than most of the Fab Four, fascinated boys with their more driving beat punctuated by the addition of saxophone and keyboard, and resonated with some parents as Clark recounted in interviews his abstinence from smoking and alcohol consumption. While the Rolling Stones were still emerging in Britain, early 1964 American pop music stations' British playlists were almost exclusively Dusty Springfield, the Beatles, and the Dave Clark Five.

Between early spring and early summer of 1964, three British male acts, with significant Beatles connections, constituted a major new transatlantic wave lapping on American shores. The three groups in this trio included the Searchers, Billy J. Kramer and the Dakotas, and Gerry and the Pacemakers. The Searchers, who took their name from a John Wayne Western of that title, relied almost totally for their initial success on covers of late fifties and early sixties American rhythm and blues and soul hits with a dash of folk music thrown in. This combination included "Love Potion No. 9," originally by the Clovers; "Sweets for My Sweet," by the Drifters; "What Have They Done to the Rain," by Canadian folk artists Ian and Sylvia; and "Needles and Pins," written and originally sung by folk-pop star Jackie DeShannon. Billy J. Kramer and the Dakotas also revealed the group's fascination with America in its name and scored a huge, double-sided hit in America with the cutely plaintive "Little Children," as sung by the exasperated boyfriend of a babysitter saddled with insomniac child charges, and "Bad to Me," which Paul McCartney had originally written for a Beatles album but provided as a friendly gift to the still-emerging group. The final member of this trio was Gerry and the Pacemakers, fronted by Gerry Marsden, who often emerged as a friendly rival to Lennon and McCartney in their formative years in Liverpool. Marsden was a talented songwriter in his own right and was actually lauded for his musical talent by a number of adult audience publications that saw songs such as "I'll Be There," "Ferry Cross the Mersey," and "Don't Let the Sun Catch You Crying" as something well beyond teen fluff.

Compared to the teen music scene of exactly a year earlier, the popular music world had undergone a seismic change by New Year's Eve 1964. Twelve months earlier, Beatlemania was still largely a European phenomenon carried to America only in grainy music clips and magazine photos. Now teen magazines not only informed their readers of the favorite snack foods of John, Paul, George, and Ringo, but offered predictions and previews of what act would be the next major transatlantic import into the domestic teen culture. On the other hand, if 1964 had been the first year in American pop music that a significant segment of the top-ten list was of foreign (mainly British) origin, the two-thirds to three-quarters of chart songs still released by American artists largely fell into categories not that different from a year or two before most Americans knew the Cavern Club or Brian Epstein even existed. The girl group genre was still huge, with new groups such as the Jelly Beans, Patty and the Emblems, the Dixie Cups, and most notably, the Shangri-Las powerful contenders for gold record status, while Motown's trio of the Marvellets, Martha and the Vandellas, and especially the Supremes were now major factors in popular music.

Acts that had emerged in the year before the onset of Beatlemania, such as the Beach Boys, the Four Seasons, and Lesley Gore were still consistent hit makers, while a surprising number of adult contemporary artists, such as Nancy Wilson, Dean Martin, Astrid Gilberto, Al Hirt, Stan Getz, and Herb Alpert, were still often hopping onto charts on top-forty teen-oriented stations as well. In fact, because of the combination of adult and teen support, "Hello, Dolly!" was seen by some chart counts to be more successful than any one Beatles single of 1964. Yet as Americans prepared for the exact midpoint of the sixties decade, the teen music scene was about to undergo a twenty-four-month sea change that would begin to fragment pop culture to such a significant extent that even the adult news media would take notice.

As 1965 began, President Johnson's Great Society educational measures—the proposed Elementary and Secondary Education Act and the Higher Education Act—were about to pump billions of dollars into adolescents' education opportunities, twenty-three thousand American soldiers were conducting primarily advisory operations in a war that had killed 147 personnel in the past twelve months, and three decidedly uncontroversial songs, "Downtown" by Petula Clark, "Come See About Me" by the Supremes, and "You've Lost That Lovin' Feeling" by the Righteous Brothers, were vying for the top spot in popular music surveys. Yet by New Year's Eve 1966, much of the Great Society would be in tatters, 385,000 Americans would be fighting in a Southeast Asian war that was now killing nearly 147 men a week, and terms like *protest song*, *folk rock*, and *psychedelic* were becoming increasingly important elements of what had once simply been labeled rock and roll. Most importantly, what had once been dismissed by adults as the "fluff" of rock and roll was now being discussed in serious articles in newsmagazines and even taught in college courses as Americans of very diverse political and cultural persuasions tried to discern whether young people would really begin to change society and to what extent that change could be tolerated or even welcomed by their elders. Whether teens were just beginning a cultural revolution or were extending much of the status quo, whatever was occurring needed a "soundtrack," and that soundtrack was heard frequently, if uncertainly, from "boss jocks" to prime-time music on television.

Most narratives of the social impact of rock music on the cultural upheavals that distinguished the late 1960s have traditionally focused on the roughly two-year period from the "Summer of Love" and the attendant emergence of Jefferson Airplane, the Doors, and the Beatles in their "Sergeant Pepper" persona to the convening of a "youth nation" at Woodstock in 1969. This period will be covered (in a somewhat revisionist mode) shortly in this chapter, but any analysis of that two years is handicapped from the start, unless the far less chronicled events of 1965–1966 are included. The enormous changes in teen music culture that had been experienced in the Beatlemania year of 1964 would accelerate even more rapidly during the twenty-four-month period just after 1964.

During the all-too-short Christmas/winter holiday of 1964–1965, tens of thousands of American teenagers temporarily left tinseled trees and new gifts behind for a two-hour movie theater experience that had been massively hyped on almost every radio or television program that any adolescent might have heard or seen. Unlike the more familiar rock movies, such as the recent A Hard Day's Night, which interrupted really good songs with really lame plots, The Teenage Awards Music International Show was nonstop music by twelve groups and artists, seven of which eventually entered the Rock and Roll Hall of Fame. Using a quartet of precursors to modern digital cameras, the director of the TAMI show used the "Electronovision" technique to jump back and forth between a packed live audience of California teenagers and much of the music royalty of their world, from the Beach Boys to the Miracles to Gerry and the Pacemakers. However, while pop princess Lesley Gore and soul king James Brown elicited huge screams and cheers from the overwhelmingly adolescent audience, the final act far outpaced any of its predecessors in causing enough commotion to spur somewhat befuddled police into action to guard against a run on the stage.

Mick Jagger and his four Rolling Stones companions burst onto the stage, and all five songs that had made the American charts up to this point, with their current hit, "Time Is On My Side," provoking the most emotional outbursts from a teen audience equally as engaged and much more numerous than the one at The Ed Sullivan Show's Beatles debut several months earlier, while the emotion spread into the "virtual" audience in the darkened movie theaters. During the next two years, as the Beatles gradually abandoned television, films, and live concerts for the creative energies of studio production, the Rolling Stones would begin to personify the complex nature of a music explosion that would set in motion a complex set of subgenres, all of which were theoretically rock music but increasingly produced very different sounds, messages, and eventually audiences. Mick Jagger and his alternately irreverent and serious comrades in music would astound and enrage adult critics and chroniclers as they moved from an almost baroque classical sound of the lutes and harpsichords in "Lady Jane" and "As Tears Go By" to satires on middle-class adult lifestyles in "Mother's Little Helper" and "Satisfaction" to blatant sexuality in "Let's Spend the Night Together," alternating between London court dates for drug charges and the mainstream, largely adult audience of multiple *Ed Sullivan Show* appearances.

Teen fans and adult critics learned in 1965 and 1966 that British Invasion music was now so diverse that fan bases became much more niche-market oriented than the early Beatles era. Some British groups brought to America a driving guitar sound that made even the Rolling Stones look a bit placid: for example, the Kinks' "All Day and All of the Night" and The Yardbirds' "Heart Full of Soul, where Jimmy Page's blaring guitar solos often marginalize the lyrics, presaged a "heavy" sound in rock music. Yet the nearly music hall sounds and fun of Freddy and the Dreamers' "I'm Telling You Now" and Herman's Hermits' "I'm Henry VIII, I Am" caused even adult viewers and listeners to tacitly admit that modern teen music might not be *all* bad. Seventeen-year-old Peter Noone and his diverse Hermits, which included a scholarly looking, bespectacled university student, added large numbers of American dollars to their British bank accounts by cornering one of the widest American demographic followings by enthralling screaming preteens on *Shindig!* one night and capturing the amused attention of a very middle-aged and even elderly audience on *Hollywood Palace* two or three nights later.

As adult journalists tried to sort out the differences between Chad and Jeremy and Peter and Gordon, the "sound" became even more complicated when the heretofore separate universes of folk and rock collided, just as young people became aware of a rapidly expanding menu of adult-generated crises that could be addressed with music. The teen music scene was now increasingly tinged with social and political edges.

During the summer of 1965, as American combat troops began to pour into Vietnam and civil rights protests swirled around an increasingly riot-torn urban home front, two young songwriters embarked on separate projects that would significantly change the teen music scene. The older of these two artists, Robert Zimmerman, better known as Bob Dylan, was listed as a marquee performer at the annual Newport, Rhode Island, Folk Festival. Dylan was the darling of the "folkies" for his forthright, unplugged anthems, such as "Blowin' in the Wind" and "Don't Think Twice," and his initial stage set went largely as the audience expected. However, Dylan was perpetually restless, always seeking a new sound, and he reappeared later in his set with that dreaded instrument of "immature rival" rock and roll, an electric guitar, backed up by percussion and electric organ. During the nearly seven minutes of "Like a Rolling Stone," while Dylan's *voice* did not sound different, the *beat* was dangerously close to rock, and at least some of his audience was less than enthralled. Contrary to the mythology of the era, Dylan was not "booed off the stage" and actually received moderate, if tepid, applause by an audience that, at least in the video available, had very few teen members.

Top-forty radio stations quickly latched on to the new Dylan sound, even though its length was interminable by current two- or three-minute record standards, and the song reached number two on the charts, just behind "Help!," at stunning speed. Yet only a few weeks after Dylan's song settled near the top, another folk-driven song moved right behind it and two weeks later dismissed the Beatles from the pinnacle of the charts. The song, "Eve of Destruction," was performed by Barry McGuire, the gravelly voiced lead singer of the nine-member New Christy Minstrels, who had rolled off a string of top-ten hits, including "Green, Green," "Saturday Night," and "Today." McGuire left the group just in time to gain the attention of record producers who had sensed pay dirt in the work of nineteen-year-old P. F. Sloan, who had just penned an anthem of teen outrage at adult perfidy, with the terminally gloomy title "The Eve of Destruction." Sloan's song equated adults with unlimited hypocrisy, as they taught teens, "You're old enough to kill but not for voting," while they "hate their next-door neighbor but don't forget to say grace." Soon McGuire was making the rounds of *Shindig!*, *Hullabaloo*, and *Shivaree* in his new "uniform"—work shirt, knee-high boots, and long hair—as music critics began to welcome the emergence of the ultimate hybrid music, folk rock.

The new genre had already begun to emerge a few months earlier as a quintet fronted by Jim McGuinn and David Crosby introduced itself as the Byrds and gained huge attention by transforming Bob Dylan folk songs, such as "Mr. Tambourine Man" and "The Times They are a-Changin'," with driving guitar and drum performances that could even attain *Hullabaloo* a-go-go status, complete with vinyl booted dancers. Now, after Dylan's Newport appearance and Sloan's surprise hit, folk rockers were everywhere from the Turtles and We Five to (by loose definition) Sonny and Cher.

Yet, if folk rock was sometimes angry, sometimes satirical, and sometimes the antithesis of romance ("It Ain't Me Babe," "Let Me Be"), it had the enormous advantage of being both introspective and often danceable. Emerging folk rockers such as Simon and Garfunkel could perform "The Sound of Silence" or "I Am a Rock" at both folk clubs and TV dance programs without skipping a beat, and as 1966 began the adult media became equally fascinated by the message of folk rock and the youthful gyrations of the emerging go-go, "discotheque" generation.

As fashion retailers began trumpeting the arrival of the new short-skirted, vinyl-booted, fishnet-stockinged teen wardrobe, the "new dancing craze" quickly made the covers of national magazines. A *Life* magazine article in the spring of 1966 was titled "The New Madness at the Discotheque," and the author warned adult readers, "To enjoy the latest thing in discotheque, you had better wear ear plugs, dark glasses and shin guards. Otherwise, you may be deafened, blinded and bruised in an electronic earthquake that engulfs you completely in an experience called 'total recreation,' and its common ingredients which are blinking lights that look like Broadway signs gone berserk, canned or live music, dancing and far out movies flashed on sand screens."

This feature article noted that many of the most successful discotheques operated in alcohol-free environments so that teens and early twentysomethings could party in an atmosphere where "dancing pandemonium takes the place of stimulants," as often after an evening in this frenetic universe "most customers go home pooped but somehow restored, as if they had undergone shock therapy."

While the sometimes self-righteous or narcissistic folk rock music and the occasionally sexually provocative go-go and discotheque scene were usually met with a certain blend of amusement and good humor by adult-oriented media and critics, by 1966 certain aspects of the teen music explosion were increasingly viewed as bordering on cultural subversion toward the existing social structure. One aspect of this cultural unease with teen music began from an initially very unlikely source. During the summer of 1966, a generally articulate, conservatively dressed group of six young men called the Association scored their first top-ten hit song, "Along Comes Mary." While the general beat and length of the song were hardly earth shattering, the lyrics revolved around a kind of Freudian analysis of romantic opportunities, where the lead singer constantly returns to the key line "along comes Mary" to solve his seemingly insurmountable problems. While members of the band officially insisted that "Mary" was simply an attractive young lady, every word of the song was parsed and analyzed, and some young listeners, as well as a number of less enthused adults sensed that there was more cannabis than feminine charm in this musical narrative and used the quite popular song as an example of the moral deterioration of adolescent-oriented music. Just as the "Along Comes Mary" furor was reaching a crescendo, the Rolling Stones' newly surging hit, "Let's Spend the Night Together," spawned debates over whether popular music had begun to cross the line into blatant sexuality, as opposed to the longer tradition of double entendre and wry hints of physical engagement.

Finally, in the last weeks of 1966, the term *psychedelic* began to enter the terminology of pop music at the same time that national magazines began running cover stories on both legal and illegal mind-expanding or mild-altering drugs. Songs just entering the pop music playlists, such as "We Ain't Got Nothin' Yet" by the Blue Magoos and "I Had Too Much to Dream Last Night" by the Electric Prunes, hinted at consciousness-altering approaches to romance. Scottish balladeer Donovan's highly popular "Mellow Yellow" was the first in a series of his hits that seemed almost incomprehensible to mainstream culture adults with obscure references and difficult-to-understand lyrics that may or may not have hinted at some form of "high." Perhaps most disturbing to culturally conservative adults and even some of their longtime teen fans was the major Beach Boys hit "Good Vibrations," which saturated the airways in December of 1966 and included a "mind-bending" video, as the formerly conservatively dressed, short-haired singers cavorted weirdly in their new persona of long hair and bushy beards with every vestige of the surfer look gone.

The last months of 1966 were clearly the portal to the often far-more-controversial, sexually explicit, or substance-altered narratives that were generally seen as the "psychedelic" final three years of the sixties music explosion that culminated at Woodstock. However, while historical narratives of the sixties as culturally and politically diverse as those by Todd Gitlin and Newt Gingrich have emphasized the impact of this less "innocent," more "rebellious" soundtrack on the social, cultural, and political upheavals, a more thorough examination of popular music of this period hints at a much more complicated reality.

Most chronicles of the social and cultural aspects of the 1960s tend to agree that much of the music of the last third of that decade was somehow strongly subversive of the status quo, even if they disagree on whether this subversion was basically laudatory or malignant. Surprisingly, both the progressive left and the conservative right of the twenty-first century tend to use the same songs, same artists, and even same concerts as proof that a sizable segment of the "kids" had somehow signed on to a children's crusade to remake America in their very new vision of reality. There is little doubt that at least *some* of the kids were embarked on *some* kind of cultural crusade, and they did have a musical soundtrack playing in the background. However, what most accounts fail to fully take into account is the reality that by the final third of the 1960s, the commonality of the teen music scene of early in the decade had atomized into numerous subgenres and music outlets to the point where the shared experience of listening to a top-forty rock station in the summer of 1963 was now, in essence, forever gone. There is little doubt that the music of the Grateful Dead or Jefferson Airplane was an invitation to an alternate lifestyle than that experienced by the parents of many young people of the era. Grace Slick's parsing of the drug-related elements of Alice's adventures in Wonderland in "White Rabbit" is a wry generational inside joke at adult-approved "classic literature," while her sultry call to expanding individual consciousness in "Crown of Creation" must have been a stunning shock to a mostly adult *Ed Sullivan Show* audience, as she wailed in front of a clearly psychedelic video background.

On the other hand, the seemingly endless process of analyzing the Beatles' iconic 1967 album *Sergeant Pepper's Lonely Hearts Club Band* as a musical invitation to "revolution," equivalent to Tom Paine's literary clarion call *Common Sense*, sometimes borders on runaway pretension. While "Lucy in the Sky with Diamonds" may or may not have been a musical cryptogram encouraging the use of mind-altering drugs, many analysts looking for a vinyl-based revolution have quickly passed over numerous songs on that album, such as "When I'm Sixty-Four," that owe far more to the British music hall tradition than social insurrection.

The music explosion of the late sixties was not so much based on a sense of insurgency or rebellion as *choice*. Rock and roll was now often called "the new rock," but the big change was that compared to the early years of the decade, there were more radio stations with more disc jockeys playing more types of playlists that meant a cornucopia of experiences and choices for almost any teen with the energy to explore a hugely enhanced musical world. *Some* teens made a voyage of discovery into the previously uncharted waters of the underground aspects of alternative FM stations that often emanated from college or university studios staffed by student announcers who could not agree on the time of day, let alone a common playlist. The sheer amateurism of college radio allowed some programming and songs to slip by simply because few people in authority knew or cared what the kids were doing. Yet while late sixties teens lobbied and sometimes protested to gain the right to attend class with long hair or facial hair or jeans or sandals, their musical tastes were far more eclectic and divergent than most narratives of the era seem willing to admit. The entire concept of this book is to chronicle the experience of sixties *teens*, rather than the more nebulous category of "young people," which in most cases tends to focus more on twentysomethings than adolescents. Teens certainly listened to "White Rabbit" and "Lucy in the Sky with Diamonds," and some of them were using drugs while they listened or even experimented with drugs *because* they had listened, but it is quite probable that this cultural insurrection was neither as wide nor as deep as often assumed, especially if focusing on the precollege age group.

The last third of the 1960s witnessed a true popular music explosion, but this process included expansion and compartmentalization, more choice, more diversity, and yet much less of the shared experience of the first third of the decade, when most urban communities had access to one (AM) top-forty radio station that theoretically appealed to demographic groups from preteens to early middle-aged parents and could play "Fly Me to the Moon," "Surfin' USA," "Fingertips, Part 2," and "Blame It on the Bossa Nova" in the same set.

Four years later, by the 1967 Summer of Love, there were discotheques in which to dance and clubs in which to listen; there were top-forty AM stations, FM album-based stations, and collegiate "alternative" stations, which would have disdained any form of rock and thus played mainly progressive jazz only three or four years earlier. The fragmentation of rock music by 1967 can easily be seen in the existence of two versions of the huge Doors hit "Light My Fire," which included a primarily vocal three-minute AM version, and a seven-minute, heavily instrumental FM version, usually played on nighttime FM programs. Even one group would no longer necessarily produce a one-size-fits-all song. Many of the chronicles of the youth counterculture of that special summer revel in the somewhat drug-oriented elements of the San Francisco music scene, spilling into the Haight-Ashbury "hippie" culture, and the "liberation" of the Beatles from mainstream rock in the continued parsing of every word in every song of the *Sergeant Pepper* album. These activities serve as great examples for later narratives of the perceived "youth quake" of that summer, and the real introduction of a widespread "hippie" culture. On the other hand, in the middle of that iconic season, a large segment of the teen population was listening to such decidedly noninsurgent hit singles as "Come on Down to My Boat" by Every Mother's Son, "Respect" by Aretha Franklin, "Little Bit o' Soul" by the Music Explosion, "Sunday Will Never Be the Same" by Spanky and Our Gang, and "Up Up and Away" by the Fifth Dimension—hardly the anthems of revolution.

A year later, in the summer of 1968, bookended by the Columbia University riots and the mayhem at the Democratic Convention in Chicago, *Life* magazine ran an extensive cover story on "The New Rock," with members of Jefferson Airplane perched in somewhat rebellious poses on the front cover. The article revealed that a music form that was seen as something between a sexual invitation and a Communist menace only ten years earlier was reaching a new maturity:

In 1958, a St. Louis radio station smashed all of its "Big Beat" records, one by one, over the air. Since then, a decade has passed, but not rock music. It has prevailed and flourished because rock was manufactured and sought after by a generation hooked on sound. That generation has bred a new rock, concerned only with now, not with nostalgia. It provides marches for their protests, lullabies for their dreams, ballads for their girls, and most of all, anthems to their freedom. It is the first music born in the age of instant communication, and it is the most popular music of all time.

This generational euphoria was not misplaced, as by 1968 something approaching 60 percent of all recorded music sales in the United States was the purchase of some form of rock music. The problem here is that while the "marches for protests" and "anthems for freedom" garnered most of the attention of later narratives that saw in those songs either the hope for a reborn society or the initiation of a steady moral and social decline, the reality is that much of the money, especially the teen spending, was more on the "lullabies for their dreams" or "the ballads for their girls" or, not even mentioned in that article, the "bubble gum" music for their cultural sweet tooth.

At the time the article was written, there was ample evidence that even the top singles lists most frequented by teens had reached a pinnacle of political or social content, but even this substantial minority of hit songs could best be described as a "revolution lite." The week of the "Battle of Grant Park," the Chicago riots paralleling the Democratic Convention that year, where protestors insisted "the whole world is watching," the singles hit list most supported by teen purchases certainly does have an insurgent tinge, if not an actual call to adolescent revolution. The top forty hits include a blatant, two-sided anti-war ballad, "Sky Pilot" by the Animals; calls for social justice in the Rascals' "People Got to Be Free" and Friend and Lover's "Reach out of the Darkness"; hints at illicit drug use in the *Easy Rider* theme song, Steppenwolf's "Born to be Wild"; and the theme from the even more generationally divisive film *Wild in the Streets*, "Shape of Things to Come" by Max Frost and the Troopers. Other hits included the theme song from the socially satirical film *The Graduate*, "Mrs. Robinson" by Simon and Garfunkel, and a number of strong hints at various forms of mind expansion in the Fifth Dimension's "Stone Soul Picnic," the Amboy Dukes' "Journey to the Center of Your Mind," and Status Quo's "Pictures of Matchstick Men." The fact that these were all mainstream, AM-radio hits demonstrates a peak level of social and political concern that had even filtered down to relatively younger teen listeners.

On the other hand, this is still a relatively small minority in a hit parade that included large elements of what was just beginning to be defined "bubble gum" music, which pushed record sales and listening back down into the middle schools and even lower. The soundtrack of the "summer of '68" includes "Indian Lake" by a family congregation called the Cowsills, "1, 2, 3, Red Light" by the 1910 Fruitgum Company, "Yummy, Yummy, Yummy" by the Ohio Express, "Sealed with a Kiss" by Gary Lewis and the Playboys, and "Choo Choo Train" by the Box Tops. Dance-oriented music was still quite popular that summer with "Tighten Up" by Archie Bell, "Mony Mony" by Tommy James, and "The Horse" by Cliff Nobles. Romantic ballads, such as "Angel of the Morning" by Merrilee Rush and "Woman, Woman" by Gary Puckett and the Union Gap, were also top hits.

Perhaps the most fascinating cultural aspect of the soundtrack of this particularly edgy summer of 1968 is the enormous number of what would generally be regarded as adult contemporary songs that gained top-five status on AM rock radio stations. As police and the kids faced off in the teargas-laced streets of Chicago, boss disc jockeys were touting the selling power of number-one hit "This Guy's in Love with You" by Herb Albert, "Grazing in the Grass" by jazz artist Hugh Masekela, "The Look of Love" by jazz group Sergio Mendes and Brasil '66, "Classical Gas" by guitarist Mason Williams, "MacArthur's Park" by singer-actor Richard Harris, and The Good, the Bad and the Ugly film theme by Hugo Montenegro, most of which rose higher in the charts than the more socially insurgent anthems. The question regarding the music explosion in 1968 is this: If the music exploded, is there any way of tracking the direction of the blast?

The last third of the 1960s featured three "event" summers, where young people and their supporting culture dominated headlines and magazine cover stories. The year 1967 was the Summer of Love in San Francisco; 1968 had the summer of the "streets of rage" in Chicago; and 1969 saw the summer of peace, harmony and understanding in the muddy fields outside Bethel, New York. The gathering of the "Woodstock Nation" has been chronicled, parsed, defined, and ridiculed almost from the moment the sound stage was put together until well into the fifth decade after the somewhat spottily paid performers retreated to drier environments and more intimate crowds. Despite the hurried time frame for preparation, the always-questionable funding, and the fact that the adult leaders of the town of Woodstock never allowed the event to occur anywhere near their community, this "Aquarian Exposition" still emerged as an iconic movement of the youth-oriented sixties experience. Just as the three hundred Spartans stopped attempting to count their Persian adversaries at the entrance to Thermopylae, the organizers and chroniclers of Woodstock likely gave up specific counts after the first hundred thousand and simply guessed how many people could squeeze into the allocated number of acres of mud-splattered fields. No matter what the head count, a sizeable part of those Aquarian revelers was most likely teenagers, even if they were almost certainly outnumbered by a more car-owning, economically independent cohort of twentysomethings. The much-less-than-high-definition film chronicles of the event often tend to depict a rather blurred sea of humanity, coping with frequent deluges and sound system problems; some middle-aged parents of the 2010s who were teenagers in 1969 can most likely point to a momentary image and explain that they are the ones being photographed. Many more of this age group may *wish* they had been given the opportunity to be part of the Aquarian exposition and received some measure of satisfaction from attending some other mass rock festival a little later in time.

However, the problem with evaluating the teen music experience in the late 1960s is determining what actually *was* the adolescent "soundtrack" of the period. Were more teens interested in Gary Puckett and the Union Gap or Jimi Hendrix, or did each artist fit a particular mood in many-mooded adolescent life? Otherwise excellent narratives of youth culture in the sixties, despite often hugely variable social and political persuasions, tend to meld twentysomethings and teens into one mass of "kids" and then promptly emphasize the older end of the cohort. Few, if any, narratives have ever addressed the discrepancy that the alleged "royal elite" of rock music playing on the stage of that Aquarian exposition seldom scored consistently in the top echelons of that era's popular music charts. While Janis Joplin was mesmerizing the Woodstock generation, huge numbers of teens were entering record stores to push Tommy James and the Shondells and Stevie Wonder to the top of that week's "Hot 100" music chart. Perhaps many of the teens who heard Joplin's set in Bethel purchased "Crystal Blue Persuasion" and "My Cherie Amour" in their local record store after they returned home, but in this still largely predigital age, there was no way to cross-reference any activity of this sort, especially with the minimal use of credit cards.

We can only know with some certainty that by the late 1960s, music was an integral part of everything that was the teen experience of the time. At the beginning of the decade, Danny and the Juniors' late fifties assertion that "Rock and Roll Is Here to Stay" looked, for a brief moment, like a hollow boast. By the end of the sixties, any adult hopes that adolescents could somehow be separated from that trashy jungle music were truly a forlorn dream. Yet on a more sobering level, the very success and permanence of this music explosion would ultimately form the background soundtrack for teens carrying their transistor radios, not on a beach or sidewalk, but in the jungles and rice paddies of an Asian war.

CHAPTER TEN

~

Teens at War

In October of 1961, as news photographers captured stunning photos of East Germans still attempting to go over or under the new Berlin Wall before it was fully completed, a cover story in *Life* warned that a whole new front in the Cold War was emerging thousands of miles from Checkpoint Charlie and the Brandenburg Gate. While the *Life* editors tacitly agreed with President Kennedy's response to the new barrier between the divided sections of Germany that "a wall is a hell of a lot better than a war," the article, "Vietnam: Our Next Showdown," hinted that after the Bay of Pigs fiasco and the fairly tepid response to the Berlin crisis, the new administration almost definitely had to draw a line in the sand against Marxist expansionism in Southeast Asia. Few of the *Life* writers or their readers could foresee that confrontation in "the beguiling, travel poster land of South Vietnam" would change the destinies of thousands of sixties teens forever.

At the beginning of the decade, Vietnam was described as

a nation cradled in Buddhism, colonized by the French and needed by the Free World. Yet today [1961], the figure of the grim visaged guerilla soldiers is almost as commonplace a sight there as the pretty girls. For the idyllic, amiable little country has become a terror-ridden battleground in this era's great global struggle. Goaded by hunger and overpopulation, the Communists to the north desperately want this land. The danger is not just from the North Vietnamese but from Red China and Russia, who, if Communists take over the country could come dangerously near to winning full control of the Orient.

It is probable that very few 1961 teens, preteens, or even adults could find Vietnam on a map, but this "idyllic, amiable little country" would become a cauldron of death for nearly sixty thousand young Americans in a war in which the average age of combat soldiers was nineteen, nearly seven years younger than the "Greatest Generation" who fought World War II, composed largely of those nineteen-year-olds' fathers. Something over two million Americans would experience some aspect of the Vietnam War "in country," in a sort of children's crusade where there were so many teenagers involved that twenty-two- and twenty-three-year-old young men would be called "Pops," and twenty-one-year-old lieutenants were designated "the old man" by teen soldiers still buying Clearasil and Stridex at the PX.

If World War II was an American conflict fought to the soundtrack of swing and Big Band, Vietnam was the rock and roll war, where even transistor radios in "the bush" of frontline activity blasted a never-ending string of top hits, including favorites such as the Animals' "We've Got to Get Out of This Place," a far cry from "There's a War to Be Won" and "Boogie Woogie Bugle Boy" of the previous generation. While World War II soldiers day-dreamed of "steak and fried onions" or "turkey with all the trimmings" when they finally arrived at the end of a victorious war, Vietnam-era teens patrolled rice paddies and jungle trails dreaming of far less generic McDonald's Big Macs and Burger King Whoppers and much less of victory than their personal calendar of 365 "in country days" followed by a jet-liner trip back to "the world." Unlike so many World War II films where the typical combat squad has one teen kid in a group of surrogate big-brother twentysomethings, entire units of troops in Vietnam could be dominated by teens, with the "adults" as the interlopers. Yet much of the film-viewing public never fully realized that crucial difference, as Hollywood continued its traditional practice of casting actors who were older than the characters they portrayed, so that Matthew Modine, Dorian Haywood, Sean Penn, and Michael J. Fox played roles in combat scenes that in real life would have featured much younger-looking teens.

The two million young men who actually did serve in Vietnam were often in Southeast Asia as participants in a giant Baby Boom–era sorting machine, in which 29 million males who turned eighteen between 1965 and 1972 were channeled into a bewildering variety of experiences, from college classroom to triple-canopy jungle, or both, due to a Universal Military Service Act that never came close to universality and, at times, could not be deciphered even by the individuals entrusted with enforcing it.

One of the historical reasons why millions of young men fled Europe for American shores was to escape the horror of either universal conscription or such quaint offshoots as naval "press gangs," most of which plucked unlucky young men from fields or taverns and deposited them into colorfully uniformed armies that battled for king or country as they were treated, according to British General John Burgoyne of Battle of Saratoga fame, as "whipped dogs, curs, and spaniels." Between the end of the War of Independence and the eve of World War II, the American republic generally avoided the worst of these outrages by almost totally avoiding a peacetime draft and granting relatively generous exemptions, even in those conflicts that necessitated conscription. The War of 1812, the Mexican-American War, and the Spanish-American War were fought almost entirely with volunteers, the Union fought the Civil War with ample escape routes for those drafted, including purchasing a substitute or paying a commutation fee, and the World War I draft was targeted primarily at unmarried men. However, in the dark days of 1940, when Hitler conquered most of continental Europe and besieged an isolated Britain, President Franklin Roosevelt broke all precedent and initiated peacetime conscription that segued into wartime conscription after Pearl Harbor.

World War II was fought without any convenient substitute purchases or commutation fees, but the emphasis on a wartime "arsenal of democracy" economy and the surprisingly poor physical, mental, and educational condition of many potential conscripts kept a relatively substantial number of younger men in civilian clothes for much of the war. A combination of war-plant employer desires to utilize as much as possible these physically durable teen workers and pressure on congressmen to limit combat duty for some length of time after high school tended to keep the average age of servicemen well up into the twenties and even thirties until fairly late in the conflict. Thus, while teens did serve in combat on all World War II fronts, they were generally only a part of a much larger pool of service personnel.

Whether Americans ardently hoped for "home alive in '45" or "the Golden Gate in '48" as a gateway back to peacetime life, the initial understanding of many citizens was that once the war ended, conscription would end with it. President Harry Truman, who presided over the termination of the war and the Axis surrenders, seemed to veer from a voluntary to a drafted postwar armed forces. At some point, draft "holidays" were declared, and conscription essentially was suspended, yet the onset of hostility between the Soviet Union and the West and the theories of American psychologists, social workers, and educators kept bringing the draft back to life.

Military officials and human services personnel had been shocked by the huge number of potentially draftable young men who brought to the induction centers poor health, questionable literacy and mathematical skills, and a shocking inability to interact with anyone particularly different than themselves. While World War II–era films repeatedly provided an image of a "rainbow" America in uniform, with Brooklyn Jews and Italians, Midwestern Nordic farmers, Southwestern Latinos, Native Americans, and to a limited extent African Americans, all pulling together to defeat Hitler or Hirohito, the reality was often a far more grim succession of taproom brawls, racial and religious epithets, and unsolved murders.

Now, in early postwar America, President Truman addressed a joint session of Congress about a possible solution to those wartime issues—Universal Military Training to "raise the physical standards of the Nation's young men, lower the illiteracy rate and develop in our young men the ideals of responsible American citizenship." The president appointed an Advising Commission on Universal Military Training, and on May 21, 1947, that body issued their report, "A Program for National Security."

This report called for universal compulsory military training for boys who were either just graduating from high school or eighteen-year-olds who had dropped out of school with a minimum of twenty-four months of active service and, at least initially, no provision to attend college until service was completed. While large numbers of college presidents supported this legislation, the result would have created an interesting age imbalance between boys and girls, with freshman classes filled with eighteen-year-old female students and twenty-year-old males. While many military leaders loved the idea of a huge pool of teen recruits, scholars who studied adolescent culture considered this experience as a perfect transition from adolescence to adulthood, "a time when teen-agers begin to question things seriously and want to argue about them; when his interest about the world begins to emerge."

Some supporters insisted universal military service was simply the logical extension of the several decades long move to compulsory education and the draft was merely the capstone experience in preparation for "full" citizenship. Also, enforced mixing of ethnic and racial groups might prove valuable in producing understanding in a multicultural society, as "one important phase of universal service is the mixing of all social groups," providing "the opportunity for every boy to mingle on a basis of full equality with other boys of all races and religions and from every walk of life and from many different parts of the country. This will teach teenage boys that they all have an obligation to serve the nation and should all share in a common responsibility for the country's destiny."

On the other hand, an equally broad spectrum of opposition began to emerge, ranging from pacifists opposed to any military service to conservative groups dismayed at what they perceived as expanding government interference in personal liberties. A wide range of opinions believed that this level of compulsion was generally an un-American principle, especially in a time of at least official peace. Just as twenty years later, when both support for the Vietnam War and opposition to the conflict emerged from a much broader political spectrum than is generally realized, the "great draft debate" formed diverse coalitions on both sides of the argument.

The next four years produced a series of stopgap conscription laws, while the universal service concept gained significant national attention. Then, on January 10, 1951, Senator Lyndon Johnson, chair of the Preparedness Subcommittee of the Committee on Armed Forces, opened hearings on universal training legislation as many of the future participants in the Vietnam War toddled across kitchen floors or curled up on the sofa to watch *Howdy Doody* on television. After considerable debate and compromise, a patchwork bill was finally passed in which theory and practice were firmly kept separate. The legislature passed the Universal Military Training Act and then promptly turned over implementation of the bill to the Selective Service System, which would effectively pick and choose which American males would eventually wear a uniform and which ones would get no closer to war than a front seat at their local theater.

One of the most substantially misunderstood aspects of the relationship between teenagers and the American military service during the decade of the 1960s is that a young person who was a teenager in the early part of that decade actually was much more likely to serve in uniform than his counterparts in the "war years" of the mid- to late sixties. Because early sixties teens were both less numerous and less attuned to avoiding peacetime military service, there existed a tacit acceptance of a military experience similar to their resignation to removal of tonsils or bouts of measles or mumps. A *U.S. New and World Report* series on the draft in the early sixties revealed a probability that a teen who had reached or would reach his eighteenth birthday in the near future faced an approximate 55 percent probability of spending at least some time in military service, with a considerably higher potential for conscription if he failed to get married soon after leaving school.

Thus, while popular films, teen magazines, and friends encouraged girls to believe that marriage soon after completion of school was both normal and expected, the Selective Service rules of the very early sixties encouraged boys who had little interest in military service to largely escape this experience through earlier matrimony. Young men attending college generally held a deferment from military service until the completion of undergraduate or even graduate school, at which point a wedding seemed the perfect complementary activity, sometimes the same week as graduation, in order to stave off the draft board on a permanent basis.

Many pre–Vietnam War sixties teens were no more enthralled with the idea of military service than their wartime counterparts, but beyond securing deferments or exemptions for school, occupation, or marriage, there was more a feeling of "getting it over with" than a genuine fear of or revulsion at conscription. Pre–Vietnam War film and television comedies, from *No Time for Sergeants* and *Sergeant Bilko* to *Gomer Pyle, U.S.M.C.*, at least partially depicted peacetime service as a kind of extended summer camp, with meddling noncoms substituting for meddling camp counselors and shared hazards, such as poison ivy or sore feet, common to both experiences. These teens had grown up in the ever-present shadow of their parents' war experiences, and a surprising number of teens joined a branch of the service based on their father's World War II experience or the manner in which that branch was depicted in the endless stream of war movies on film and television. A neighborhood filled with World War II Marine veterans could often become a happy hunting ground for recruiting sergeants from that service, although more than a few teens may have had only the vaguest idea of exactly what a peacetime Marine actually did.

Those teens who grew up in the more peaceful first half of the sixties and did not seem likely to secure a marriage, career, or school exemption in the near future sifted through glossy color brochures and compiled experiences from older friends, fathers, and recruiting personnel to attempt to secure the best "fit" between themselves and a particular branch of the peacetime military. Since no branch of the military was particularly dangerous before late 1965, decisions often revolved around length of enlistment, areas of possible assignment, or a special feature of a particular branch.

The largest, but in some cases least glamorous, service was the United States Army, which was the only branch in the peacetime sixties reliant on a mix of volunteers and conscripts. The army faced a split-identity issue at this time because Selective Service policy generally favored drafting the oldest eligible draftees first, while many of the volunteers were teens who had just graduated or dropped out of high school. A typical army barracks could easily feature numerous bottom bunks of jaded, resigned twenty-seven-year-old men with enthusiastic, immature seventeen- and eighteen-year-old teens directly above them. Even the length of service could be quite variable. While many teen volunteers were expected to enlist for three or four years, depending on assignment and specialty, almost all draftees would be discharged after twenty-four months. The size of the army offered some recruiting advantage as the large number of both combat and support branches offered training from driving a tank to programming an early computer.

The Marine Corps, which somewhat paralleled the ground-combat mission of the army, was still totally volunteer, a situation that would be enormously complicated by the induction of conscripts at the height of the Vietnam conflict. The Marines emphasized their relatively small and selective nature, which featured a grueling basic training experience that both fascinated and terrified potential recruits. The Corps tended to attract very young recruits who, despite preference for high school graduates, often included seventeen-year-olds who saw the Marines as much more exciting than senior physics or English. Surprisingly, despite the promotion of the Marines as the "toughest" and "most demanding" service experience, a self-selection of generally motivated and physically fit recruits and a training program that terrorized many, but actually dismissed relatively few, produced few disgruntled "rejects," discouraging teens from trying their hand at becoming sea soldiers.

The Marines' parent service, the U.S. Navy, was an all-volunteer service that was now combining its traditional "Join the Navy and See the World" promotion with the lure of serving aboard a fleet that was increasingly becoming a nuclear-propelled flotilla. Teens who had barely ventured from their neighborhood or city were quick to sense the opportunity displayed by recruiting posters showing both exotic locales and exotic means of reaching them. For many adolescents, the major adjustment to a three- or four-year hitch in the navy would be leaving the sensory stimulus of sixties teen life for an experience where the excitement of ports of call were relatively short intervals in a much more mundane life on or under the sea, where much of the twenty-first-century entertainment and communications array was still largely science fiction.

At the beginning of the 1960s, the United States Air Force had existed as a separate entity for little more than a decade but was receiving extremely generous funding due to its projection of power in the "high ground" of aerospace and missile deployment. This relatively new service emphasized a certain cerebral nature in its recruitment policies and especially welcomed teen recruits who had been science fair enthusiasts, excellent math students, and amateur futurists in high school. The air force generally demanded the most extensive time commitments for enlistees but in turn offered a possible gateway to the civilian "knowledge industry" that was exploding outward during the sixties decade. Unlike the golden days of the Army Air Forces in World War II, where plucky teens who dropped out of high school to enlist early could end the war as officers and fighter aces, almost all pilots were now recruited from the ranks of twentysomething college graduates. Yet teens were still offered fairly impressive consolation prizes, as a high school diploma holder with the proper courses could still gain entry into the emerging world of computers, missiles, and the maintenance aspects of the jet air fleet, with corresponding postservice opportunities in an early high-tech America.

Until the midpoint of the 1960s, most male teens who entered the armed forces experienced a military career still largely in the shadow of World War II, which loomed over the early sixties as the great adventure of modern times. Significant numbers of fathers of teens either consciously or unconsciously compared their experiences in "The Big One" to their sons' far less dramatic service lives, even if a substantial number of those parents had actually been in no more danger in 1943 than their children were in 1963. Even fathers who had been file clerks, construction workers, or food-service personnel in World War II often ramped up their stories to fit into a television and film world of *Combat!*, *The Gallant Men*, *The Longest Day*, and *The Battle of the Bulge*.

Then, sometime during the summer and autumn of 1965, Americans evolved from advisors to combat troops in Vietnam, and World War II history competed with current events in Southeast Asia. Unlike the reminiscences of their parents, there was no Pearl Harbor, no outrage over the day of infamy, no "we're all in this together" feelings. An inexorable chain of events—the Diem assassinations, the Gulf of Tonkin raids, the attack of Pleiku Air Base, the battle for the Ia Drang Valley—sent ever more Americans into harm's way and even more draft boards scrambling to meet their monthly quotas. During the last summer of John F. Kennedy's tenure, there were 16,000 troops in Vietnam, with a death rate of roughly one a week; June of 1965 found 184,000 Americans deployed there, with twenty-five weekly fatalities. At the same point in 1966, the total had more than doubled to 385,000, and the death rate had reached triple figures each seven days; by the tumultuous summer of 1968, 536,000 men and women were deployed, and fatalities had reached nearly fifty a day.

The Vietnam War, even at its peak intensity, would never reach the carnage American young people endured in the Civil War, with three thousand combined Union and Confederate weekly fatalities, and World War II not far behind at an average of two thousand deaths each week. But the empty spaces on some high school memorial plaques were still gradually filling in, and unlike the newspaper and magazine war maps that showed Allied forces a little closer to Berlin and Tokyo each week, the paradoxically alien yet familiar battleground names in Southeast Asia seemed to be fought over with numbing repetitiveness.

The United States never formally declared war in Vietnam, but the nation went to war just the same, even if the conflict was in a very different place than the armed clash with communism had been expected. The American armed forces spent most of the 1950s and the first half of the 1960s preparing to contest control of Western Europe against a possible Soviet military juggernaut. War along the plains, forest, and rivers of Germany would have been horrific, but it would have been a conflict in a relatively temperate country with a backdrop not totally unlike the experience of many Americans from tidy farms to town shopping centers. Soldiers who grew up in Pennsylvania, Iowa, or Tennessee who might have been sent to defend the Fulda Gap against Russian tanks might have been enmeshed in an environment of violence, but it was an environment of temperatures in the thirties and forties in winter and seventies and eighties in summer, not battling in some seemingly alien universe. One of the less developed themes of the Vietnam experience is that by a strange coincidence, a combat environment in which only very young people could function was largely fought by exactly those very young Americans.

Diaries of Americans fighting in the Civil War or the European theater of World War II are replete with tales of torrential rainstorms, snow- and frost-covered uniforms, and tramping in the heat on dusty roads. Yet those same accounts often describe cloudless, cool autumnal mornings, placid spring afternoons of brilliant sunshine, and picture-postcard fields of snow seen from warm and cozy huts. Quite simply, Vietnam was an experience without anything most American participants could even begin to describe as "pleasant" weather. It was a season, or actually a year, in hell, with the only variation of this infernal place being mind-numbing sunny days with temperature and humidity racing together toward the hundred mark and equally mind-numbing torrential rain that seemed to re-create a near-drowning experience without the release of death. The thousands of teens at war in Vietnam were hardly immune from these trials, but in general they could survive and even function in a battle zone that would have been a supreme challenge for anyone from Achilles to Audie Murphy.

Americans who experienced the second half of the 1960s as teens were probably more aware of the battleground of their generation's war more than any similar group before them. For several generations before the sixties, adolescents who were too young to engage in battle if their society was at war eagerly read accounts of slightly older warriors who were actually fighting as their letters reached the home front. By the 1940s, teens could sit in the comfort of theaters and see both documentary films and feature-length movies chronicling the war against the Axis. Yet the actual films were both relatively brief and grainy, and the commercial films were invariably filmed on a Hollywood lot where rain, snow, and tropical humidity were all little more than props. As the Vietnam War escalated and reached lead-story status on the network news, many adolescents could see the war up close and personal, in stunning lifelike videotapes that were also increasingly shot and telecast in "living color."

The Vietnam War was experienced by sixties teens in a variety of ways, from viewing combat footage on the nightly network newscast to participating in pro- or antiwar rallies to actually serving in combat in Southeast Asia. Yet however little or much it was experienced, the Vietnam War was so long and significantly publicized that it served as a backdrop to many other aspects of teen culture during this volatile decade.

For the hundreds of thousands of teens who actually experienced the conflict firsthand, it was as a participatory event almost always based around a series of time frames that somehow ended up totaling a magic number of 365. Most nations that raised armies to fight wars generally expected their either volunteer or conscripted soldiers to fight on until major injury, death, or peace ended the need for their services. Some Union regiment personnel who had enlisted for three years at the beginning of the Civil War were able to honorably disband almost a year before Appomattox with government blessing, and as the Korean conflict settled into stalemate, a point system was established that allowed soldiers to go home before the termination of the conflict. However, during the Vietnam War, the vast majority of participants were automatically rotated home after 365 days (or thirteen months for Marines), even as battles were still raging below their climate-controlled jet airliner now heading out to sea. Thus a tour of duty for an American teenager was a time span largely equivalent to one year in the high school experience, the same time frame as the first day of summer vacation after eleventh grade up to commencement day the following June.

For more than a few American teens, the Vietnam experience was essentially "thirteenth grade," a sort of very extended field trip in an enormously exotic locale. Like many adolescents entering a new grade or a new school, new arrivals quickly sized up potential new friends, potential adversarial relationships, and probable neutral entities. Since the war and expanded draft calls had recently propelled thousands of twentysomething male college graduates into the badly understaffed sixties high schools, the platoon and company officers tended to be about the same age as the classroom instructors these adolescents had just left behind. Like the teacher counterparts, these teens at war were able to categorize junior officers from those who merited substantial respect to frauds and bullies who would become reviled.

Many of the World War II–era television programs and films had depicted the noncommissioned officers, such as platoon sergeants, as gruff, grizzled leaders who resembled middle-aged coaches or gym teachers. Yet this image quickly proved to be largely a myth for the teens in Vietnam. A combination of the twelve-month duty limit and extremely rapid promotion to NCO ranks meant that grizzled sergeants were far more common on Hollywood war movie sets than in the real conflict. In reality, many bright adolescents who quickly adapted to military life were channeled into rapidly expanding NCO schools, which meant that some highly motivated teenagers could earn sergeant's stripes before they needed to shave regularly.

Those very young captains, lieutenants, and sergeants would ultimately constitute the surrogate high school "faculty," and the teen enlisted men would use the same powers of observation and intuition that helped them navigate the high school corridors to maximize the chances of a reasonably tolerable tour of duty. Incompetent leaders and "chicken" officers were quickly detected by teens who had been appraising superiors for years in school, and even in very diverse units a surprisingly rapid consensus developed regarding who merited respect and who incurred disdain. In a climate and environment where every action was either enervating, dangerous, or both, when to follow and when to "sham" was an extremely important decision for an adolescent "grunt."

Most teens in Vietnam had arrived recently from a high school experience in which it was quite possible to have more responsibilities and assignments than could comfortably fit into a normal day or week. Whether the term is to "sham" or to "play the system," many adolescents needed survival skills to wend their way through the labyrinth called high school, which in some respects carried over into the jungles and rice paddies of Southeast Asia. Just as in high school, teens at war quickly learned how to pick new friends and allies that could, in turn, produce both a more pleasant, or at least tolerable, experience and perhaps negate the threat of deserved or undeserved adversaries in either the mock battle of group living or real combat against the enemy.

High school friendship often developed based on residence in adjacent houses, streets, or neighborhoods or shared interests, both in and out of school. Some of these same forces could often develop in military experiences. For example, some platoon or company friendship developed over residence in geographically relatively similar environments. Relationships could develop based on attendance at the same high school or even a neighboring school that contained friends of friends. Common interest in the same sports or sports teams could create bonding, while the increasingly diverse genres of sixties popular music could create a common platform. On the other hand, adversarial relationships could easily develop from mocking the regional accent of another platoon member, heaping sarcasm upon favorite teams or musicians, or less-than-complimentary comments concerning pictures of family members or girlfriends. A combination of an extremely demanding environment, casual transition from peace to gunfire, and adolescent inability to understand the need to "cool it" could be a volatile brew, with additional kindling added by a racially, ethnically, and religiously diverse American military.

Just as in many modern wars, the teens who served in Vietnam faced a wide range of in-country experiences. On any given day between 1965 and 1972, one teenager could be complaining about the failure of the air conditioner in a Saigon military office building, a second could be conducting a mind-numbing count of ammunition boxes in a base camp warehouse, and a third young man could be trapped in an ambush beneath a triple canopy of jungle vegetation. As teenagers, all of these kids may have been more easily bored than older adults, and the question whether the firefight participants would change places with the office clerk is more complex than it might initially seem. Yet all of these teens shared the same rhythm of the 365-day calendar, which seldom ran from January 1 to December 31. In some respects, this individual calendar was a bit closer to the school-year calendar, which runs roughly from early autumn to late summer, with moderate difference from school district to school district and state to state.

Much like the school calendar many of those teens had just left behind, the yearlong Vietnam experience had a rhythm of its own, peppered with peaks of anxiety, frustration, and even anticipation. Transition from combat patrols to base camps and passes from base camps to major cities temporarily placed the teens at war in a less anxious, more carefree environment. The Vietnam experience even mirrored the school calendar in providing a much-anticipated "midterm vacation," roughly halfway through the tour of duty. This was the eagerly awaited R & R (rest and recreation) experience, which allowed American service personnel to sample exotic, peaceful venues such as Australia, the Philippines, or Hawaii for several days in which hooches and fox holes were traded for hotel dining and some brief semblance of a civilian social life.

This relatively brief military equivalent of midyear Christmas vacation often sharpened anticipation of the major goal of the year in country, which was the long flight from Southeast Asia back to "the world." Paralleling their high school experience, these adolescent warriors eagerly began a final countdown as "short timers" that roughly paralleled the final weeks before summer vacation in school. Just as teens often experienced a noticeable easing of the academic workload on the part of many teachers as the vacation dismissal date loomed larger, a significant number of adolescents in Vietnam discovered a less intense duty regimen as their date of transfer edged downward from weeks to days. Then the magic 365th day of service arrived, with an anticipation surpassing even that golden June morning when teens entered school for the last session of the year or, if seniors, nervously adjusted their caps and gowns for commencement exercises that symbolized a major transition in their lives. The teens at war enjoyed their own equivalent to a commencement in Vietnam.

Service personnel still on combat operations as DEROS day (date of expected return from overseas) approached enjoyed many of the honors or concessions equivalent to high school seniors between the end of final examinations and the reception of their diploma from the school principal. For example, in some Marine companies engaged in field missions, the arrival of DEROS day meant the ability to pop your own smoke grenade to signal to the helicopter coming to pick you up where to land. Other field personnel gave a last thumbs up or two-fingered peace symbol as they gained height on their lift out of the jungle. Just as students anticipating graduation or summer vacation almost ritualistically handed in their textbooks as a symbol of academic finality, teens at war went through a military equivalent of handing in their weapons in preparation for departure. While DEROS candidates lost their weapons, they gained amenities not unlike the experience of soon-to-graduate high school seniors: more freedom to come and go, less petty harassment for real or imagined misdeeds, and more respect from formerly skeptical associates.

Then, in the final hours in Vietnam, a military version of high school commencement evolved. Olive-drab equivalents of school buses transported eager DEROS adolescents to an air terminal where the names on the flight manifests were called off one by one. Then, in a version of a graduation procession, these teens boarded jet liners and took seats, after the military equivalent of school dignitaries, the higher-ranking officers, had formed the head of the line and settled into the front rows. As the air conditioning engaged and stewardesses prepared to take orders, the planes left the tarmac behind, and in most cases the cabin erupted in cheers, screams, and hugs worthy of any graduation ceremony across the nation to which they were now returning.

Contrary to popular myth, the vast majority of these warrior teens did not land in stateside airports bulging with war protestors shouting obscenities and spitting in their faces. The demonstrations that did occur were generally orderly and relatively polite and seldom targeted returnees. Ironically, due to the substantial lag time between the end of World War II hostilities and the return of most servicemen from the European and Pacific theater, there were seldom welcoming crowds and brass bands for most GIs as well. However, unlike that earlier conflict, the teens who survived the Vietnam experience returned to a country deeply divided about the war, and from a conflict that was not rapidly edging toward either a triumph or a defeat. For most of these young people, their major victory was simply that they were alive when roughly one in fifty of their counterparts was dead. And they were free to return to a "normal life" in an affluent, prosperous society.

Only about one in fifteen of the teenage boys who turned eighteen during the sixties ever served in any capacity in Vietnam, and among those young men who went to college and graduated, the percentage was even lower. Twelve hundred seventeen- and eighteen-year-old male members of the high school class of 1965 entered Harvard that fall; only twenty-six served in Vietnam, and every one returned home alive. Yet even if most teens never saw Vietnam in person, the war was seldom far from sight, even for teen girls not subject to conscription.

While Vietnam placed hundreds of thousands of teenagers on tropical battlefields, it altered hopes, expectations, dreams, and even relationships for millions of other sixties adolescents. Support or opposition could become an instant or longer-term litmus test determining the future of a new teen relationship. A couple sitting across the table from one another eating fast food burgers and fries might find their long list of commonalities made ir-relevant if the conversation turned toward opposite viewpoints concerning the war. Teen protestors and adolescent supporters of the war could carry toxic feelings, from social studies class discussions and lunchroom tables to after school activities, as political discussions could sour more-immediate shared interests and talents. Otherwise popular teachers could appear in a far less positive light if class discussions, or even offhanded remarks, revealed a position contrary to that of the student admirers. While most of the battles and deaths during the Vietnam War would occur during the sixties, teens would in many cases still be "at war" over it as the conflict spilled over into the seventies, and traces of rancor still survive in their twenty-first-century middle age.

CHAPTER ELEVEN

~

Visualizing Teens,
1964–1969

One of the ironies of the teen experience in the 1960s was that while the rapidly expanding medium of television ran numerous features on that decade's "youth quake" and ran a substantial number of commercials that had a strong teen presence, most of the sixties video experience still ran primarily on a three-network system in which even programs enjoyed by adolescents needed a strong preadolescent or adult viewership interest in order to survive demographic realities that seem incredibly primitive in the cable, satellite, and digital universe of hundreds of channels five decades later. The impact of the ongoing need for networks to balance teen interest and the viewing habits of both younger and older viewers appears in particularly sharp focus on the night of one of the iconic teen visual experiences of the sixties decade.

On Sunday, February 9, 1964, the Beatles made their television debut in the CBS New York studio, which was the primary base for *The Ed Sullivan Show*. Almost every visual recounting of the Beatles' impact on America in the 1960s shows clips of the Fab Four singing along with rapid cuts of screaming teenagers in near hysteria at each lyric of the British band's miniconcert. What is less commonly realized is that the Beatles' historic American television debut actually occupied only one-fourth of the Sullivan program on that cold winter evening. There was an initial segment consisting of the poker-faced host's transmission of good luck wishes from Elvis Presley, a caution to the "youngsters" in the audience to maintain some level of decorum, and a seven- or eight-minute segment that featured the Beatles singing "All My Loving," "Till There Was You," and "She Loves You," while on-screen graphics helpfully identified each member of the group and apologetically informed female viewers that John was already married.

However, as Sullivan reminded a near-hysterical young segment of the audience that the Beatles would return "later," much of the next forty minutes belonged to the adult studio and home audience, as the "sacred ground" on which the Beatles had performed was now given over to Fred Kaps performing magic tricks, the Broadway cast of *Oliver* doing a medley of their songs, impressionist Frank Gorshin spoofing Hollywood actors, Tessie O'Shea singing show tunes, and comics McCall and Brill performing a skit on office life. At the point at which many teen eyes were probably glazed over as they parsed what Sullivan's promise of "later" really meant, John, Paul, George, and Ringo reclaimed the stage for another five minutes of pandemonium as they performed their double-sided single hits "I Saw Her Standing There" and "I Want to Hold Your Hand," which returned studio and home living rooms to adolescent frenzy mixed with adult bemusement and befuddlement at how "Yeah, Yeah, Yeah" could be more enjoyable than cute *Oliver* cast urchins or Tessie O'Shea singing show tunes. Then, in a moment of unbelievable network producer cluelessness, this historic telecast ended, not with a final crescendo of Beatles singing and the audience entering a new level of enthrallment, but with a final act of "acrobatic comedy" by the Four Fays, *not* the Fab Four, in a symbolic triumph of vaudeville over rock and roll.

The Beatles would eventually score nearly an hour of *Ed Sullivan* prime time that February, but it would be over the course of three programs, alternating between New York and Miami, and always interspersed with comedic unicyclists, "The Pinky and Perky Dog and Cow Routine," and cameo audience bows from heavyweight boxing champion Sonny Liston. However, once it became clear that the Beatles, or even anything *like* the Beatles, could jack up television ratings, the two networks that did *not* land the Beatles' initial U.S. shows began investigating how they could at least indirectly hop on the Beatlemania bandwagon. The American Broadcasting Company moved a bit faster than rival National Broadcasting Company when soon after the *Ed Sullivan* ratings triumphs, network executives began negotiating with British producer Jack Good to create some form of American version of English hits such as *Oh Boy!* and *Ready Steady Go!* The frenetic pace of these programs was very much in evidence in early summer of 1964, when ABC ran a pilot of *Shindig!*, hosted by a top Los Angeles radio disc jockey, Jimmy O'Neill. *Shindig!* was in some respects *Ed Sullivan* without the ventriloquists and acrobats, but with a huge, enthusiastic audience primarily composed of very vocal teenagers who magically seemed to give frenzied welcomes to even second-tier performers.

Shindig! ran in successive versions as a weekly thirty-minute program, then as an hour-long show, and finally as twice weekly half-hour segments, but always at the same frenetic pace, which included rapid transitions and somewhat abridged versions of some songs to maximize the total number of performances. While O'Neill generously introduced virtually every guest as a "major" recording star, the reality was a bit less sensational. Most of the songs were performed by either individuals or groups who were having their first real hit or were otherwise just emerging, or by a somewhat revolving succession of house performers such as the Blossoms, the Wellingtons, and the Shindogs, with special billing given to a trio of regular acts—the extremely attractive and talented teenager Donna Loren, the handsome young "pop idol" Bobby Sherman, and the soulful duo the Righteous Brothers, who had the great good fortune of having several of their biggest hits just after *Shindig!* went on the air.

Most episodes of *Shindig!* featured one or two major acts in midsixties pop music through a creative mix of strategies. First, Berry Gordy's just-emerging Motown empire cheerfully furnished rising stars such as the Supremes, the Temptations, and the Four Tops to promote new songs; second, Los Angeles was already home to both star musical groups such as the Beach Boys and the singer-actor hybrid performers such as Shelly Fabares and Patty Duke, who also just happened to star on ABC situation comedies; and finally, Jack Good simply taped major British teens substituting for their American counterparts, with particularly popular acts, such as the Rolling Stones, Gerry and the Pacemakers, and Marianne Faithful, always finding their way to network studios on American tours.

Shindig! was a solid enough success in the fall of 1964 to warrant expansion to an hour-long episode slated for the following January, which in turn prompted rival NBC to initiate its own pop music series titled *Hullabaloo*, which premiered the same month. This rival program featured a relatively similar musical format with some variations, such as an absence of in-house acts; use of both male and female dancers; a weekly *Hullabaloo* "A-Go-Go" segment that mimicked the rapidly spreading discotheques that featured female dancers with short skirts and vinyl boots gyrating in cages above the dance floor; and finally, a culminating "Top Pops" segment in which virtually all of the musical guests sang abbreviated versions of top-ten hits from that particular week.

One of the major variations on the *Shindig!* format was to replace the regular program host with a weekly guest host or hostess with substantial name recognition. These individuals included some of the younger stars of NBC weekly series such as David McCallum of *The Man from U.N.C.L.E.* and

Michael Landon of *Bonanza*, pop music stars such as Petula Clark and Chad and Jeremy, and film/music hybrids such as Annette Funicello and Frankie Avalon. A second program innovation was to replace *Shindig!*'s "stealth" presentation of British groups as if they were in Los Angeles, when they were actually in England, with a highly publicized British segment from "Hullaba-loo, London," which featured a parallel audience of screaming British teens and was hosted by Beatles impresario Brian Epstein, who was now more than willing to introduce his second-line acts to American audiences with the hope that those acts would tap into the lucrative teen market on the other side of the Atlantic. The NBC program also gained a small but significant advantage when, relatively early in its run, the program was transmitted in color, which added a whole new visual dimension for the lucky minority of viewers who had color television sets.

While *Shindig!* and *Hullabaloo* executives were always aware that their most loyal audience segment would be American teenagers and preteens, in a world of only three networks virtually no prime-time program could hope to survive without some level of adult viewer interest. The two programs fol-lowed somewhat divergent paths to lure those indispensable adult viewers to their channels on a regular basis.

From the very first pilot episode of *Shindig!*, it became clear that the program's senior personnel viewed the twentysomethings or even early thir-tysomethings who had been teenagers back in the 1950s as the most valu-able demographic supplement to the current young audience. Twenty-first-century adults who were preteens or teens in the midsixties heyday of *Shindig!* and who view DVD replications of that program are often surprised to dis-cover that what they remembered as a program focusing almost entirely on current hits of the era, actually offered nearly as many 1950s oldies as sixties songs. The pilot episode alone gave major billing to guest star Little Richard and included fifties hits such as "Tom Dooley," "La Bamba," "Shout," and "Whole Lotta Shakin' Going On" intermingled with contemporary hits such as "Hard Day's Night," "Don't Hang Up," and "Chapel of Love." Within the first few weeks of the regular season, oldies acts, such as the Everly Brothers and Jerry Lee Lewis had already appeared twice, and young series regulars Donna Loren and Bobby Sherman were regularly performing songs that had been hits when they were in elementary or junior high school. Much of the advertising alternated between adolescent grooming ads and the detergents, sandwich wraps, and food products that would regularly be used by mothers with children.

Hullabaloo seemed to develop an even more ambitious demographic en-hancement for its audience as it trolled for viewers who were even well into middle age. For example, a significant minority of the program's hosts had demonstrated almost no interest in rock and roll in their careers and often looked clearly uncomfortable attempting to stir up enthusiasm for musical acts that seemed truly alien to their own preferences. For example, crooner Jack Jones, band leader Skitch Henderson, and Mitch Miller alumna Leslie Uggams seemed on the verge of wincing as they forayed into musical duets with midsixties rockers, while Jerry Lewis actually announced the wrong title to his own son Gary's performance of "Everybody Loves a Clown."

The decidedly nonrock guest hosts were given moral support by a generous supply of easy listening performers who were far more familiar on adult-oriented, middle-of-the-road radio stations than teen-oriented music explosion formats. Vicki Carr, Lola Falana, Barbara McNair, and Lanie Kazan paired off in medleys with Peter Noone of Herman's Hermits, the Lovin' Spoonful, or the Byrds, which was a valiant attempt to maximize audiences that probably aided in the ratings wars but somehow never appeared to be totally enjoyable for the performers.

A decade and a half later, the surging number of television channels and networks created by the spread of cable services allowed the fledgling MTV operation to largely feature youth-oriented videos introduce by young "veejays" who did not have to either explain or defend Adam and the Ants, the Buggles, or Duran Duran to their audiences. Yet during the sixties, *Shindig!* and *Hullabaloo* were essentially two-year experiments in fusing teen and postteen audiences into profitable television. Many more adult series died much quicker deaths, and in an era where African Americans were generally on the margins of series television, the teen pop music programs were models of integration and racial harmony. Once television left its own adolescence of limited networks and limited channels, the soundtrack of the teen experience would have its own platforms that did not need to import musical outsiders to survive. Meanwhile, in the summer of 1966, as the teen music shows left the air, two new programs, each highly original in its own way, would create a vast new market for bedroom posters and create a new dimension in teen idols.

During the runs of *Shindig!* and *Hullabaloo*, program writers occasionally tried to experiment with combining several commonly themed songs into a miniepisode that had at least a minimal plotline. For example, one episode of *Shindig!* recreated a malt shop in which Donna Loren, seated at a table with "boyfriend" Bobby Sherman, sang the assertive new-couple ultimatum "90 Day Guarantee," the Righteous Brothers, dressed as soda-counter workers, sang "Charlie Brown," and Sherman and the *Shindig!* dancers did a finale around "High School Confidential." Other minidramas centered around racing-car songs, beach-oriented hits, or school-related music performed on minimalist sets. By mid-1966 NBC program executives approved a more formalized concept based on the combination of sight gags and music performances of the spectacularly successful Beatles films *A Hard Day's Night* and *Help!* Auditions were held to produce a network-generated rock group that would incorporate the minimalist plotline and catchy music of the Fab Four in a thirty-minute American setting. Even the title, *The Monkees*, was a thinly disguised takeoff on the British superstar quartet, and the producer selections—Mickey, Mike, Peter, and Davy—had the required combination of musical talent and comic instinct to make the idea feasible. First-line songwriters and comedy scriptwriters were soon onboard, and before the program even hit the fall network premiere, "Last Train to Clarksville" was on its way to the top of the pop music charts.

Each episode of *The Monkees* featured an almost laughably thin plotline, lots of sight gags, dream sequences, and slow-motion segments backed by platoons of mod-fashioned girls and villains straight from an early twentieth-century movie serial. Young viewers loved the irreverent dialogue, the great fashions, and the steady stream of pop hits that were almost painfully squeezed into the plotline, while a fair number of adults enjoyed the nearly slapstick comedy that was part vaudeville and part *The Honeymooners*. As the Beatles increasingly dodged public appearances to concentrate on their musical craft, the funny, cute, reasonably talented Monkees became accessible substitutes for more than a few teenagers.

While *The Monkees* thrived on bizarre plots and caricature villains, an ABC soap opera that debuted that same summer snared a huge teen audience by treating the always-engrossing struggle between good and evil in an entirely different way. At about the same time that the Lovin' Spoonful was musically depicting the urban experience with "Summer in the City," producer Dan Curtis was moving the action far away from the concrete and asphalt to a tiny fictional community in Maine. *Dark Shadows* was a fascinating hybrid of the daily soap opera format combined with a new spin on the classic figures in horror: ghosts, werewolves, witches, and vampires. Much of the storyline revolved around Victoria Winters, a late teen who journeyed from an orphanage to a strange job appointment in a gloomy mansion rising on the cliffs along the Atlantic coastline. Vicki became the teacher to a deeply troubled preteen boy, a new friend to his bored teenage cousin, and as the series fully hit its stride, the object of romantic affection for an "older man," a two-hundred-year-old vampire who has been accidentally released from the family crypt.

While conventional daytime dramas were quite capable of drawing teen audiences, *Dark Shadows* drew a huge following of adolescents in the way

Twilight and *True Blood* connect with twenty-first-century counterparts. Similar to these modern phenomena, *Dark Shadows* offered three parallel realities to young viewers: young believers like Victoria, David Carolyn, and Maggie Evans who feared, envied, and sometimes loved the parade of supernaturals; a cynical, relatively nonbelieving adult cast whose cynicism sometimes brought their destruction; and finally, the supernaturals who were far more complex and multidimensional than most film or television equivalents of this period.

The series also offered a strong element of time travel, with surprisingly detailed and accurate replications of American life in times such as 1795, 1840, and 1897, which made history "come alive" for some teens in a way far more vivid than their school textbooks. The exaggerated reality that teens often craved, the onset of seemingly impossible romances, the ability to travel to another time or reality, the ability to ignore mainstream adult authority—all produced an adolescent fascination with *Dark Shadows* that parallels the different forms of exaggeration inherent in the plotline of *The Monkees*. The teen-friendly air time of *Dark Shadows* and the music and plot content of *The Monkees* ensured that both of these programs would have a generous teen audience share. However, producers of many more conventional prime-time series were aware that tens of millions of teenagers were potentially on the other side of those program sets, and thus a number of what might best be called "teen friendly" programs made a large enough impact on the sixties teen experience to warrant discussion. These programs can very roughly be divided into action/adventure shows and comedy/fantasy offerings.

Four of the most popular action/adventure programs for teen viewers of the mid to late sixties were *The Man from U.N.C.L.E.* (and its spinoff, *The Girl from U.N.C.L.E.*), *Lost in Space*, *Star Trek*, and *The Avengers*. Taking them chronologically, the first of these series was the saga of the seemingly never-ending duel between the fictional United Nations Command for Law Enforcement (U.N.C.L.E.) and its diabolical mirror image, THRUSH. The program largely owed its genesis to the enormous American movie audience response to the third installment of the film adventures of James Bond, based on Ian Fleming's book series. While the first two films in the series, *Dr. No* and *From Russia with Love*, were substantial hits, during the summer of 1964 *Goldfinger* became an international sensation that particularly engaged young audiences with its almost comic-book villains, Auric Goldfinger and his henchman Odd Job, large-scale car chases and fierce battles, and especially the introduction of far more gadgetry than in the earlier Bond films. The NBC network quickly decided to cash in on this huge interest in spy action thrillers and premiered *The Man from U.N.C.L.E.* that September.

The surrogate James Bond role initially went to Robert Vaughn's character, Napoleon Solo, who in turn was supported by his stuffy British superior, Alexander Waverly (Leo G. Carroll), and his much younger partner, Ilya Kuryakin (David McCallum), who was a native of Soviet Georgia and was a cool, cerebral, and phlegmatic contrast to Solo's hot-blooded, nervous, and sarcastic character. However, as the series unfolded, network executives were shocked to discover that McCallum was receiving far more attention among young viewers than Vaughn, and the scriptwriters quickly began to revise plots to provide a more equal division of labor between Solo, who seemed to resonate with older segments of the audience, and Kuryakin, who was now appearing on numerous posters and in virtually every teen magazine. In fact, one plotline of the award-winning twenty-first-century chronicle of the sixties *Mad Men* features series lead Don Draper's preteen daughter, Sally, experiencing a sexual awakening as she watches McCallum in action on the den television.

Two years later, as the series scored solid ratings among adults and virtual must-see status among teens and preteens, the network launched a spinoff, *The Girl from U.N.C.L.E.*, featuring even more mod fashions and music, pairing Stephanie Powers as agent April Dancer and teen heartthrob singer Noel Harrison as her partner, Mark Slate. For many teen magazines, the September 1966 premier of this series saw a bonanza of features in which the young and stunningly attractive Powers became a role model for girls as she defeated villains, gave orders to Mark Slate, and scampered from one set to the next in a seemingly inexhaustible succession of fabulous wardrobes. For example, two weeks before the premiere episode, *Seventeen* ran an extended photo spread in which, in between costume changes, April labels Mark a "Bungler," orders him back to the office in disgrace, and breaks up a spy ring, supplemented by effusive comments on her activities from the article writer.

While NBC reaped huge advertisement revenues from its *U.N.C.L.E.* series, rival ABC began to tap into the Bond mania sweeping American youth by following a somewhat different strategy—purchasing the rights to a real British television spy series. Soon after the original Bond feature, *Dr. No*, was released in 1963, British producers began airing a hybrid police/spy series titled *The Avengers*. Initially, the series focused on plots featuring a male police physician and an amateur female sleuth, with a mysterious government agent named John Steed hovering around the edges of the storyline. The series writers eventually wrote the doctor out of the plot, pushed the series more toward espionage, and formed a team between Steed (Patrick Macnee) and the amateur sleuth, Cathy Gale (Honor Blackman). However, in an interesting coincidence, just as ABC began considering the series viability on American television, Blackman left the show in favor of the female lead opposite Sean Connery in *Goldfinger*, and a young Shakespearean actress, Diana Rigg, was brought in as the new "talented amateur," Emma Peel. As *The Avengers* reached the point where it might enter the far more lucrative American market, the series writers largely dropped the serious, often pretentious plotlines and made the program more exaggerated, humorous, and to many viewers in the United States, a depiction of what they thought British society and culture *ought* to be—a land of bowler hats and umbrellas, eccentric characters, quaint villages, and gorgeous castles. At the same time, the writers managed to include the increasingly youth-centered mod, swinging London part of the "New Britain," and thus Steed's formally dressed, bowler-hated, and umbrella-carrying character was played off against Mrs. Peel's unlimited supply of one-piece jump suits, plastic boots, and fast sports cars.

As soon as *The Avengers* appeared on American television in June 1966, young people raved about a series that had almost nonstop action, enormously original villains, and an ongoing backdrop of mod fashion and clubs, all done with wickedly funny dialogue. Teens debated about the "real" relationship between Steed and Mrs. Peel, who never called each other by their first names yet exuded a sensuous chemistry. At that point in time, many American teens believed that anything British was somehow more "with it," or "in," and *The Avengers* was television headquarters for this visual experience.

The counterpoint to teen-friendly secret agent adventures was the emergence of prime-time science fiction series in the mid- to late 1960s. Science fiction was not completely new on TV, as networks had already featured child-oriented series such as *Space Patrol* and *Flash Gordon* outside the prime-time schedule and fantasy/science fiction anthologies such as *The Twilight Zone* and *The Outer Limits* on nighttime television. However, beginning in 1964, producers such as Irwin Allen, Gene Rodenberry, and others began to develop series that concentrated on either an individual or a small group of regulars often engaged in some form of exploration in space or time. The two series most discussed in high school home rooms or cafeterias were Allen's *Lost in Space* and Rodenberry's *Star Trek*, which debuted in 1965 and 1966, respectively.

Lost in Space emerged on CBS, largely due to Allen's success on ABC with the television version of his hit 1961 film *Voyage to the Bottom of the Sea*. *Voyage* attracted a substantial young audience but had an almost exclusively adult cast, as the submarine *Seaview* alternately encountered enemy agents and bizarre creatures. Allen followed this effort with what essentially became *Swiss Family Robinson* on a spaceship, as it followed the adventures of a family attempting to reach Alpha Centauri in the overcrowded future of 1997. The cast initially centered around two brilliant professors, John Robinson, played by Guy Williams of *Zorro* fame, and Maureen Robinson, played by June Lockhart of *Lassie*. They were accompanied by three children—nineteen-year-old Judy, eleven-year-old Penny, and nine-year-old Will—as well as Judy's eventual on-and-off love interest, young Major Don West, the spacecraft pilot.

The vast majority of the plots focused on some combination of the three children, whose ages conveniently paralleled most of the preteen, early adolescent, and late adolescent viewing audience. However, what turned an initially relatively ordinary space opera into a much discussed program among young people was the addition of two characters who were not even in the original pilot.

One of those "characters" was actually a robot, usually identified only by that title but officially designated B-9. This entity was essentially the reappearance of Robbie the Robot from the lavish film *Forbidden Planet* a decade earlier, and he quickly emerged as the primary protector and one of the two main companions for Will and Penny. Robot's help was always needed, and his often-repeated tagline, "Danger, danger, Will Robinson," was based on the exploits of the second surprise hit character, Dr. Zachary Smith. Smith, played by Jonathan Harris, was originally envisioned as a disposable cast member and played an enemy agent who gained access to the rocket in order to plant an explosive device and then failed to escape before liftoff. Smith was despised by all of the older members of the crew but somehow gained the sympathy of the children, while simultaneously throwing them into one crisis after another. Lockhart and Williams were never entirely marginalized, but for most of the series the action revolved around Judy's exasperation with Don's interest in nubile female aliens in a play on school romances, and Will and Penny's adventures as they were caught between Smith's bumbling and cowardice and Robot's last-minute interventions. This combination of comedy, fantasy, and science fiction and the central role of the preadult cast often confused both critics and parents, but for children and adolescents the bizarre saga of the Robinsons was a highlight of the viewing week.

While *Lost in Space* essentially remained forever fixed in its 1960s version of the late twentieth century with only a single uninspired twenty-first-century film to continue its traditions, the other significantly teen-viewed science fiction series spawned one of the most far-flung franchises in entertainment history. Gene Rodenberry often envisioned *Star Trek* as a twenty-third-century *Wagon Train*, and a 1963 pilot came close to producing a series. Finally, three years later, with significant cast changes, the U.S.S. *Enterprise* magically found itself in deep space with no premier episode to explain how the vessel got there. This romp through the cosmos was far more violent than *Lost in Space* and was fortunately experienced by a crew of over four hundred men and women, as in several early episodes the death toll flirted with double figures.

Unlike the members of the Robinson expedition, none of the original core crew members of the *Enterprise* would ever experience adolescence again, but Rodenberry and his talented stable of scriptwriters were quickly aware that teens and preteens were a vital part of the audience. Two popular early episodes, "Charlie X" and "Miri," focused almost exclusively on the emotional roller coaster of adolescence, even in not-quite-human aliens. By the second season, the array of second-tier, late-teen "cadets" and "yeomen" drifting around the edges of the plotlines were joined by a similarly aged, relatively long-haired member of the inner circle, Ensign Pavel Chekov. The final season brought a number of youth-centered plots, most famously the appearance of a circle of teenaged twenty-third-century hippies.

On the other end of the age spectrum, one of the older members of the cast gained fame on posters and in teen magazines, very much like *The Man from U.N.C.L.E.*'s Ilya Kuryakin. Leonard Nimoy's character, the two-hundred-year-old Mr. Spock, became the darling of "hip" sixties teens who quickly identified with his stoic yet brilliant presence as a counterweight to the emotional, sometimes immature Captain James Kirk. Many teen boys admitted that they identified with Spock's frustration at being the object of romantic affection by numerous characters on the series, yet unable to respond emotionally to the overtures, while more than a few adolescent girls viewed that same stoicism and logic as enormously sensuous traits for this permanently unattainable individual.

This quartet (plus a spinoff) of action/adventure programs that resonated with significant numbers of sixties teens was matched by at least four (plus one "clone") of that era's comedy/fantasy offerings that became a part of adolescent conversation and mostly debuted within a few days of one another in the autumn of 1964. The most geographically fantastic of these series moved Bob Denver—Dobie Gillis's beatnik friend Maynard—to a tropical island with six other castaways in an improbable television plotline.

Gilligan's Island would, on paper, seem unlikely to last even a full season given the extremely narrow plotline with only seven characters tethered to a tiny, unchanging "desert island" stage. Yet the show proved to be an instant and sustainable hit with a huge teen and preadolescent audience. While none of the main characters were teens, much of the action had a decidedly adolescent feel. The two twentysomething female castaways, Mary Ann and Ginger, were Betty and Veronica–like surrogate high school students in a never-ending duel for female supremacy on the island, with an implied first choice of the motley collection of male companions. This was a duel between class president (or honor student) and aspiring actress/model, with a rivalry that at least included occasional self-interested truces. Episodes that featured their rivalry often alternated between interest in the only other twentysomething on the island, Gilligan, who was kind and understanding but very bumbling, and the surrogate teacher and adviser to the whole contingent, the early middle-aged Professor, whose intelligence and ingenuity were largely responsible for the castaways' continued survival. Other characters Thurston Howell and his otherwise unnamed wife Lovey were fabulously rich but usually acted like particularly clueless teenagers who seemed to believe that they were in a bizarre dream from which they would wake up conveniently close to their bank vault. Gilligan's nominal superior, the Skipper, was Gilligan's roommate in a thatched hut, yet also mentor and dispenser of advice, and additionally a surrogate parent who seemed largely responsible for stranding the castaways in the first place.

While audiences from children to adults seemed to enjoy the constant sight gags, contradictions, and bumbling that provided much of the comic content, the fact that Bob Denver had played high schooler Maynard only a year earlier may have created a seamless transition from the conflicting excitement and boredom of high school life to this open-air equivalent on an isolated tropical island. Even teen or preteen viewers in a more inquisitive moment wondered how the short distance covered by a "three-hour tour" could dump the castaways on an island beyond search range of rescue agencies but regularly visited by British rock groups, famous explorers, and film stars seeking privacy, all of whom are rescued as the seven regulars remain stranded, much like teens who must repeat a grade as everyone else is either promoted or graduated.

The same month of September 1964, ABC premiered another type of fantasy/comedy that, while it featured no adolescent regular characters, quickly emerged as a favorite teen viewing experience. *Bewitched* was the brainchild of Beach Party film series producer William Asher, who cast his wife, Elizabeth Montgomery, as a seemingly normal twentysomething young woman who just happened to be a witch. By the end of the first episode, she had married junior advertising executive Darren Stevens (Dick York) and settled down as a suburban housewife who can never quite refrain from using her magical powers in ways that comically complicated her befuddled husband.

Despite the lack of major adolescent characters in the series, Samantha Stevens emerged as an enormously popular role model for teenage girls because of her intelligence and ability to handle crises, even if few of those teens were going to be able to handle marital issues through twitching their noses and reciting magical incantations. Many teen boys perceived Elizabeth Montgomery as an exotic, enormously attractive "older woman" who, despite her mischievous activities, positively adored her husband and actively aided his career rise by the end of each episode, in spite of the interference of Samantha's more traditional witch mother, Endora. Many teen girls gained a sense of female empowerment in watching a program that, on the surface, seemed to show a typical sixties middle-class household, but was actually dominated by the female trio of Samantha, daughter Tabitha, and Endora, all of whom led varying kinds of exciting lives, while Darren's character was so bland that when Dick York left the show and was replaced by Dick Sargent, many viewers humorously suggested that they did not really know the difference. In a sense, *Bewitched* was a sixties answer to the fifties *Father Knows Best*, as the male characters, such as Darren and his boss, Larry Tate, were almost always reacting to situations, while Samantha, and even Larry's wife, were largely dictating the plotlines and the outcome.

While William Asher fashioned a hit comedy on the premise of making an archetypal suburban residence into a (comic) haunted house, a new CBS comedy that debuted the same month, *The Munsters* (along with ABC "rival" *The Addams Family*), placed a much more traditional haunted house in the same type of suburban subdivision as *Bewitched* and used the very eccentricity of the home and its resident family as the basic plotline.

Unlike *Bewitched*, much of *The Munsters'* plotline revolved around adolescent or preadolescent themes developed in the characters of Herman and Lily Munster's preteen son, Eddie, and teenage niece, Marilyn. Much of the teen audience attraction to this series was the incongruous "normalcy" of a family where Herman was a Frankenstein monster clone, his wife some sort of ghoul, and resident in-law Grandpa a vampire, while Eddie was a werewolf and Marilyn was an attractive, typical teenage girl with almost no recognition that her family is somewhat "different." Much of the plotline that teens particularly enjoyed and with which they were able to identify was the satire of sixties suburban lifestyles, as Marilyn nonchalantly brought new boyfriends home to meet the family and was clueless when they ran back out in terror, or when Eddie tried out for the local Little League team and Herman volunteered to be the coach. Teenagers of the period were often quick to pick up the wicked humor poked at adults interfering with adolescent lifestyles, even when the adults were clueless that they, themselves, were largely outside the "normal" culture. At the same time, many adolescents also understood the basically upbeat nature of the series as, despite the enormous diversity among the Munster family members, they were actually more caring, loving, and united than their more mainstream neighbors.

Almost exactly two years after the Beatles' first appearance on *The Ed Sullivan Show* dominated next-day conversations in school home rooms and cafeterias, a decidedly nonmusical event produced similar shock waves in teen culture. During the winter of 1966, ABC initiated a twice-weekly television series based on the legendary DC Comics franchise Batman. While action hero rival Superman was present on fifties television as a low-budget serious drama, *Batman* debuted as an entirely different type of television program that almost ideally fit a new term being introduced in popular culture studies: *camp*. The series concept produced two relatively unknown actors, Adam West and Burt Ward, playing Batman and his young apprentice, Robin, while far more recognizable Hollywood figures lined up to secure guest villain roles as the Joker, the Riddler, Catwoman, and other nemeses of the superheroes. The combination of carefully arranged overacting on the part of stars such as Caesar Romero, Frank Gorshin, and Julie Newmar, and their villainous contrast with the absolute innocence of the superhero pair, defied reality, and then devolved into slapstick as the producers superimposed animated comic book exclamations such as "Pow" and "Splat" as the adversaries tussled in a totally choreographed, totally bloodless climactic battle.

American teens frequently seemed able to appreciate the inside humor and satire of this wildly successful series more quickly than adults, and they used series phrases, such as the "Same Bat Time, Same Bat Channel" used at the end of the initial segment "cliffhanger" episode each week, as a form of code when secretly laughing at some adult phrase or action that seemed hopelessly pretentious or uncool to adolescents, who were daily attempting to navigate a society where adults still held the reins of power but young people increasingly recognized that they were part of a rapidly expanding subgroup. *Batman* was too different from mainstream programming and too heavily based on a more-or-less single plotline to remain very long as a major hit program. However, during the last eighteen months of the sixties, the network that launched the *Batman* phenomenon also launched a trio of teen- or-youth oriented programs that revolved in very different ways around the emerging demographics of the Baby Boom generation.

The first entry in securing a substantial segment of the *Batman* population debuted in the autumn of 1968 and was developed by actor-producer Danny Thomas and his partner, Aaron Spelling. Their plan was to infuse the traditional police-procedural format with lead characters that, at first glance, would seem to be the antithesis of traditional cops. The program was called *The Mod Squad* and featured three college-aged undercover operatives who had only avoided imprisonment due to the intercession of a sympathetic police captain who wanted to use them as the nucleus of an undercover team that would blend into late sixties youth culture. Peter Cochran (Michael Cole) was a rich, rebellious, long-haired prep schooler who seemed to have an endless supply of equally, rich, rebellious male and female friends who became the centerpiece of action in more than a few episodes. Lincoln Hayes (Clarence Williams) was an emotional, highly intelligent African American with barely suppressed loathing for the "establishment" that he was now, at least indirectly, attempting to aid. Julie Barnes (Peggy Lipton) was the epitome of the late sixties television "love child" or "hippie," with obligatory long blond hair, a seemingly endless supply of hip wardrobes, and a youthful appearance that permitted her to go undercover in either college or high school settings.

Much of the real counterculture community of the late 1960s either did not own television sets or laughed at what they saw as contrived hippie dialect that sat incongruously within more traditional dialogue, but for millions of teens who viewed much of the period through the prism of the traditional home, family, and school, there was a certain excitement to watching Julie blend in as a traditional high school student, or Pete or Linc pounce on school drug dealers from their covers as hip young teachers. Ironically, most of the plotlines featured older villains, with the teens depicted primarily as either victims or involuntary accomplices to criminals who were little different from adult-oriented crime dramas, while the Mod Squad trio had enough young relatives or former love interests in peril to supply half of the series plots.

While the high schools and teens in trouble were major components of *The Mod Squad* formula, producer James Brooks, a future creator of *The Simpsons*, emerged a year after the initial episode of the police drama with a series in which the secondary-school experience became the focal point of the action. *Room 222* centered around a fictional Los Angeles high school, Walt Whitman High. On one level, Brooks developed the series along the general character theme of the still relatively recent *Mr. Novak*, in the sense that the faculty members were the principal regular stars who, in turn, interacted with a changing cast of students who became the focal points for each storyline. However, the program took a major step beyond the earlier series by placing the action in a very culturally and socially diverse institution and casting African Americans in two primary character slots. The four most frequently featured faculty roles were popular history teacher Pete Dixon (Lloyd Haynes), equally popular young guidance counselor Liz McIntyre (Denise Nicholas), their principal Seymour Kaufman (Michael Constantine), and an idealistic, youthful student teacher, Alice Johnson (Karen Valentine).

Though *Room 222* never seriously contended for the most popular program on television, its ability to successfully merge drama and comedy, its talent pool of teenage actors in believable student roles, and its sense of the pulse of the high school experience at the turn of the decade won the series an Emmy for best new program for 1969 and a five-year run in which Valentine's character finally became a full-time teacher, the Haynes and Nicholas characters expanded their romantic feelings for one another, and critics applauded the realism of this window on the teen experience. However, while this program garnered artistic plaudits, the third series in ABC's youth-oriented, late sixties trio gained an iconic status well into the twenty-first century.

Within days of the fictional opening of school at Walt Whitman High, a fictional wedding brought together a group of siblings that would gain the long-term attention of kids from preschoolers to teenagers. This was the debut of *The Brady Bunch*, which in the Boomer era of large families was the not-totally-unreasonable melding of the three sons of a young widower and the three daughters of a similarly aged single mother (whether widowed or divorced, we're never told). The plotline effectively paired off three boy-girl couples in the melded family of Mike and Carol Brady in which early adolescents Greg and Marcia became intermediaries between adult parental authority and the four younger children, Bobby, Peter, Jan, and Cindy, all of whom would move toward becoming seventies teens as the series continued. While the number of melded families was still far below the numbers that would be reached three or four decades later, a series plotline featuring step-siblings in male-female dynamics added a sense of the mildly exotic to the much more familiar reality that many late sixties teens faced in dealing with younger siblings who ranged from cute and cuddly allies to small-statured monsters in the complicated dynamics of relative large households. For many teens of the era, viewing *The Brady Bunch* was a sort of guilty pleasure that was the polar opposite of the Woodstock experience, and yet it was viewed by far more teens than went to the music festival in Bethel, New York.

While the television networks of the late 1960s offered a wide spectrum of preteen and adolescent experiences, ranging from the comedy of *The Brady Bunch* and the mixed humor and drama of *Room 222* to the action-adventure of *The Mod Squad*, the film industry seemed increasingly averse to portraying the humorous side of adolescence as the *Gidget* and *Beach Party* movies of the early sixties gave way to almost exclusively dramatic fare, which placed the teens in quite different environments than earlier in the decade.

For example, the ever-popular teen high school film, represented in the early sixties by *Because They're Young*, *The Explosive Generation*, and other films, underwent substantial transformation in two important late 1960s treatments: *Up the Down Staircase* and *To Sir with Love*. Each of these films emerged as a classic example of what social historian Robert Bubon defines as the "teacher hero" genre. In the first of these two films, Sandy Dennis portrayed an idealistic neophyte teacher coping with rampant bureaucracy, overcrowded classes, and often-exasperating students in a culturally disadvantaged New York City high school, while in the second, Sidney Poitier played a slightly less idealistic, career-switching engineer who was teaching adolescents in a secondary school in London remarkably similar to the one in New York. Both Dennis and Poitier played masterful roles as new outsiders attempting to interact with and mentor essentially good but misunderstood kids. However, unlike the two films mentioned from an earlier era, the audience learns very little about the teens outside each teacher's classroom. In the earlier films, Dick Clark and William Shatner played teachers that were essentially first among equals in storylines that devoted considerable time to the teens' social relations among themselves and with their families. These two elements are noticeably absent in the two 1967 dramas.

Another significant stylistic change between the earlier and later segments of the sixties decade can be seen in the only significant beach films of the late 1960s. As the *Gidget* and *Beach Party* comedies disappeared into a less-complex era, in 1969 director Frank Perry placed one final group of sixties teens on a beach and largely disposed of surfboards and innocence. *Last Summer* was based on Evan Hunter's novel of a group of teens discovering themselves and each other during the course of a summer by the sea. Richard Thomas, Barbara Hershey, Bruce Davison, Cathy Burns, and Frank Perry shed inhibitions and to some extent clothes, as they alternately frolicked and meditated during a summer that evolved from sexual awakening to the manifestation of adolescent evil in a film that, in its initial cut, had a rare X rating for a relatively mainstream production. For better or worse, Sandra Dee, Frankie Avalon, and Annette Funicello's innocent frolics by the sea had now been supplanted in dramatic fashion.

Two other teen-oriented late sixties films, one sumptuous and somewhat highbrow, the other low budget and sensationalist, initiated both interest and criticism during the final two years of the decade. The artistic success was Franco Zeffirelli's lush, exquisite 1968 version of *Romeo and Juliet*. Zeffirelli's project is not only quite possibly the best cinematic version of Shakespeare's narrative of tragic romance, it signaled an awareness of the importance of youth culture in the era by placing major emphasis on a haunting musical score and by casting real teenagers, seventeen-year-old Leonard Whiting and fifteen-year-old Olivia Hussey, as the doomed couple. In typical late sixties "generation gap" style, *Seventeen* magazine made the film a centerpiece of a parent-teen forum on modern movies in which, relatively predictably, the very youth of the actors and the brief nudity that attracted the younger viewers generated outrage among adults who as teens had experienced the pre–World War II version, which was both far less suggestive and starred the much less age-appropriate Leslie Howard and Norma Shearer in the protagonist roles.

If *Romeo and Juliet* could ignite a generational dispute, a far more hurried and cheaper release in that same year of 1968 generated even more fireworks. Director Barry Shear's low-budget dark satire about generational conflict, *Wild in the Streets*, starred Christopher Jones as a young singing idol, drug pusher Max Frost, who was elected president of the United States after manipulating Congress to lower the voting age to fourteen. While a number of film critics loved the concept of the satire on pressure politics, and teens enjoyed a movie with a great soundtrack, highlighted by multiple versions of the song "Shape of Things to Come," a rollicking youth threat to adults, many parents groups were outraged by a plot that included teen rebels contaminating the Washington water supply with LSD and placing anyone over thirty in adult concentration camps where they were forcibly exposed to hallucinogenic cocktails.

While the late 1960s still offered American adolescents a menu of interesting dramas that feature a significant teen presence, the really high-profile narrative of young people as separate from adult culture brought plotlines primarily involving characters who had left their teen years behind. Widely discussed, commercially successful films such as *The Graduate*, *Bonnie and Clyde*, and *Easy Rider* clearly flaunted adult conventions in either passive or violent revolt, from the resistance and wry sarcasm of Benjamin Braddock as a new college graduate to the roaring engines and flying bullets surrounding 1930s car chases to contemporary motorcycle adventures. By the late 1960s, teens could see themselves on screens as the adolescents they were or the potentially rebellious young adults they might become, but if the action was often great and the dialogue increasingly sophisticated, much of the early sixties innocence of school dances, going steady, and high school high jinks was essentially on hiatus and would not fully return in a contemporary view of adolescence until the 1980s.

CHAPTER TWELVE

~

Yesterday Once Again

The Sixties Teen Experience as History

Only a week after the sixties ended, *Life* magazine announced that its traditional forecast for the upcoming ten years was essentially canceled, as "the unpredictable 60's cracked the crystal ball too badly and proved perhaps all we can prophesy with certainty is that what will occur in the Seventies will be unpredictable." Ten years earlier, predictions about the upcoming "soaring sixties" focused on moving sidewalks, videophones, and futuristic cars. Yet now, "The experience of the 1960's shook us all so deeply that few easy assumptions can still be made about our basic beliefs, about our opinions of ourselves, about our social divisions, fears or hopes. Now the Seventies loom as a sobering time of diminished expectations amid unsustainable population growth." A subsequent cover story, "Squeezing into the Seventies," asked rhetorically,

> Can 200 million Americans tolerate each other to survive like this? Americans today face a new frustration, for all their prosperity, they are unable to buy their way out of the crowd. Wealth is now judged by how much privacy it can buy; the next decade will begin the fatal math—the doubling and tripling of national population to levels that present day science predicts will be impossible to support without violence and constant pushing with our fellow space usurpers as part of an ugly new social adjective—"mass." In the 70's, we may not need a President who can bring us together, so much as one who can pull us apart.

The sixties began with almost every media outlet trumpeting the long-term benefits of the high birthrate in America with features on how families with six children often led a more satisfying lifestyle than those unfortunate households limited to a single child. Magazine articles and television specials assured citizens that the onset of communications wonders such as closed-circuit television and computers would create innovative ways to instruct teenagers in ever-more-populous high schools, while the adolescents in turn would become reliable consumers, ensuring the economic growth of the republic.

Now, ten years later, the decade began with apocalyptic films concerning the long-term impact of rapid population growth as sixties adolescents would somehow run amok in producing babies who would produce twenty-first-century dystopias, as portrayed in Hollywood features such as *Z.P.G.* (*Zero Population Growth*), *The Omega Man*, and *Soylent Green*, where scientific attempts to feed outrageously inflated populations backfire into turning Americans into vampires (*The Omega Man*) or cannibals (*Soylent Green*). The new made-for-TV film industry quickly developed a profitable new genre of movies set in the relatively near future of the early twenty-first century, where sixties Baby Boomer teens match or exceed the fertility rate of their parents, thus creating emergency fertility limits on couples in the 2010s and 2020s, and babies are often black-market items and pregnancy limited to the favored few.

By the early 1970s, a seemingly unlikely coalition of liberal and conservative middle-aged writers, film producers, and pundits were developing a loosely organized theory of sixties youth culture as the launching pad to Armageddon in the twenty-first century. Scientist-demographer Robert Ehrlich became a staple of the television talk show circuit with his best-selling book *The Population Bomb*, which predicted that the Baby Boom would ultimately spark massive overpopulation and resultant catastrophe in the early next century. Film director Richard Fleischer's 1973 movie *Soylent Green* begins with placid scenes of early twentieth-century amber waves of grain gradually devolving into a chaotic montage of a socially explosive youth population of the 1960s that, in turn, morphs into a New York City dystopia of the early 2020s where forty million people are packed into a nightmare world of deadly smog, permanent one hundred degree temperatures, and food riots over the only appetizing food remaining: green biscuits of "soy and lentils," which are actually the processed remains of dead humans.

However, while middle-aged pundits already viewed the sixties as the antechamber of a twenty-first-century ecological hell, a number of younger individuals who had spent at least part of the previous decade as teenagers viewed the present as a shadow of the sixties simply because that's era's culture had *not* been sufficiently replicated in the seventies. By the summer of 1973, one of the nation's most popular recording acts and one of the most talented young filmmakers had issued invitations to sixties teens to return with them to a more innocent and pleasant time, at least for the length of the record album or film.

One of the first truly successful music acts that emerged with the new decade of the seventies was formed around a young brother-sister team, Richard and Karen Carpenter. This twosome essentially ignored the growing sexual and drug innuendo of much of early seventies music and secured huge amounts of radio and television airtime through excellent songwriting and the instantly recognizable attraction of Karen's singing voice. With an audience ranging from *Brady Bunch*–fan preteen listeners to now-married fifties and sixties teens who wanted rock music that had some links to their own younger days, the Carpenters dominated the upper echelons of the top-forty charts of the early seventies with such huge hits as "Close to You," "We've Only Just Begun," and "Superstar." By 1973 the group was a regular feature on prime-time network television, and Richard Carpenter was engaged in developing a concept album that would link the music of the early 1960s with the period a decade later.

The album, titled *Now and Then*, emerged on the music scene in the summer of 1973, an era in which the start of the Watergate scandal and the downslide of the American economy made the world of the early sixties seem particularly attractive. The major single from the album was titled "Yesterday Once More" and was essentially centered around Karen Carpenter's bittersweet lament that the songs of the seventies were increasingly failing to strike the responsive chord of the teenage condition to nearly the same extent as the songs of her own early teens had a decade earlier. She insisted that even the widely panned repetitions and nonsense verses of that era actually meant something to the emerging social awareness of young teens as every "sha la la la" and "wo, wo, wo" really comprised an essential part of the larger song, even its singability, on a trip with the blaring of the car radio for company.

The *Now and Then* album then segued into an extended medley of Carpenter covers of familiar songs that became hits between 1962 and 1964, including "Johnny Angel," "One Fine Day," "The End of the World," "Fun, Fun, Fun," and "Dead Man's Curve," followed by a reprise of "Yesterday Once More" in which Karen Carpenter insisted that although it made her sad that the early sixties were now a decade past, the magic of that era was now reemerging as "oldies but goodies" in the growing number of radio stations utilizing that musical format.

Just as "Yesterday Once More" was peaking at number two on the Billboard pop music chart, print ads in newspapers and magazines began enticing potential film patrons with the catchy question, "Where were you in '62?" A rapidly expanding advertising campaign invited both young adults who had experienced the early sixties as teens or preteens and current adolescents to be whisked away to a single night in September 1962, in the theoretically typical American community of Modesto, California. The setting was actually the hometown of young filmmaker George Lucas, who had scored enough attention from the artistically acclaimed but financially failed *THX 1138* to develop a more high-profile film. While *THX* was Lucas's vision of a dehumanized underground culture five centuries in the future, *American Graffiti* pushed the time machine in the opposite direction and into the recent past.

Lucas emerged with an intoxicating film effort in which he surrounded himself with young actors and relegated adults to the periphery for the entire journey. The film gave top billing to its most visible star, Ron Howard, who had played Andy Griffith's son, Opie, in the long-running comedy series *The Andy Griffith Show*, and then introduced a gathering of talented but not immediately recognizable actors including Richard Dreyfus, Paul Le Mat, Cindy Williams, Charles Martin Smith, Mackenzie Phillips, Harrison Ford, and Suzanne Somers, who all shared a career-launching experience in the shadow of the early sixties teen experience.

As early seventies audiences alternately gasped, chuckled, and reminisced at a now-ended teen world of crew cuts, bouffant hairdos, madras shirts and blouses, letter sweaters, and penny loafers, the plotline combined, separated, and paired off its multiple actors in a succession of drive-in diner, sock hop, car cruising, and "parking" sequences set against a time frame from sundown to the next dawn. The action unfolded against a musical backdrop of late fifties and early sixties hits that were virtually continuous, from the rollicking "Rock Around the Clock" in the opening drive-in restaurant scene to the Beach Boys' "All Summer Long" in the closing credits. Lucas's decision to use a substantial portion of his relatively limited budget to secure rights to dozens of period songs proved to be a wise one, as the film produced one of the most popular and extensive soundtracks in film history.

In many respects, *American Graffiti* was a relatively typical coming-of-age narrative of the adolescent experience. The major plotline revolved around the conflicting emotions of excitement and fear as newly graduated high school seniors Howard and Dreyfus prepared to leave the next morning for a college located on the East Coast. Howard was torn between the prospect of separation from his comfortable steady relationship with Williams (Dreyfus's sister) and the enticement of new social opportunities in college, while Dreyfus had just discovered that the almost phantomlike Somers, whom he had viewed as an unobtainable object, was actually equally interested in him, providing he went out with her the following evening.

Lucas constructed a narrative that was both genuinely funny and achingly realistic to most teens caught in a battle between security and independence, and the secondary plotlines involving relationships between Smith and Clark, Le Mat and Phillips, and Williams and Ford spanned teen roles from those bursting with excitement at their newly discovered adolescence (Phillips) to the looming prospect of imminent adulthood at the end of the teen experience (Le Mat). The future creator of *Star Wars* challenged his early seventies audience to decide which of the two teen experiences a decade apart was more exciting or more worth experiencing, while in turn peppering the film with both dialogue and costumes that were already appearing either quaint or old fashioned by 1973. Yet whatever each member of the audience decided, Lucas was insisting that the sixties were not about to simply disappear anytime soon, at least in the consciousness of those who had experienced adolescence in that decade.

The enormous success of *American Graffiti* would produce two major effects in the seventies entertainment industry. First, Lucas himself would use the film's profitability as a wedge to pry open the door at Twentieth Century Fox for funding another dimension of the coming-of-age genre. Cruising cars and drive-in restaurants gave way to sand speeders and exotic cafés in Lucas's next venture, *Star Wars*, in which teenage Luke Skywalker was plucked from small-town farm life, while equally young Princess Leia was forced to give up literal adolescent-princess standing in an attempt to save her home planet against a backdrop where, especially in this first film, far more adults are villains than heroes.

In turn, the ABC television network utilized *American Graffiti* as a vehicle to launch a nostalgia-oriented family comedy, initially set in the period about six years earlier than the time frame for the Lucas film. *Happy Days* began airing only a few months after *Graffiti* came out, and much of the plotline revolved around Ron Howard's character, Richie Cunningham, who was almost an exact clone of Steven in the film, with the addition of an on-camera house and parents, largely absent in the movie. Ironically, *Happy Days* became one of the highest-rated shows on television, and the series ran for so long that it gradually caught up with the *American Graffiti* time line— so Richie Cunningham eventually became a sixties teen after all.

The success of *Happy Days* encouraged the network to develop a spin-off based on teen working girls, Laverne and Shirley, who occupied the more blue-collar elements of the plotline through their common friendship with the surprise icon of the show, Arthur (Fonzie) Fonzarelli. The producers of the two hit programs tended to be a bit cavalier with the need for a common time line. After five seasons, *Laverne and Shirley* developed a plotline set in Los Angeles in the Beatlemania era of early 1964, while the characters remaining on *Happy Days* were still in 1960 or 1961, as Cindy Williams (Shirley), who had successfully enticed Ron Howard's character to remain behind as her boyfriend in *American Graffiti*, never fully connected with his almost identical character in the television program.

At about the same time that *Happy Days* scriptwriters moved three male leads, Richie, Potsie, and Ralph from fifties high school students to early sixties college freshmen, *National Lampoon* magazine fronted a far more raucous and sexually suggestive early sixties college adventure titled *Animal House*. This 1977 film focused on the antics of two rival fraternities at 1962-era Pennsylvania college Faber University.

While college-themed movies might be technically characterized as young-adult films, *Animal House* emerged as a much more teen or adolescent movie, as most of the major characters are depicted as either real teens or twentysomethings who still have never really left adolescence. In essence, *Animal House* viewed early sixties youth culture through two parallel prisms: seniors Otter, Boone, and Bluto, who were aghast at the thought of imminent graduation and could easily spend several more semesters in what was essentially adolescent high jinks; and freshmen Pinto and Flounder, who were shocked, then delighted, to see their "older brothers" living out a semipermanent teen lifestyle with far fewer restrictions than high school.

While *Animal House* was nominally promoted as a virtual death dual between the fun-loving Deltas and the more mature, but essentially sadistic, Omegas, most of the action centered around the senior/freshman divide at Delta, which produced adolescent-like surprises for most of the characters, as well as for the viewing audience. Fifteen years after the time frame of the movie, the writer initially depicted sixties college life as a placid cocoon just before the emergence of social and political activism in the mid- to late sixties. Yet behind that placid front, nothing about late adolescence proceeded according to plan. Pinto discovered that the high school student / checkout-counter clerk with whom he was about to have an affair was thirteen, not seventeen, and the daughter of the virulently antifraternity mayor; the rotund, socially inept Flounder, who had been assumed to be capable of no social relationships, appeared at a party with his strikingly attractive steady from high school; Boone, who assumed that his girlfriend Katy was totally loyal despite his own roaming, discovers that she was actually having an affair with a popular professor. In turn, the movie audience was reminded that time cannot stand still, the placid early sixties must soon give way to the most turbulent part of the decade and the seventies beyond, in that nothing ended exactly as it seemed. Boone and Katy did get married but divorced before the end of the sixties; the Gestapo-like ROTC leader ended up being killed by his own men in Vietnam; Bluto, who had been in college seven years and had all Fs, emerged as a U.S. senator and married the insufferable coed who snubbed him for most of the film. Yet, like *American Graffiti* four years before, the late seventies views of the early sixties re-created "yesterday's" adolescent life with enormous authenticity. Every song in the soundtrack had been a major hit during that era, from Pinto and Katy doing an off-key duet of "Hey Paul, Hey Paula" to Bluto initiating a food fight choreographed to Chris Montez's "Let's Dance"; for two hours in a darkened theater, it was indeed "yesterday" once again.

A year after *Animal House*'s enormously profitable run, Paramount Pictures utilized a large budget and major stars to link elements of the late fifties, early sixties, and late seventies teen life into one of the most popular film chronicles of teen culture of all time. For several years previously, Broadway theater cash boxes had filled regularly from the smash hit play *Grease*, which was a musical time machine trip to a 1950s New York–area high school inhabited by almost every form of stereotypical teen that decade could produce. Yet when Paramount decided to produce a film version of the play, the end product was a fascinating amalgamation of three eras. On the surface, at least in costuming and some other visuals, the film was clearly in the fifties, but while the play took place in an unspecified year of that decade, the film version placed the action at the portal of the next decade, in 1959. Standard fifties teen garb from black leather jackets to poodle skirts were clearly in evidence, and teen idol Frankie Avalon, who scored most of his signature hits in 1959, was cast as the "teen angel" in the hilarious "Beauty School Dropout" dream sequence.

On the other hand, while during much of the film the late fifties were clearly in evidence, the next two decades were never entirely absent. For example, the gritty, urban fifties feel of the Broadway hit, which had a *West Side Story*–like forbidden romance between Italian American Danny Zuko and Polish American Sandy Dumbrowski, largely faded away in the film as Olivia Newton-John's Sandy was a far-less-controversial Australian exchange student/immigrant. John Travolta's Danny keeps his leather jacket and comb, but the California beach scenes of him meeting and dreaming of Sandy looked much more like a sixties *Gidget* or *Beach Party* venue than fifties "mean streets." Newton-John, who emerged as a superstar in the early seventies, added an authentic musical dimension to the role, but her styles went back and forth among three decades for the soundtrack, while Frankie Valli's rendition of the title song was a noticeable disco-era beat by a performer who had most of his hits during the 1960s.

Grease was an enormously successful attempt to combine nostalgia for fifties and sixties teen culture, while utilizing the talents of the contemporary film star Travolta, just coming from the equally huge contemporary success *Saturday Night Fever*, and Newton-John, who maintained an enormous fan base while playing a teen girl from the reality of a thirtysomething woman. While *Grease* re-created a teen yesterday that was essentially a hybrid of the fifties and sixties, attempts to re-create the adolescent culture of a bygone era through popular music and film would eventually focus considerably more on the latter decade, even if the 1950s were hardly forgotten.

When Karen Carpenter assured nostalgic sixties-era teens in "Yesterday Once More" that their music would live on in "the oldies but goodies," she very likely had little inkling of the future medium that would turn this dream into a full-fledged revival. Eight years to the week after "Yesterday One More" dueled Jim Croce's "Bad, Bad Leroy Brown" for the top spot on the Billboard pop music chart, at midnight, August 1, 1981, a formerly blank television screen flashed a picture of an astronaut standing on the moon holding a flag with the letters MTV embossed on it. A few seconds later, the picture segued into a videotape of a British band dressed in futuristic silver lamé jump suits, ironically mourning the loss of a disappearing entertainment form, as "Video Killed the Radio Star." The video cut from the Buggles album *The Age of Plastic* initiated the Music Television Network, on which five photogenic young "veejays," Alan Hunter, Nina Blackwood, J. J. Jackson, Mark Goodman, and Martha Quinn, spent twenty-four hours a day hyping a new amalgamation of television and music. Just as seventies-era disco was in full retreat, it became readily apparent that the teen music of the 1960s was going to become an influential element in the new music genre of the emerging eighties.

Many of the prominent British groups of the sixties now reemerged with videos that merged the contemporary world with the teen experience of twenty years earlier. The Kinks' "Come Dancing" and the Moody Blues' "Once Upon a Dream" featured nostalgic shots of British rock and roll of the sixties and used quick cuts to a rediscovery with contemporary teens dancing to what was, in effect, their parents' music. Mick Jagger and the Rolling Stones jumped quickly into the realm of music videos as a logical next step in their seemingly never-ending musical morphing. British talents who had emerged after the end of the 1960s now utilized that era's musical mood to enhance their pop standing in the present. For example, Phil Collins scored an enormous video hit with the Supremes' "You Can't Hurry Love" and then starred in the movie *Buster*, in which the 1963 British Great Train Robbery was interspersed with both a period soundtrack and period music sung by

Collins. Eighties teen heartthrob Kim Wilde, daughter of fifties and sixties pop star Marty Wilde, blended sixties and eighties dance styles in her video "Kids for America," and then reprised another Diana Ross hit, "You Keep Me Hanging On." British girl group Bananarama produced an elaborate video of the late sixties hit "I'm Your Venus," while Billy Idol's "Mony Mony" originated from that same era.

Eighties artists on the American side of the Atlantic showed equal enthusiasm for covering sixties hits and turning them into top-ten sellers for a new generation of listeners. For example, David Lee Roth's "California Girls," Juice Newton's "Angel of the Morning," the Bangles' "Hazy Shade of Winter," and Tiffany's "I Think We're Alone Now" all emerged as major hits on both MTV and pop radio stations.

Another popular trend in this new MTV culture was for artists to record videos that essentially bridged teen culture and music between the two decades. This trend included Jefferson Starship's tribute to their sixties San Francisco roots with "We Built This City," ABC's acknowledgement of the impact of Motown in "When Smokey Sings," and Tracy Ullman's huge album *You Broke My Heart in 17 Places*, which featured a cameo by Paul McCartney as her dreamy boyfriend in the video for "They Don't Know" and Ullman's covers of such early sixties favorites as Marcie Blaine's "Bobby's Girl" and Doris Day's "Move Over Darling." Some artists went even further with sixties tie-ins, essentially pairing off with a major sixties singer, such as Eddie Money and Ronettes lead singer Ronnie Specter in "Take Me Home Tonight" and a British merger of the Pet Shop Boys with Dusty Springfield in "What Have I Done to Deserve This?"

Three of the most influential artists of the eighties, Bruce Springsteen, John Cougar Mellencamp, and Billy Joel, all used a combination of records, videos, and live concerts to successfully meld their common sixties adolescence and the new music technology of the contemporary decade to produce huge mixed audiences of teens who had grown up in the 1960s and current adolescents to join in a new, even more visual music explosion. For example, Springsteen's "Dancing in the Dark," "Hungry Heart," and "Glory Days" evoked the memories of a Jersey Shore adolescence that, in turn, spawned productions of the hit movie *Eddie and the Cruisers*, which, like Springsteen's music, journeyed seamlessly between the two decades. Mellencamp brought a slightly different perspective of the sixties teen life to MTV generations, as his world had been a small-town Indiana that provided a social intimacy that was both comforting and boring to restless adolescents. Major hits such as "Jack and Diane," "Pink Houses," and "Cherry Bomb" dealt with this duality, which was not that enormously foreign to the eighties teen generation, while the video for "R.O.C.K. in the U.S.A." was essentially a reshot miniversion of *Shindig!* that at times pined for the social and stylistic diversity of sixties rock and roll, which Mellencamp believed had become increasingly difficult to experience a generation later.

Joel, who was one of the earliest performers to successfully meld records and music videos, brought the most urban sixties experience to his music, but it was an experience made less gritty by his own desire to become a high school history teacher. Joel's videos were more frequently set in the 1960s than Springsteen's or Mellencamp's, with "The Longest Time" a time-travel trip between a contemporary high school reunion and the same (younger) characters roaming the same halls in the early sixties. "Keeping the Faith" was a fanciful montage of early sixties iconic images from finned cars to sharkskin sports coats in a mock trial of rock and roll. Two of Joel's most popular videos, "Tell Her About It" and "Uptown Girl," depicted the same Sunday evening in July of 1963, with Joel as a teen idol singing on a mock *Ed Sullivan Show* in the first video and then playing a garage mechanic wooing a rich girl, Christie Brinkley, beginning with the service station personnel watching the end of "Tell Her About It" on a small office television. Thus, unlike most of the 1970s, in which new artists and sixties arts that still maintained some popularity tried to take pop music in a new direction that frequently lurched toward disco, much of the music world of the following decade acknowledged and publicized sixties influences. Sometimes this produced situations, such as in October 1987, when remakes of "I Think We're Alone Now," "Mony Mony," and "Hazy Shade of Winter" were all vying for the top spot in the pop charts, while songs with a significant sixties "flavor," "Got My Mind Set on You" by George Harrison, "I've Had the Time of My Life" by Bill Medley and Jennifer Warner, and "Lost in Emotion" by Lisa Lisa and Cult Jam, made up much of the remainder of top-ten hits.

If the emergence of MTV made both Boomer parents and their adolescent children wonder if sixties teen culture had ever fully ended, a trip to the local movie theater could easily encourage the same feeling. One of the fascinating realities of teen-oriented films of the 1970s was that most teens were either depicted frolicking their way through high school in an earlier decade or in mortal danger in the present. During the seventies, teens had fun and adventure in World War II (*Summer of '42*), the fifties (*Grease*), or the sixties (*American Graffiti*, *I Want to Hold Your Hand*, and *The Wanderers*), but once they arrived in their own decade, teens were routinely stalked by child slashers (*Halloween*), out of control telekinesis (*Carrie*), or if they made it to the freshman year of college, paranormal, jealous ex-boyfriends (*Black Christmas*). On the one hand, contemporary film teens were not always safer in the eighties as *Terror Train*, *Prom Night*, and several *Halloween* sequels would prove, but unlike the seventies, the new decade brought a revival of contemporary teen comedies and dramas that in many respects rivaled and sometimes surpassed the golden age of teen pics driving the fifties and sixties. *The Breakfast Club*, *St. Elmo's Fire*, *Pretty in Pink*, *Sixteen Candles*, *Ferris Bueller's Day Off*, and numerous other films brought contemporary teens back into the spotlight, even without knives or chain saws. However, parallel to prolific strings of contemporary teen films, the narrative of Boomer adolescence was an equally appealing theme for movie producers of the eighties.

Almost certainly, the most successful portrayal of growing up in the Boomer era was a blockbuster film (and sequel) set five years before the dawn of the sixties. Robert Zemeckis's initial film in his time-travel trilogy, *Back to the Future*, was a zany romp between the eighties and the fifties that rocketed television personality Michael J. Fox into film stardom as an eighties teen, Marty McFly, thrown back into his parents' high school years by a crazed scientist (Christopher Lloyd). Most of the first two films operated on an exact time sequence of thirty-year intervals in a sort of time-transport commute back and forth between 1985, 1955, and 2015, even though Marty's birth date of 1967 or 1968 could easily have placed his parents' high school experience in the early to midsixties. Yet if the sixties was *not* one of the decades depicted in this sensationally popular film, a year later the next teen time-travel film satisfied that oversight by moving the primary scene of action to the very early 1960s. Francis Ford Coppola, who had been substantially involved in the production of *American Graffiti*, returned to the small-town America of the pre-Beatles era in the comedy/fantasy *Peggy Sue Got Married*. Kathleen Turner portrayed Peggy Sue, a middle-aged mother of two who runs her own business in the face of a crumbling marriage to high school sweetheart Nicholas Cage. At her twenty-fifth high school reunion, a freak mishap sends her back in time as a teenager who was just in the process of developing a steady relationship with Cage. She is then torn between the golden opportunity of countering adolescent crises with the mind of a mature adult while intensely missing her own children in the now relatively distant future. She also faces the Cassandra-like dilemma in which her predictions about the numerous changes that will occur in the next quarter century are seen as signs of mental illness by most of her friends and relatives. Like Marty McFly, Peggy Sue eventually returns to the 1980s, with the ability to use knowledge gleaned as a teen in the sixties contributing to a probable reconciliation with Cage.

While *Back to the Future* and *Peggy Sue Got Married* viewed the past through the premise of time travel, a trio of late 1980s films focused on teen culture in the sixties in a more conventional plotline of simply setting the action in the past. All three of these films essentially focused on teen social life within a single year from the early summer of 1962 to the summer of 1963, the high point of John F. Kennedy and the New Frontier. Within this rather tight time frame, the earliest in terms of sixties chronology was John Waters's *Hairspray*, which centered around teen fascination with the multiple dance crazes that followed the twist. The main scene of action was a mostly socially segregated Baltimore TV dance party, *The Corny Collins Show*, where bouffanted teen girls and their equally hair-spray-addicted male partners vie for camera time while gyrating to the Fly Bird, Mashed Potato, and Pony. Plucky, overweight Tracy Turnblad (Rikki Lake) bluffs her way into the show, astounds everyone with her spectacular dance moves, and falls in love with the boyfriend of the resident teen witch of the dance floor. Somewhere among the dance contests, beauty pageants, and high school politics Waters shows Lake and her small group of black and white teen friends as adolescent change agents attempting (somewhat successfully) to get the white adults onboard with the campaign to integrate the dance show as a first step toward social justice.

Class tensions more than racial issues dominated the other two films in this trio of eighties chronicles of the early sixties teen experience. Both *Dirty Dancing* and *Shag* were set in the identical time frame, summer 1963, in what more than a few scholars see as the last innocent time before the series of crises that began with the assassination of John F. Kennedy a few months later. In essence, these two films are chronicles of a nominally idyllic summer in two rather different geographic locations, the Catskills of New York and Myrtle Beach, South Carolina.

The more northerly venue, the primarily Jewish resort camps of upstate New York, focused on the vacation of a well-to-do heart surgeon (Jerry Orbach), his wife, and two teenage daughters. Much of the plot centers around an emerging forbidden romance between daughter Jennifer Grey (with the odd nickname of Baby) and the very working-class dance instructor, Patrick Swayze. The film produced a fascinating blend of sixties and eighties teen culture as the soundtrack interspersed authentic "summer of 1963" hits with much more 1980s-oriented tunes, while also veering between a plotline based on the relatively more conservative social mores of 1963 and steamy romantic scenes that would have ended up on the cutting room floor for *Bye Bye Birdie*.

While *Dirty Dancing* focused primarily on the Jennifer Grey–Patrick Swayze romantic entanglement between a spoiled teen princess and a working-class employee, the narrative of Dixie teens on the South Carolina seashore somehow ties together four concurrent relationships with the backdrop of a major dance contest that in some respects was strikingly similar to its Catskill counterpart. *Shag* follows four recent high school graduates from well-to-do families who steer their hot new convertible to a teen-laden beachfront after telling their parents that they were headed for a tour of Fort Sumpter. The narrative then follows Phoebe Cates, Annabeth Gish, Page Hannah, and Bridget Fonda as they collectively gather assorted boyfriends, most of who seemed shockingly unsuitable for the girls' wealthy uptight parents. Cates seems the least likely to be seeking romance as she is engaged to hometown rich kid Tyrone Power Jr., yet she is the first girl to feel romance in the salt air in her attraction to a nominal "bad boy" who at first appears to be only a working-class "townie" who also happens to be a good dancer. Like *Dirty Dancing*, much of the plotline could easily have developed against an eighties backdrop, but the perceived innocence of the early part of the sixties had obvious allure as the film plays out in a series of mistaken identities and couple switches. Both Cates and Gish are certain they are cavorting with working-class "bad boys" from a totally different social universe than the girls. Yet as the plot unfolds, Cates discovers that her love interest is actually about to matriculate at Yale, while Gish's prospect is soon to be en route to the U.S. Naval Academy. Much of the last third of the film is set against the backdrop of an Independence Day "shag dance" contest, which is ultimately won by Gish and her "midshipman," with a climax in which Cates eagerly explors the possibility of enrolling at a Seven Sisters college to be near her new beau. Fonda, the most rebellious, actively pursues the celebrity judge, who is a womanizing twentysomething pop idol, and Hannah latches onto Power, who has come to Myrtle Beach looking for Cates but leaves equally content with a new girlfriend. Beyond being able to tap into the phenomenal level of interest in teen dance contests in the 1960s, the 1963 setting provided the *Shag* scriptwriters with plot devices less easily developed in their contemporary era. For example, by the late 1980s, both Yale and Annapolis were coeducational, which reduced some of the mystique of the all-male social setting, and a bit more of Old South adult conservatism would have been evident in 1963 than a quarter century later.

Unlike the 1970s, trips back in time were not the only outlet for nonslasher teen-oriented films, but comedies such this trio, and dramas such as *The Outsiders* (which featured a cast replete with "regulars" of eighties teen films), largely placed the contemporary teen experience in a broader perspective for both adolescents and parents of that era.

An analysis of the impact of sixties teen culture over a period of several decades after the era of the Beatles and Woodstock seems to indicate that by 2011, the 1980s was the period of highest interest in the adolescent experience of the 1960s. One of the possibilities here is that the eighties represented a unique point in which very large numbers of Boomers had teenage children of their own, which created a special link between the two decades. Teens of the 1980s seemed fascinated by the era in which their parents spent their adolescence, and adults were flattered that their kids still cared about a culture that was not of their own time. Also, the novelty of the emergence of MTV and music videos cannot be overstated. Far more thirtysomethings of the 1980s watched MTV on a regular basis than is generally realized, and many of them were enthralled by the clear connection between the sixties and eighties in this visual portal.

During the two decades that followed the 1980s, interest in teen culture of the sixties would continue to be a potent media force but never quite to the same level as the first decade of the MTV generation. The Hollywood film industry of the 1990s continued to produce an only slightly scaled-back volume of movies dealing with the 1960s teen experience. At the very beginning of the decade, actor Richard Benjamin turned director in *Mermaids*, which featured Cher as a somewhat beleaguered single mother from early 1960s New England who is dealing with her teen daughter Winona Ryder's sexual awakening and the rivalry between Ryder and preteen sibling Christina Ricci. Three years later, director Joe Dante focused on the social life of junior high school kids against the backdrop of the Cuban Missile Crisis and a parallel plotline in which a horror movie *schlockmeister* attempts to premier a new low-budget film to the alternately enthralled and skeptical adolescents in *Matinee*. Later in the decade (1996), Tom Hanks released a chronicle of the impact of Beatlemania on the emergence of four Erie, Pennsylvania, teens as pop idols in *That Thing You Do*. The last major twentieth-century view of teen life in the 1960s belongs to Sarah Kernochan's *All I Wanna Do*, which brought together emerging, turn-of-the-millennium teen talents such as Gaby Hoffman, Rachel Leigh Cook, Kirsten Dunst, and Vincent Kaithesen in a clever comedy about a 1963 girls' boarding school that is split into rival camps as the trustees decide on a possible merger with a boys' academy.

The first decade of the new century featured somewhat of a shift of base for sixties teen culture outlets from film to television. In 1999, NBC studios commissioned Lynda Obst, executive producer of *Sleepless in Seattle*, to produce a miniseries chronicling the experiences of a group of high school students from adolescence to early adulthood in a sixties production complete with a significant musical score from groups such as the Beach Boys and Jefferson Airplane. Four years later, that same network and Dick Clark collaborated on a more extended venture in which 1960s Philadelphia and the *American Bandstand* television program would be the backdrop for interplay between adolescents and adults, centered on the Prior family: a small-appliance shop owner, his somewhat bored stay-at-home wife, and four children, including a teenage son and daughter, a preteen daughter, and a young boy. Just as *American Dreams* was completing its run, the movie-dominated American Movie Classics channel and producer-writer Matt Weiner, a young fan of sixties popular culture, combined to produce one of the most highly touted dramatic series of the first dozen years of the new century. *Mad Men* revolves around two primary themes, the adventures of Madison Avenue advertising executives during the 1960s and their relationships with a diverse array of spouses, companions, and children. As the series has progressed, a more extensive part of the plotline has revolved around the emerging adolescence of series star Don Draper's daughter, Sally, and her difficult relationship with her newly divorced mother and a new blended family. This teen-culture aspect of the series will no doubt continue to expand as Don's three children begin their individual adolescent adventures.

On the other hand, while visual representations of the sixties teen experience have continued unabated for most of the more than four decades since the 1960s ended, the musical connections to that time, which flared most brightly during the 1980s, are somewhat of a different matter. Sixties music is in some respects more available than it was in the decade it was created. Devices such as CDs, iPods, and other forms of digital downloading, large numbers of specialty music channels or digitalized television services, satellite radio, and related media, all mean that anyone interested in the soundtrack of the sixties can access any song at any time in almost any place—a dream unbelievable to a sixties teen carrying his or her transistor radio. Yet the audio, as opposed to the visual, representation of teen culture in the sixties has never quite matched the tempo of the 1980s. Shortly after the end of the eighties, popular music began to fragment at such an accelerating level that much of the previous commonality of experience ended permanently in an ever-more-vast series of niche markets.

Americans who spent much or most of their teen years during the decade of the 1960s now have an access to a media revolution where they can replay their adolescence through both visual and audio devices on a level unimaginable in that now increasingly distant era. In this respect, it is now *always* "Yesterday Once More," for anyone who chooses to virtually return to that era for a brief or extended visit. Yet for contemporary teenagers, now often the grandchildren of the Boomers, the teen culture of that time four or five decades ago, while still worthy of some level of interest, is now part of a much larger teen culture history where the term *sixties* may or may not be as magical as some other point in a collective experience called adolescence.

~

Conclusion

The teen experience of the 1960s is, in many respects, a fascinating cocktail of the wonder and trepidation that face the adolescents of most modern societies and a magical journey through a unique period when just the right mixture of innocence and excitement hovered, suspended briefly in time, and would never be entirely repeated. Proportionally, there would never be as many teenagers as a component of the whole American population, and in a still-predigital world of communications and entertainment, teen-oriented music, literature, and films simply loomed larger on the stage of the national lifestyle than before or since.

These millions of young people who experienced the sixties did not inherit a perfect environment for their adolescent experience. Teen boys were liable for compulsory military service in a time of war that saw far less popular support than World War II and was far more dangerous than the conflicts of the early twenty-first century. These teens were so much better educated than their parents that even their most rational opinions were often dismissed by their elders as narcissistic, yet they were exposed to massively overcrowded high school classes and a college admissions system that had not yet created enough capacity to accept even all of the very qualified candidates.

On the other hand, these kids lived in a culture where teen fashion was a unique combination of casual and dress-up styles that neither made them look like miniature adults nor were so nondescript as to be largely unworthy of attention by anyone who was not a teen. Their music was clearly their own soundtrack of adolescence, different enough from adult-oriented sounds to be clearly their own yet still not so toneless and vulgar to never entice their elders to surreptitiously listen in.

Teens of the sixties generally lived in a society where intact families were still the norm, and families could eat meals together and enjoy viewing television in a villagelike atmosphere, where their elders would offer a reasonably polite audience for the Beatles on *The Ed Sullivan Show* and the teens would reciprocate with some level of decorum as they sat through the Broadway show tunes that bracketed the Fab Four's sets. Every family was not the Cleavers, the Stones, or the Nelsons, but there was enough relevance in these programs to make them more than live-action cartoons. Much of the chronicle of youth culture in the sixties has emphasized the divisiveness between the adult and adolescent cultures, and there certainly was shouting, from school protests to heated conversations at the kitchen or dining room table. Yet at least most families *did* sit down together for meals on a regular basis and even shared the same living room or den as they watched programs of moderately common interest.

My research of both adult- and adolescent-oriented media of the sixties shows that while there were cracks in the intergenerational institution, most teens and adults at least tacitly admitted that their juniors or elders had something intelligent to say and that their society was not hopelessly doomed.

Yet, if most teens of the era evolved in rather normal patters for emotionally active adolescents, the stage on which they acted and interacted with each other, with adults, and with their younger siblings was simply more colorful, more charged with energy, and more interesting than many other earlier or later decades. It is no accident that teens garnered a substantial proportion of adult media cover stories and network news and features specials. Teens were interesting, photogenic, opinionated, and extremely numerous, a perfect target for anyone in the news or entertainment industries. In turn, if sixties teens were a good topic for contemporary narratives, it seems reasonable that a chronicle of their culture in a historical genre is not without merit.

Since I personally experienced the 1960s primarily as a preteen and teenager, I possess both the advantage and disadvantage of being very close to the topic that I have undertaken. Yet I was only one of millions of teenagers, and I have learned far more about sixties teens than I could have originally imagined with the added benefit of being able to process the information as a semidispassionate, middle-aged adult. Even as a teen, I suspected, and now I know, that the vast majority of 1960s adolescents never affected the hip TV-series teen slang spoken by Pete, Linc, and Julie in *The Mod Squad*, never became as musically proficient as Lesley Gore or Stevie Wonder, nor were able to chronicle their own adolescence at a single point in time like George Lucas. Yet what they *did* do and accomplish is still pretty impressive. They challenged adults to view, and change, a world that for many teens across a wide political spectrum often produced rules that made little or no sense. Teens who campaigned for Richard Nixon and those who idolized Bobby Kennedy more often than not agreed that conscription needed to be massively reformed or discarded. Adolescents of both conservative and progressive persuasions argued for more freedom of expression, dress, and outlook in the nation's high schools. Their hope and belief was not a small cabal of adolescent Robespierres or Trotskys or Francos but a surprisingly broad-based hope and expectation far more thoughtful than nihilistic, argued with a background soundtrack among the coolest in history. These teens are worth remembering, and I hope that you, the reader, found this literary journey "groovy" and "boss."

~

A Note on Sources

From the time I first envisioned a project devoted exclusively to the teen experience during the 1960s, I was convinced that the best way to understand that adolescent world and the adults who interacted with it was to tap into the wide variety of popular periodicals that made up so large a part of their informational experiences. I was also personally insistent that the best way to experience that time was to opt out of the twenty-first-century technology of online searches that would produce bland excerpts from sixties-era magazines and, instead, peruse the real copies from cover to cover, including letters to the editors, advertisements, and articles that I would not have originally believed pertinent to my project. Therefore, I have spent much of the past year alternating between teaching, parenting, and watching twenty-first-century sports, movies, and television, and immersing myself in the adult and adolescent magazines of a world four to five decades in the past.

The adult-oriented magazines of the sixties were still available in their original form at the University of Pennsylvania and Rosemont College and represent one of the main informational outlets to huge numbers of American families in a predigital age. I focused primarily on eight magazines that were read by a very substantial number of adults and more than a few adolescents as a secondary audience. This included the two major illustrated news and popular culture journals, *Life* and *Look*, which devoted very substantial space to teen issues in the sixties; the two primary newsmagazines, *Time* and *Newsweek*, which often viewed the teen experience a bit more sardonically; *U.S. News and World Report*, which was a hybrid of news and analysis and featured more articles on the adolescent experience than *Time* and *Newsweek* combined; *Fortune*, which was invaluable in understanding the business and financial aspects of the burgeoning teen consumer society; *McCall's*, which was a women's magazine that featured fairly extensive material on teen life from the perspective of parenting; and *T.V. Guide*, which carried valuable articles on teens as consumers and as members of a growing international audience in the wake of Telstar.

While original, bound issues of period adult-oriented magazines were readily available in at least two area libraries, teen magazines are more often found in either specialty archive shops or online through eBay, which generally offers a fairly wide selection. I focused my primary attention on ten of the most widely recognized magazines that targeted a teen reading audience, and through store purchases and online bidding, I became the proud possessor of scores of these journals.

The two most widely read youth-oriented journals for teens in senior high schools were *Seventeen* for girls and *Mad* for boys, although some teen girls would openly purchase the latter, and some teen boys would less openly read the former when a sister or girlfriend was not paying attention. While these two journals seem very different on the surface, each provided a prism though which to understand both the adult world and the opposite sex, and the letters to the editors from two seemingly disparate audiences actually converged at some points. The two most representative general-reading magazines for preteen junior high school audiences were *American Girl* and *Boys Life*, each an outlet of the huge scouting movement of postwar America. *American Girl* had far fewer color fashion ads and photos and clearly younger teen-oriented fiction and career features but still held a very loyal audience and could be read in combination with *Seventeen* by many midteen girls. *Boys Life* was in many respects a male version of *American Girl*, with less fashion but equal amounts of grooming tips and advice on the dating world just emerging for its readers.

Glamour and *Mademoiselle* magazines were perused to obtain a better feel for the world of girls who were either near the end of their high school experience or very early in their career or college worlds, with less advice on coping with parents and more on male-female relationships and prospects for marriage in a world of young brides. *Teen Age* and *Teen* magazines offered many of the career and fashion tips seen in *Seventeen* but included far more material on the teen entertainment scene and, interestingly for a twenty-first-century author, substantial material on the regional difference among teens from North to South and Atlantic to Pacific. The final pair, *Teen Screen* and *Teen Time*, were primarily entertainment magazines filled with artificially generated "dates" between a male and female actor or pop star, "inside scoops" on new and fading relationships and careers, and after 1964, frequent insider "views" of the myriad British Invasion groups.

The journals of the era formed the primary source material for this book, given my intent to chronicle the sixties teen experience as the adolescents and adults of that time viewed it. I supplemented those written sources with long (and generally pleasant) hours spent watching dozens of films and television series from that era and listening to hundreds of period songs, while attempting to analyze them in a mixed adolescent and middle-aged mindset. While virtually all of the analysis of teen experiences in this book is based on my own opinions, which of course may be at odds with readers, I still utilized several dozen books, both from the sixties and from more contemporary periods, to gain a better global view of the culture and mindset of this fascinating period.

The section on 1959 as portal to the sixties can be further explored by accessing period works such as James Herlihy's *Blue Denim* (New York, 1959) and Enid Haupt's *The Seventeen Book of Young Living* (New York, 1959). A general cultural and social view of the fifties is the magisterial work by David Halberstam, *The Fifties* (New York, 1993), while Fred Kaplan's *1959: The Year That Everything Changed* (Hoboken, 2009) is an excellent chronicle of the year from an adult perspective.

The home life, school life, and social life of sixties teens is explored in D. J. Walde's memoir *Holy Land: A Suburban Memoire* (Boston, 2005) and Homer Hickman's award-winning retrospective, *Rocket Boys* (New York, 1999). Also helpful were James Conant's proposal for restructuring American secondary education, *The American High School Today* (New York, 1960); Thomas Hine's cultural panorama, *Populuxe* (New York, 1986); and parental point of view in Peter Stearns' *Anxious Parents: The History of Modern Childrearing in America* (New York, 2003). The transition from high school to college receives attention in Gerald Gutek's *American Education, 1945–2000* (Chicago, 2009), Lynn Peril's *College Girls* (Boston, 2006), and John Thelin's *A History of American Higher Education* (Baltimore, 2004).

The impact of popular music, film, and television on the teenage experience of the sixties has received scholarly and popular attention from Glenn Altschuler in *All Shook Up: How Rock and Roll Changed America* (New York, 2000), Tim Neely in *The Roots of Rock and Roll* (Iola, WI, 1999), Robert Bulman in *Hollywood Goes to High School* (New York, 2005), and Thomas Doherty in *Teenpics* (Boston, 1986). Excellent reference sources for popular music of the 1960s are Joel Whiteburn's *The Top Ten Single*

Charts of Billboard Magazine: 1955–2000 (Menominee, WI, 2001) and Joel Whitburn's *Billboard Hot 100 Charts: The Sixties* (Menominee, WI, 2010).

Teens as sixties consumers receive attention in Thomas Hine's *The Rise and Fall of the Teenager* (New York, 1999), Kate Burns' *The American Teenager* (Farmington, MI, 2003), and Yvonne Connikie's *Fashions of a Decade: The 1960s* (Philadelphia, 2007). The issues of the generation gap are treated in Maurice Isenan and Michael Kazin's *America Divided* (New York, 2008), Max Lytle's *America's Civil Wars* (New York, 2006), and Todd Gitlen's *The Sixties* (New York, 1987).

The relationship of conscription, universal military service, and the Vietnam War to young Americans is treated along a variety of themes, including the genesis of peacetime conscription in Joel Spring's *The Sorting Machine* (New York, 1976), the role of the combat infantryman in Vietnam in James Ebert's *A Life in a Year* (New York, 1993), and the national debate over the conflict in Michael Lind's *Vietnam: The Necessary War* (New York, 1999) and James Torr's *American Views About War* (San Diego, 2002).

The role of sixties popular culture in succeeding decades receives attention in Steve Gillon's *Boomer Generation* (New York, 1986) and Howard Sounes' *The Seventies* (London, 2006).

Index

~

About the Author

Victor Brooks is professor of history and education at Villanova University. He is the author of ten books, including *Boomers: The Cold-War Generation Grows Up*; *The Fredericksburg Campaign*, nominated for the Virginia Literary Prize; and *Hell Is Upon Us: D-Day in the Pacific*, a feature selection of the History Book Club.